THE
ENGLISH
GARDEN

Ursula Buchan

Photographs by **Andrew Lawson**

THE ENGLISH GARDEN

FRANCES LINCOLN LIMITED
PUBLISHERS

PAGE 1 A beguiling glimpse into the old cider orchard beyond the garden at Tintinhull in Somerset. The gate is flanked by the shrub rose 'Duplex'.

PAGES 2–3 Cothay Manor in Somerset is a glorious medieval manor house, restored in 1925 by Colonel Reginald Cooper. He made a garden consisting of a long yew seventeenth-century-type walk with 'conversation arbours', parallel to the house, which links a number of hedged compartments. This is an example of an early twentieth-century garden harking back to the formal gardens of the seventeenth century. The present owners have restored and replanted the garden.

THIS PAGE The lake at Gresgarth Hall in Lancashire, a garden created by the owner, the garden designer Arabella Lennox-Boyd. The sundial was designed by her husband, Mark.

Frances Lincoln Ltd
4 Torriano Mews
Torriano Avenue
London NW5 2RZ
www.franceslincoln.com

CONTENTS

INTRODUCTION

'Our England is a garden' wrote Rudyard Kipling and so it is, to be sure. Gardens take up more than one million acres in this country, and there are an astonishing three thousand gardens which are considered of sufficient quality (and with owners of a sufficiently charitable frame of mind) to open to the public at least once a year. More than five hundred are open far more often, either on their own or as part of a house and garden package, to provide the owners with an income, or at the very least to help pay for the maintenance of the garden. These numbers are easily taken for granted, because open gardens have been part of our mental landscape all our lives, but they are most remarkable all the same.

This is a Golden Age for gardens; of that I have no doubt. The restoration of important gardens in the last thirty years, intellectually powered by the scholarship of the Garden History Society, founded in 1965, as well as by the energy of fundraisers and the generosity of the Heritage Lottery Fund, has meant that some very fine gardens which seemed lost have been regained – in glorious style, too, thanks to the work of a whole army of experts and craftsmen: historical landscape specialists, archaeologists, geophysicists, stone masons, tree surgeons, hydraulic engineers and so on. And the high levels of taxation, especially inheritance tax, which looked, in the 1950s and 1960s, as if they might finish off the old, large garden-owning classes, were tempered in the 1980s, so that the prospects for the country house garden are still quite bright, while rising prosperity means that houses and gardens are generally well cared for and often imaginatively laid out, sometimes but not necessarily by professional designers.

As for design, this is truly an exciting moment for gardens in this country, as we finally throw away the Arts and Crafts comfort blanket and move towards a more relaxed style which suits our modern world. That is why it is so important – as well as highly enjoyable – for all gardeners seeking inspiration and knowledge, as well as spiritual refreshment, to visit open gardens. Only pressures on land, which may rule out the creation of a great many large gardens in the future, the present shortage of professional gardeners as well as the pervasive bane of traffic noise, have the power to spoil our fun.

My aim in this book is to give a sense to the reader of the extraordinary richness and diversity of the English domestic garden, seen through the prism of my own interests and tastes, as well as the

OPPOSITE Contemporary designers are often called in to change gardens which have existed for many years, when they must be sympathetic to the context but not shackled by it. At Eaton Hall, Cheshire, a very large garden with grand Victorian terraces, Arabella Lennox-Boyd was asked to redesign the garden when a new house was built. This is the Rose Garden, laid out as a geometric parterre of hedged enclosures.

BELOW The lake at Garsington Manor in Oxfordshire, an Italianate garden laid out by Lady Ottoline Morrell from 1915.

camera lens and artistic sense of Andrew Lawson, principally though by no means exclusively in gardens that are open to the public. The book is intended as an approachable introduction to the English garden; it does not pretend to be a scholarly work. The subject is treated thematically, as being (it seems to me) a very good way of showing that richness and diversity, while at the same time (I hope) making the subject both comprehensible and enlightening. The theming into chapters may feel at times rather arbitrary, since it is employed partly for convenience and partly to try to make some sense of what is a huge subject. I hope you will feel that it is generally helpful, however. Treating it thus has required me to say quite a lot about the history of English garden styles, since frequently it has a direct bearing on how a garden looks today and why. Obviously, many gardens open to the public have a long, varied, even chequered history, often going back several hundred years, and this history dictates how some have been renovated or conserved. The book does not allow more than a brief overview. Anyone who wishes to dig deeper into the history of gardens – a subject very well served by scholars in recent years – will find a number of suitable books in the Select Bibliography on page 378.

It is important to understand how society and culture have shaped English gardens. This is not the book in which to explore social history in depth, but I would refer readers to the excellent books by Jane Brown and Charles Quest-Ritson on the subject (see page 378). Knowing something of this adds enormously to the enjoyment of visiting gardens, I believe. It certainly does to mine. Garden visiting becomes not just a sensory pleasure but an intellectual one as well.

Gardens are not static, of course. They are a process. They scarcely stand still for a day, let alone a year, a decade or a century. The dynamic of growth and decay is inexorable, for both plants and structural elements. They blossom and flourish as leaves on a tree. But they also wither and perish. One of the most fascinating aspects of the study of English gardens, uplifting and touchingly sad by turns, is how one garden retains its continuity of existence through good times and bad, while another will burst on the scene like a bright firework and almost as quickly die away.

Even when gardens somehow survive for many years, they change. Often many times. The best gardeners never leave their gardens quite alone, never consider them finished and complete. They endlessly strive to improve, even if nature does not force them into it (which it so often does) by blowing down a stand of trees or ensuring a shrub grows beyond its allotted space. I may describe a garden, or part of a garden, in this book which, scarcely has the print button been pressed, will have changed ownership or been altered in some radical way. What I am attempting to describe is the English garden in the early years of the twenty-first century, using examples that I consider typical or exceptional. Please don't fret, or feel cheated, therefore, if some feature I extol in a garden is lost or overlaid by the time you see it in person.

Photographs, for all their positive qualities, are unwitting accessories to this, for they can freeze a garden at one moment in the mind of the observer. Moreover, it is impossible for any photographer, even one as hard-working and meticulous as Andrew Lawson, to chronicle every change in every garden.

I have tended to describe in detail only a few gardens in each chapter: those that seem to me to be highly representative or particularly good of their type. A litany of descriptions would have been wearisome for the reader and, in any case, this book is designed not as an alternative to visiting gardens but rather as a resource to make the visiting more enjoyable. Some gardens find a mention in more than one chapter, especially if they have been developed, or grown organically, over time, or have a number of important elements to them.

Most of the gardens mentioned are on the larger side. That is inevitable, since they tend to be the ones which can withstand the pounding feet of visitors, and the ones that need the money which those visitors bring. But there are some much smaller gardens that are less than an acre/half a hectare in extent, which are full of fascination, and well worth a visit on the days when they open. There are many examples in both the *The Daily Telegraph Good Gardens Guide* and the National Gardens Scheme's 'Yellow Book' (see page 378).

The gardens described date mostly from the eighteenth century and later. That is because there are relatively few gardens which are from the sixteenth and seventeenth centuries: either rare Elizabethan survivals like Lyveden New Bield, Northamptonshire, or reconstructions such as Westbury Court, Gloucestershire, and Hatfield House, Hertfordshire. However, included in the book is some representative of most recognized garden styles: the Tudor, the French, the Dutch, the eighteenth-century 'landscape tradition', the Victorian fashion for bedding out, the Italianate, the Japanese, the Arts and Crafts garden, the twentieth-century cottage garden and the much more modern phenomenon, New Naturalism. Fashion is a very strong factor in garden making, as in all art forms: both slavish adherence to it and bloody-minded denial. I have even mentioned the twentieth-century nostalgia for seventeenth-century gardens. Sometimes, that expression 'What goes round, comes round' seems very apt, even if history does not repeat itself exactly because, in the intervening time, society has changed.

It is inevitable in a work of this limited length that many readers' favourite gardens will have been left out. For this I apologize, of course, with all sincerity, but to be comprehensive not only is impossible but would be self-defeating. (I have added, at the end of each chapter, a list of some other fine gardens for which there was no space in the text itself.) It is inevitable that I shall not have pleased everyone. I have pleased myself, however, and am content to allow that to be my guide. As for public parks, botanical gardens, educational establishments and display gardens, important as these are on the English horticultural scene, descriptions cannot really be justified, except *en passant*, in a book essentially on the English domestic garden. There are a few exceptions which find a place here: although they are not strictly attached to a house, they illustrate points I wish to make. The David Austin rose garden near Wolverhampton and Pensthorpe Waterfowl Park, Norfolk, are two such.

I must also mark my regret that there is no room in a book called *The English Garden* for so many wonderful gardens in Scotland, Wales, Northern Ireland and Eire. Perhaps another time.

Although most of the gardens mentioned and illustrated are open to the public, there are some private gardens which were just too interesting, beautiful or important in what they tell us about the English garden to miss out, yet are firmly closed to visitors. But these cases are not common, since I am conscious that to mention too many closed gardens would be frustrating to the reader. Which of the gardens mentioned are open is indicated in the index. This also gives the counties in which they reside, so that anyone with a copy of *The Daily Telegraph Good Gardens Guide* and the National Gardens Scheme's 'Yellow Book', both published annually (see page 378), should be able to find them easily.

As I write, a genteel debate is raging (perhaps whispering would be a better word) amongst garden commentators concerning why it is that there is so little adverse criticism of gardens open to the public. It is a debate worth having, since it is possible to argue that if you open your gates to visitors and expect them to pay good money to see your garden, it is only just that, if standards fall short, they should be publicly noticed. Moreover, without criticism, how can garden making be called an art form, as it deserves? I agree wholeheartedly with that, and occasionally have written something critical where I thought it justified. However, in a book of this restricted size, I have just not mentioned gardens which I consider do not offer visitors their full money's worth. There are so many good gardens in this country that I have been spoiled for choice and have not had to resort to mentioning anything which was not absolutely first-rate. That said, if your favourite garden is not in this book, it is more likely that its omission is a matter of space or lack of knowledge on my part rather than disapprobation.

On the subject of choosing gardens, I must pay tribute to all those who have written gazetteers of English gardens in recent years (see page 378). Their meticulous care and assiduous toil have made my task a very much easier and more pleasant one than it might otherwise have been. I feel like a small dwarf perched on the broad shoulders of some very tall giants.

Finally, and most importantly, I should like to record what a pleasure it has been to collaborate with Andrew Lawson on this book, and to have had the run of his wonderful photograph library, representing some of the finest images of many of the finest gardens that England can offer. I have been supremely fortunate, and I know it. His pictures are central to the book. They say very much more than I ever could, and give the reader the opportunity closely to study and observe, often more than is possible when actually standing in a garden.

I hope very much that this book will spur you to go out to visit gardens you have never seen before, or to revisit with renewed pleasure those which you do know. If it does, do take time when you go. Many gardens, which may seem simple in my perforce terse descriptions, will reveal themselves best and most fully to those who have the time to stand and stare.

I have been a writer on gardens and gardening in this country for more than twenty-five years and, in that time, I have seen many and various gardens, and many and various developments and trends. It has been the most tremendous fun and I count myself extremely fortunate. And it has given me a lasting and sincere admiration for all the individuals who have made the creation and maintenance of a beautiful garden a very important – sometimes the most important – aspect of their lives. When they feel that they can share that garden with fellow gardeners, stranger and friend, we are truly blessed. The commonplace nature of garden visiting does not blind me to the privilege which these people bestow on me. I try to remember and respect the many, many hours (much of it in the bath, no doubt) that they, and sometimes their forebears too, will have spent dreaming up the schemes before going outside to realize them. It is to all these gardeners that this book is respectfully dedicated.

FORMAL BONES

If asked to imagine the quintessential English garden, most of us – I would willingly put money on it – would come up with a description along the lines of 'informal and generous planting within a formal layout'. That is because a great many English gardens have been laid out in this way over the centuries, using geometry as the guiding principle but with plants undermining, ever so slightly, the purity of line. For both practical and aesthetic reasons, garden owners have found it convenient and satisfying to mould their gardens into geometrical shapes – circles, squares, rectangles and parallel lines – as a way of organizing and making sense of the space available. Moreover, for the same reasons, they have usually (though not invariably) plumped for symmetry as well. The architectural elements may be man made, they may have originally been dug out of the ground or they may be composed of growing plants; it does not matter. What matters is the shapes those materials make.

All gardens, if they can be described as such, have ultimately to do with the desire of their makers to control their surroundings. And as we know, nature abhors not only a vacuum but also a straight line, so geometry is a specific rejection of nature – or at least one important feature of it. For many people, however, geometry is what defines a garden, as opposed to a small slice of landscape. What is more, it is for many the most satisfactory way of unifying house and garden, since the rules which govern architecture can be used to govern the immediate garden, too. And a strong structure in the garden means it has something to offer all year round.

At times in our history, there have been intentional rejections of this geometry, indeed a wholesale reaction against it; I will come to those later (see Chapters 3 and 11). Right now, let us look first, briefly, at the structural elements that make up the English formal garden as we see it today.

We are lucky enough to be able to see an unearthed and reconstructed version of a Roman garden at Fishbourne Palace in Sussex. When excavations began in the 1960s, it was found that there had been a very large (240 feet/83 metres by 300 feet/90 metres) enclosed formal garden in the centre of the main palace complex, and a less formal one to the south side of it. The formal garden was surrounded by a colonnade and divided by a broad path, with smaller paths running off it. The archaeologists even discovered that there had been a geometric pattern of clipped box hedging on each side of the broad path, and it is very possible

OPPOSITE The massive yew hedges guarding the entrance to the Bathing Pool Garden at Hidcote Manor in Gloucestershire. An example of a 'tapestry hedge' (see page 38) can be glimpsed behind the topiary birds. The garden was made between the wars by Lawrence Johnston.

BELOW A rustic arch at The Grove in Oxfordshire, covered with the Wichurana Rambler rose 'American Pillar', a confection of bright pink in early July. The use of both round and pointed arches is interesting.

The Fuchsia Garden at Hidcote Manor in Gloucestershire, in winter, demonstrating the value of 'good bones', as well as the inherent jolliness of representational topiary.

there was also a pergola and fountains. All this has been reconstructed. As Christopher Thacker puts it: 'Fishbourne is an inspiring yet perplexing statement that the great tradition of formal garden design, which was to reappear in the late 16th century . . . was already there, full-fledged, in the first century A.D.'[1]

There are a few gardens (probably market gardens) mentioned in the Norman Domesday Book, and later in the Norman period scholars believe that there was considerable horticultural activity, especially to do with orchards, vineyards, herb gardens and productive types of garden, generally. As the Middle Ages progressed, it is apparent that royalty, aristocracy and religious orders were firmly engaged in gardening, albeit often on a smaller scale than what was to come, and using a very restricted range of plants. The small, enclosed garden, *hortus conclusus*, often in a courtyard, was widespread, but there were also larger gardens attached to castles and large houses, surrounded by palings or hedges, say, and with turf benches, flower beds, fruit trees and clipped shrubs. As for monasteries, they probably had ornamental, recreational gardens as well as the more obvious herbal and medicinal ones. Sadly, no medieval gardens remain, but there is no reason to think that these did not present aesthetic, as well as horticultural and scientific, satisfactions to both those who worked in them and those who observed them.

After the Dissolution of the Monasteries, the formality remained, but gardens became pleasure grounds with flowers grown extensively as well as useful herbs. The formal garden, from its inception, lent itself to compartmentalization into what we now call 'rooms' and this is a facet which remains important to this day. These rooms gave shelter and sometimes shade, of course, but in later centuries also ensured that plantings could be coherent, encompassable and, if necessary, separated

in colour or atmosphere. Gardeners discovered early on that nothing makes a garden look bigger or more interesting than dividing it up.

In the sixteenth and early seventeenth centuries, knot gardens and simple raised parterres, with mounds, galleries, pleached avenues, topiary and statues, were *de rigueur*.

A knot was, and is, a formal arrangement of dwarf hedging, where the hedging is grown in a pattern, sometimes an elaborate one. It is possible to have both 'open' and 'closed' knots. This hedging has most often consisted of dwarf box but lavender, santolina and thyme were also used. A good example is the knot garden created from 1981 by the Marchioness of Salisbury in what had been a nineteenth-century rose garden in front of the Tudor Old Palace at Hatfield House in Hertfordshire. There is also a reconstructed Tudor knot at Little Moreton Hall, Cheshire, and a re-creation at the Tudor House in Southampton. Of modern knot gardens, there is one in the garden of The Abbey House, Malmesbury, Wiltshire, where the garden is partly on the site of the Benedictine abbot's garden in the days before the Dissolution of the Monasteries. Made by the present

ABOVE The knot garden close to the house at Barnsley House in Gloucestershire was created by Rosemary Verey from 1970 onwards, using two types of dwarf box, *Buxus sempervirens* 'Suffruticosa' and *B.s.* 'Aureomarginata', as well as *Teucrium* x *lucidrys*, the grey-green germander in the far knot. There are two patterns, the nearer one of which is the true lovers' knot. Note how cleverly the interlacing 'threads' have been clipped to give the impression that they go over and under. Rosemary Verey was inspired to do this after visiting the grand formal garden Filoli, in California. The sentinel hollies are *Ilex* x *altaclarensis* 'Golden King'.

FOLLOWING PAGES The knot garden at Antony in Cornwall, consisting of dwarf box and teucrium. The pattern is cleverly echoed in the seat back.

LEFT The Tudor Garden next to the Old Palace (c.1485) at Hatfield in Hertfordshire, which replaced a nineteenth-century rose garden. It was laid out in 1981 and 1982 by the Marchioness of Salisbury, and consists of three knots and a maze, with plant species dating from Tudor times. The fountain in the middle has recently been replaced by a new one, a copy from a drawing to be found in a 500-year-old book on gardens called *Hypnerotomachia Poliphili* of a gilt boy standing on a sphere and blowing an equally golden trumpet.

LEFT BELOW The open knot at Helmingham Hall in Suffolk, interplanted with pinks (*Dianthus*), *Lychnis coronaria* 'Alba' and love-in-a-mist (*Nigella damascena*). This is a modern knot, designed in 1982 by the Tudor house's chatelaine, Xa Tollemache, a professional garden designer.

RIGHT The Ladies' Garden at Broughton Castle in Oxfordshire, with fleur-de-lys box shapes and height provided by standard hawthorns (*Crataegus* 'Paul's Scarlet'). Camomile is growing in the centre to enhance the period look. The infilling is provided by roses, 'Gruss an Aachen' (pinkish white) and 'Heritage' (darker pink).

FOLLOWING PAGES A Nesfield-designed Victorian Italianate parterre at Eaton Hall in Cheshire. Particularly striking is the Dragon Fountain in the pool. The planting is in keeping but is by Arabella Lennox-Boyd. The spring planting consists of red tulip 'Landseadel's Supreme' and deep burgundy 'Queen of Night'.

owners, the garden includes a knot garden in the shape of a Celtic cross.

Knots are supposed to be looked at from above, in particular from a mound or the windows of the house, and that is true also of the parterre, a grander and more spacious affair, imported from France in the seventeenth century, when it was sometimes called *parterre de broderie* (embroidery parterre). The parterre was probably invented by the French royal gardener Claude Mollet, who worked for the French queen Catherine de Medici in the sixteenth century. Parterres were usually laid out on terraces close to the house, and often composed of much more intricate and ornate patterns than knots – ribbons, curlicues, scrolls – using thin lines of dwarf box, on a bed of gravel.

In English gardens, these days, knot gardens and parterres are words often used loosely, with a parterre being larger and in the open and a knot garden smaller and enclosed, but the distinction has to do really not only with size but also with the shape of the patterns.

After the Restoration of the monarchy in 1660, the influences on smart gardens were also French, the Court having been in exile in

RIGHT Westbury Court in Gloucestershire is a rare seventeenth-century survival in the Dutch style. The 4-acre/1.5-hectare garden, created by Maynard Colchester from 1696, mainly consists of a walled garden, with a long canal, terminated by a pavilion, and a parallel T-shaped canal. The yew hedges have clipped hollies on top.

FOLLOWING PAGES The 2-acre/0.8-hectare Privy Garden at Hampton Court Palace in Surrey, soon after the reconstruction work was completed. This garden dates from the early sixteenth century, but has been restored to how it would have looked in William III's day (late seventeenth century). It has been called 'a spectacular and unique example of the Baroque'.

France); André Le Nôtre (of Versailles fame) had a notable impact. Parterres in front of the house became more extensive and intricate, and tree *allées* radiated from a central point, or the house, in a *patte d'oie* or goose foot. Narrow flower beds were planted in a *plat-bande* style – that is, with shrubs clipped into balls and repeat patterns of flowers, with the tallest in the middle and the shortest on the edge.

Bramham Park in Yorkshire and Melbourne Hall in Derbyshire are survivors of this late seventeenth-century French style, having parterres in front of the house (replaced now at Melbourne Hall by lawns, it is true). Melbourne Hall was the work of the most fashionable design team of the time, George London and Henry Wise (who supplied plants from their Brompton Nursery). They also worked at Hampton Court Palace, Longleat and Chatsworth, as well as Kensington Palace.

Bramham Park was probably the work of its owner, Robert Benson, who had travelled in France and was very influenced by Le Nôtre. His garden, begun around 1710, is laid out on a different axis from the house, with one of the main paths, the Broad Walk, running along in front of it, which historians say is evidence that the house was becoming just one feature in a garden rather than the garden providing the setting for the house. In front of the house is an Edwardian formal rose garden, once a parterre, with a waterfall at the end into which water debouched down a cascade from a hidden pond, now dry, above.

But what gives this garden its special atmosphere are the *allées*, lined with very tall beech hedges, through woodland trees, and containing eyecatching garden buildings and monuments (some by James Paine) of exceptional quality in magnesian limestone (see pages 129–31). The trees, and the grassy glades, spangled with wildflowers in spring, are a delight. Moreover, there are thrilling formal water features, including a set of five ponds, at different levels, called the Cascades, and the T-Pond, over which the eye skims to another far temple, in an oak wood called Black Fen. Rides were cut through this wood and the native trees were augmented in the mid-nineteenth century by exotic ones such as the monkey puzzle (*Araucaria araucana*). It is a very great pity that there are not more survivals of this French style, since Bramham provides such an invigorating experience – not to mention a good long walk.

The Dutch style (similar to the French but generally simpler and with avenues rather than radiating *allées*, and topiary) arrived with King William and Queen Mary in the 1680s. The most complete extant gardens in the Dutch style are Westbury Court in Gloucestershire, and Castle

The formal garden designed by W.A. Nesfield at Broughton Hall in North Yorkshire, c.1855. He was known for using coloured gravels instead of plants in his parterres, incurring William Robinson's derision.

Bromwich Hall, Birmingham, although the best known must be the Privy Garden at Hampton Court Palace, in Surrey, now restored to as it was in William's day. Water, in the form of severely rectilinear canals, was important, as were statuary, fountains and garden pavilions. These gardens have a strong axial design, as well as plantations.

The formal gardens of the seventeenth and early eighteenth centuries were mainly swept away from about 1720 onwards (see Chapter 3), but formality made a comeback in Victorian times, thanks to well-known architects such as W.A. Nesfield, Sir Charles Barry (who also designed the Houses of Parliament) and Sir Reginald Blomfield (the latter writing *The Formal Garden in England* in 1892). Nesfield often went for a rather French parterre style (as at Somerleyton Hall, Suffolk, and Witley

A tunnel of the Judas tree (*Cercis siliquastrum*) in the walled kitchen garden at Buscot Park in Oxfordshire, designed by Tim Rees. A pleached avenue of hop hornbeam (*Ostrya carpinifolia*) intersects it. The garden dates mainly from the twentieth century. Harold Peto worked here from 1904, but there have also been substantial additions by the owners since the 1960s.

Court, Worcestershire), sometimes using coloured gravels instead of plants in the parterres, as had been common in the seventeenth century, while Italianate influences can be seen in his parterre at Broughton Hall, North Yorkshire. Also Italianate are highly structured and architectural gardens such as Trentham Gardens, Staffordshire, Buscot Park, Oxfordshire, Iford

Manor, Wiltshire (see also page 67), Port Lympne, Kent, and Blenheim
Palace, Oxfordshire, where a Frenchman, ironically, called Achille
Duchêne created an Italian Garden, finished in 1910, and the Water
Terraces, completed twenty years later. The garden at Hever Castle in Kent
was also partly made over in the Italian style (see page 218).

The parterre at the French-inspired 'chateau' of Waddesdon Manor in Buckinghamshire, in its spring glory, with tulips and wallflowers, edged by pansies. This garden was originally laid out by Élie Lainé in the 1880s. Just visible in the far left of the picture is a pool and fountain by Mozani. There is statuary in this garden of Italian, French and Dutch origin. Waddesdon is one of the few gardens where 'carpet-bedding' is practised in summer. To the left and right of the fountain are beds set at an angle and planted in early June with alternanthera, sedums, echeverias and sempervivums, just as they would have been in Victorian times. In 2006, the picture picked out was that of a fan owned by Charlotte de Rothschild c.1885. The number of plants required, and their placing, must first be worked out by computer. In past years designs have been by John Hubbard (2000) and Oscar de la Renta (2001).

The boldest parterre in the country must surely be the remarkable one on the south side of the house at Waddesdon Manor in Buckinghamshire. The house was built by the Baron Ferdinand de Rothschild in the French chateau style and finished in 1889. At the same time, elaborate terraces, parterres and pools were laid out, as well as an extensive formal garden. (The whole garden estate stretches to 165 acres/67 hectares.) In Victorian times, the south parterre was bedded out elaborately and exuberantly, but grassed over in 1931. However, in the 1990s, it was restored to its former splendour. In 1997, 'carpet-bedding' was reinstated north and south of the fountain. The millennium display was designed by the artist John Hubbard. The number and placing of the plants each year is worked out by computer.

The Italian Gardens at Trentham Gardens in Staffordshire, restored by the owners, a property company, with the advice of garden historian Dominic Cole, whose Land Use Consultants really set the standard of high-quality historical restorations at Stowe (see page 133) in the 1980s. The Lower Flower Garden (above), designed by Tom Stuart-Smith (with input also from Piet Oudolf), is a contemporary take on Victorian bedding-out, using perennials instead of annuals. These gardens are on such an heroic scale that even 'Capability' Brown's mile-long lake, seen in the distance, cannot dwarf them.

The equally magnificent parterres at Trentham Gardens, Staffordshire, laid out originally for the 2nd Duke of Sutherland by Sir Charles Barry from 1833, have been restored and replanted: the Upper Flower Garden is faithful to the spirit of George Fleming, the Duke's innovative head gardener from 1841 to 1860, but the Lower Flower Garden is planted in a contemporary take on Victorian bedding-out, using perennials instead of annuals (see also page 361). The layout is the same, however, except that paths have been cut between beds so that the public can walk amongst them, and sit by the fountains – something not encouraged in the nineteenth century. These parterres are on an enormous scale; even 'Capability' Brown's mile-long lake, which abuts the Lower Flower Garden, cannot dwarf them.

By the Edwardian era, especially in the gardens of what we now call period houses, the Arts and Crafts garden had gained hugely in popularity. Nostalgia and romanticism were respectable and the style harked back in many ways to the formal seventeenth-century garden. (It is a feature of English garden history how many times the formal garden style finds itself reinvented, adapting to changes in culture and society.)

The Great Court at Athelhampton in Dorset, which was designed by F. Inigo Thomas in the 1890s. The twelve 30-foot/10-metre-high pyramids have been clipped every year by the present owner since he was fourteen years old.

Its most famous exponent was the Edwardian architect Sir Edwin Lutyens, designer of a number of gardens in the Arts and Crafts or Old English style (often in collaboration with the plantswoman/designer Gertrude Jekyll), but W.D. Caröe, Inigo Triggs, Thomas Mawson and H. Avray Tipping were other designers who worked in the style. At Athelhampton, Dorset, in the 1890s, for example, Francis Inigo Thomas designed a garden that would happily accord with the fifteenth- and sixteenth-century house.

So much for a brief history of the formal garden in England, but what do we see today? Like middle-aged women everywhere, English gardeners still extol the virtues of good bone structure. Just as the body needs bones to prevent it lying flat and flaccid on the ground, it seems we still appreciate that gardens need bones to make the aesthetics work. As James van Sweden puts it, 'The architecture is what bounds and focuses the space. A garden may have different kinds of bones, but it's the architectural elements that are the spine.'[2] However exuberant the flowers in gardens are allowed to be, garden owners know that it can make eminent sense to contain them within an enduring, dependable,

FORMAL BONES

A scene which shows clearly both the versatility of yew as a hedging material and Vita Sackville-West's attachment to 'the strictest formality of design, with the maximum informality of planting'. This is the view from the Tudor tower of the Rondel and Rose Garden at Sissinghurst Castle in Kent.

defined structure. You have only to think of a colourful, profuse herbaceous border placed in front of a deep green smooth-textured English yew hedge – a sight to be seen in very many gardens – to appreciate this point. The hedge provides stiffened sinews and muted contrast. The lax and unruly flowers acquire definition thereby.

The twentieth-century garden at Sissinghurst Castle, in Kent, is a prime example of this. Its success, according to its maker, Vita Sackville-West, resulted from a combination of 'the strictest formality of design, with the maximum informality of planting'. She knew perfectly well that structure ensured that the natural informality in habit of many plants could be contained, so that plantings did not risk degenerating into a messy confection. (It would be as well to point out here that many gardens which we consider formal have informal elements to them, especially in the furthest reaches away from the house. I will discuss that further in Chapter 3.)

Formal structural elements also serve many practical purposes, such as providing the quickest and most efficient way of getting from one part of the garden to another, as well as shelter from the elements, which is equally important to us and to the plants we wish to grow, not to mention privacy and seclusion.

Structure takes many forms in English gardens: not only clippable hedges (both evergreen and deciduous) but also 'hard landscaping' – the inelegant phrase used for all materials used in gardens which are inert, rather than alive: walls, fences, both freestanding and retaining, terraces, trellis, pergolas, and soft and hard paths. These are all permanent features, which change little, if at all, in the course of the year and act as boundary or backcloth to the changing scene

A circle cut in an evergreen hedge frames the view of the Walled
Garden at The Garden House, Buckland Monachorum in Devon, laid
out originally by the plantsman Lionel Fortescue.

of flowers and fruit, as well as eyecatcher, eye-leader or viewpoint.
Within that overall structural layout, there are often what one might call
sub-structures: clipped evergreen shrubs in borders, say, or tripods to
support climbing plants.

Structural planting has a long and honourable pedigree. Since medieval
times, and probably earlier, gardens have contained at least some
evergreen plants, ensuring that the shape of the garden is not blurred or
lost between November and April, when deciduous plants are usually
denuded of leaves. In earlier times, those winter bones were provided by
the few hardy evergreen trees and shrubs which were native to England:
juniper, box, holly and yew. John Evelyn claimed to have popularized
yew as hedging: 'I do name them [English yew] for hedges, preferable for
beauty and a stiff defence, to any plant I have ever seen and may . . .
without vanity be said to have been the first who brought it into
fashion.'[3] Well, I don't know about 'without vanity'. In the late
seventeenth and early eighteenth centuries, when foliage reigned
supreme over flowers, these natives were augmented by the

Mediterranean phillyrea and other imported 'greens', in order to help promote 'a green thought in a green shade', in Andrew Marvell's phrase. This can be seen clearly at, for example, the restored Castle Bromwich Hall Gardens, near Birmingham, laid out between 1680 and 1740. In the twentieth century, other conifers, besides yew, became extremely common for hedging and specimen planting, in particular the often dreaded (because it is so quick growing) Leyland cypress (× *Cupressocyparis leylandii*), as well as western red cedar (*Thuja plicata*) and Lawson cypress (*Chamaecyparis lawsoniana*). It is no exaggeration to say that the existence of evergreens, which have the capacity and amenability to be trimmed tightly into solid, enduring hedges, has influenced the direction of English garden design right up to the present day. Without those eminently clippable shrubs, it would simply have not been possible or economic to lay out gardens in a way that was both visually satisfying and enduringly practical. Important as stone and brick walls are, they are too expensive and too heavy to be used more than sparingly, except in very large garden spaces.

At The Grove in Oxfordshire, David Hicks made a parterre of box squares and rectangles, with only a minimal infill of flowers. At the top of the grass slope, a hornbeam hedge on stilts is backed by a second one clipped to ground level, creating an interesting effect. To the left of the ornament, the mown grass is allowed to grow long.

The top end of the Long Walk at Hidcote Manor in Gloucestershire. The walk is interrupted by a bridge and stream which flows across and makes it even more interesting. It is a smooth, restful space between two busy parts of the garden. Lawrence Johnston, its creator, saw it as a 'breathing space'.

Recently, *Ilex crenata* 'Convexa' has been added to the list of dwarf shrubs useful as hedging, as an alternative to dwarf box (*Buxus sempervirens* 'Suffruticosa') in some of the gardens where the fungal disease box blight (*Cylindrocladium*) has become a problem. The shock/horror reaction of garden owners (such as Sir Roy Strong, who recounts his experience in his book on The Laskett – see page 42) when they encounter box blight indicates clearly just how important dwarf hedging is for the compartmentalization and definition of spaces in formal gardens, as well as the means of ornamentation in knot gardens and parterres.

It is also possible (as at Hidcote Manor, Gloucestershire, Great Dixter, East Sussex and Herterton House, Northumberland, for example) to have 'tapestry' hedges, which contain more than one evergreen species (often variegated hollies as well as yew and box) and coloured-leaf deciduous beech to add muted colours and textures to the mix (see page 12).

Hedging does not necessarily have to be evergreen, of course. There is plenty of deciduous hedging used in gardens, but it must be said that the two most common species used – beech (*Fagus sylvatica*) and hornbeam

(*Carpinus betulus*) – can be persuaded to retain their brown dead leaves through the winter, if clipped in early summer. This propensity makes them very useful to the gardener, since the hedges can act as windbreaks in winter and retain solidity for design purposes, yet give pleasure and variety with their new green foliage in spring.

Straight lines of deciduous hedging became an important feature of the English countryside in the eighteenth century, with the implementation of the Enclosure Acts. Although that was a painful time for country dwellers, as anyone who reads John Clare's poetry will know, it has meant that in the last two centuries the beauty and congruity of the straight hedge has become fixed in our psyches. Although not natural, it has come to seem so, and this may partly explain why straight hedges have remained popular in the design of English gardens ever since.

Double straight lines, separated by path or grass, are also used sometimes to create a false perspective, if the gap between the lines is narrowed as they stretch away into the distance. Evergreen hedging is an excellent medium for this, since it is so malleable and relatively cheap, in comparison to hard materials, at least.

The double serpentine hedges at Chatsworth in Derbyshire create an unusual vista to the statue of the 6th Duke of Devonshire at the far end. These hedges date from 1953.

ABOVE 'Armchair' topiary shapes at Knightshayes in Devon. This garden also boasts topiary hounds tirelessly chasing an equally fit fox along the top of a hedge.

OPPOSITE Yew buttresses break up the plantings in the border at Packwood House in Warwickshire, making the eye accept more readily the mixed-colour planting of roses and perennials.

Hedging – evergreen or deciduous – need not be straight, of course, even in the formal garden. Because it comprises so many plants set close together and usually has a narrow width, it is possible to clip hedging into many different shapes, including serpentine (beech hedges at Ascott, Buckinghamshire, and at Chatsworth, Derbyshire) and circular, as in the massive yew Rondel at Sissinghurst, with its meeting of four paths in the middle (see pages 34–5).

Evergreens can be used as visual door stops, as for example, at Arley Hall, in Cheshire, where clipped yew 'buttresses' define areas of the immensely long herbaceous borders, creating *cordons sanitaires* to prevent colour clashes, and to allow the eye to wander less frenetically and more comfortably down the border. And at Knightshayes in Devon, something of the same effect has been achieved using yew 'armchairs'.

This column stands at one end of the Elizabeth Tudor Avenue at The Laskett in Herefordshire, the garden made by Sir Roy Strong and his late wife, the stage designer Dr Julia Trevelyan Oman. The plaques at the bottom commemorate both Elizabeth I and Elizabeth II. At the time of the present Queen's Golden Jubilee (2002), a golden crown was added to the sphere at the top of the column. At the end of the walk is a monument to Shakespeare. Most of the ornaments in this highly structured garden are painted blue and gold, and gold leaf is used liberally.

Perhaps the most famous of contemporary formal gardens, which uses hedging extensively for shelter, space definition and knots, is that at The Laskett in Herefordshire. Since the garden is rarely open to visitors, it is a good thing for us that one of its two creators, Sir Roy Strong, has written an entire book about it.[4] This is a garden made over more than thirty years, since 1973, by Strong and his late wife, the stage designer Dr Julia Trevelyan Oman. As befits a garden created by an historian and a theatre designer, it is ultra-formal, consisting of a great number of small gardens, walks, avenues, knots, vistas and orchards, with sculpture, garden buildings and decorative features, like obelisks, at many suggestive points. It is unusual in two ways, in that it is so intricate and elaborate, when the movement in the late twentieth century has tended to be towards simplification, and in that it is also a 'memento' garden, full of references to stages in its makers' lives (for example, areas with names such as Nutcracker Garden and a memorial to a much-loved cat).

It is punctilious in its historicism. Strong admits to being much influenced by his scholarly research on Tudor and Stuart gardens, as well as late Victorian ones. 'In creating The Laskett I was following an

historicist impulse, the desire to go back, first to the gardens of late Victorian England and then, reaching even further back, to those of the age of Gloriana or, rather, those that masqueraded as re-creations of them.' He acknowledges his debt to the champions of formality Blomfield and H. Avray Tipping. And when he writes, 'All of them embodied that vision of a timeless England whose values and roots lay in the soil of the countryside, as opposed to the squalor, grime and commercialism of the industrial city,'[5] it is impossible not to be reminded of William Morris, father of the Arts and Crafts movement.

Almost as important as their use for the delineations of space in formal gardens is the fact that evergreens – especially yew and box – have also proved to be amenable to being cut into singular shapes of almost infinite variety, which give verticality, balance and solidity to formal gardens. Examples are the perfectly symmetrical and spaced domes of clipped yellow yew (*Taxus baccata* 'Aurea') each side of the path leading away from the house at Tintinhull, Somerset.

This is what we call topiary. As an idea, it was introduced by the Romans into this country; indeed, the Latin word for a gardener was

ABOVE One of the parterres in the walled garden at West Green House in Hampshire. There are dwarf hedges of box in heart and oval shapes, decorated by topiary balls, boxes and conical shapes. West Green House also delights in an 'Alice in Wonderland' garden, with a chequerboard parterre filled with flowers mentioned in the story. There are, for example, red and white roses, apparently painted at the Red Queen's direction.

FOLLOWING PAGES Identical golden yew domes in the Eagle Court at Tintinhull in Somerset. They are symmetrical, promoting an atmosphere of orderliness and purpose and encouraging flow through the garden.

topiarius, which suggests how important clipping evergreens must have been. Although topiary has gone in and out of fashion, over the years, it remains a strong visual element in many important and influential formal gardens: Athelhampton in Dorset, whose Great Court has twelve monumental and remarkable pyramids of yew, 30 feet/12 metres high; Lytes Cary Manor, Somerset, with its individualistic squat, cone-headed topiary, like a march of green aliens to the front door; and, best known and loved of all, Levens Hall in Cumbria. Here the enormous shapes, originally planted by a Frenchman, Guillaume Beaumont, at the very end of the seventeenth century, have become more abstract and gigantic over the past 300 years. They are mostly of green yew, but some golden yew figures were added in the nineteenth century.

At Great Dixter, East Sussex, the late Christopher Lloyd's father, Nathaniel Lloyd, not only planted yews and topiarized them but wrote a book about it, entitled *Garden Craftsmanship in Yew and Box*, published in 1925. These topiary shapes have now been *in situ* for more than eighty years, and consist of a number of truncated pyramids, topped with squat peacocks.

OPPOSITE Some of the extraordinary – and random – shapes at Levens Hall in Cumbria, many of which were originally planted by Guillaume Beaumont at the very end of the seventeenth century. Although topiary has gone in and out of fashion over the centuries, it has remained a constant at Levens, with many shapes increasing in size and singularity as the years have passed. Some have picturesque names: the Judge's Wig, the Howard Lion, the Great Umbrella, the Jug of Morocco Ale amongst them. The shapes are trimmed in mid-autumn, the job taking at least two months.

ABOVE Individualistic cone-headed topiary shapes, marching like aliens down the house lawn at Lytes Cary Manor in Somerset. The attractive 'dovecote' in the distance is actually a cleverly disguised water tower.

At Garsington Manor, near Oxford, which in the early twentieth century belonged to Lady Ottoline Morrell, friend and benefactor of the Bloomsbury Group, the garden she made depends heavily on yew and box shapes. They have been used both to create contrast of light and shadow, to add verticality and deliberately to reinforce the formal, Italianate feel of the garden. Trimmed narrowly, the yew columns give the impression of the Italian cypress (*Cupressus sempervirens*), which, of course, is not reliably hardy in England.

At Brodsworth Hall in Yorkshire, clipped evergreens are a major feature of the restored 1860s garden. The borders on both sides of the formal and colourful flower beds in the Formal Garden are filled with clipped balls, bobbles, spirals and mounds. Although not a cheery sight on a rainy day, they none the less provide an important insight into the Victorian Gardenesque style.

Topiary has also long been employed in English gardens, grand and humble, to express the owners' creativity and sense of humour. Gardeners, especially cottagers, have shaped evergreens into hens, pheasants, even battleships. At Knightshayes, you see a marriage of two concepts in a structural hedge, in this case yew, where the top has been

clipped to show a fox being chased by hounds. This is pure fantasy topiary, worthy of a cottager's fertile imagination and lack of self-consciousness. At Nymans, West Sussex, in the walled garden, there are carefully crafted topiary 'crowns' in the centre, acting as a very effective focal point.

At Ascott in Buckinghamshire, there is a sundial laid out in clipped box and yew, with a yew gnomon and the charming inscription 'Light and shade by turn but love always' in

The remarkable Sermon on the Mount at Packwood House in
Warwickshire. Here we see the Multitude in the foreground, with the
twelve 'apostles', four 'evangelists' and 'Christ' in the background.
The figures date from the mid-nineteenth century and are one of a
comparatively few examples of explicit Christian imagery in extant
English gardens.

golden yew. At Groombridge Place in Kent, there is a garden of crazy
'drunken' topiary shapes contrasting sharply with a line of ultra-formal,
neatly clipped yew 'drums', on either side of a walk in the central garden.
At Haseley Court, Oxfordshire, there is part of a chess set laid out as if
in the middle of a game, with the yew chess pieces surrounded by
clipped Portugal laurels. There was topiary here in the early sixteenth
century, according to John Leland, but the chess set dates from about
1850, the same time as the truly astonishing and dramatic Sermon on the

ABOVE A 'pot-pourri' of topiary shapes at The Grove in Oxfordshire, designed by David Hicks. Although they look as if they are in containers, in fact most are planted in the soil below. The climbing frames by the hornbeam hedge are for roses.

FOLLOWING PAGES The maze at Chatsworth, Derbyshire, which looks old but was actually planted in 1963. At Chatsworth there is also a 'bedroom' garden with a 'four-poster bed' in ivy and a 'dressing-table' of privet.

Mount and Multitude at Packwood House in Warwickshire. The Sermon on the Mount yew figures grow on an eminence in the garden and are reputed to consist of Christ with, below him, twelve apostles and four evangelists. The Multitude, consisting of conical shapes in yew, are gathered below them on the lawn.

Topiary has also found a place in very small gardens, particularly in towns, where it is used in pots, which can be moved around, thus providing a mobile geometry when and where required.

ABOVE Perhaps the most famous (or infamous?) and certainly the oldest hedge maze in England. This is at Hampton Court Palace in Surrey. The half-mile of yew hedges was planted by 1686. It is trapezoid in shape – and fiendish. Mazes or labyrinths, which probably originated in the Near East, were a feature of medieval gardens, when they were often treated as a symbol of man's tortuous and confused journey through life.

RIGHT The asymmetrical cherry laurel (*Prunus laurocerasus*) maze of 1833 at Glendurgan in Cornwall. Unusually, the maze was planted on steeply sloping ground on one side of this valley garden, so it is possible to see it from the other side.

A species of topiary which seems to have an enduring fascination for us is the living maze. There is much mythology and symbolism (some of it rather suspect) attached to mazes but, at the most basic level, the idea of getting lost or puzzled (but not really) seems to be always popular, with adults and children alike.

Famous examples include those at Hampton Court Palace, Chenies Manor in Buckinghamshire (which has both a yew maze and a turf maze) and at the other Hampton Court, in Herefordshire. At the latter, there is a maze planted with 1,000 yews, leading to a Gothic tower at its centre, which acts as a viewing platform. Glendurgan in Cornwall has a maze of 1833, consisting of cherry laurel (*Prunus laurocerasus*), and there is a yew maze at Hever Castle as well, not to mention a topiary chess set.

One of the best contemporary exponents of the art of maze-making is Adrian Fisher, who has created a number, notably at Escot Park in Devon, Leeds Castle in Kent and Blenheim Palace in Oxfordshire, where the design was inspired by the stone carvings by Grinling Gibbons on the palace. The Bamboo Maze at The Alnwick Garden in Northumberland is his, and he has also designed brick-paths-in-grass mazes at Greys Court, Oxfordshire, and Parham Park, Sussex.

ABOVE The iconic Stilt Garden at Hidcote. These are hornbeams. Enclosing a space in this way, as Lawrence Johnston did after he bought the house in 1907, had a profound effect on many English twentieth-century formal gardens.

OPPOSITE Relaxed formality at The Stone House, Wyck Rissington in Gloucestershire, with a diamond pattern of grass and stone making the simple path. The designer is Katie Lukas.

FOLLOWING PAGES Chenies Manor in Buckinghamshire exhibits many of the classic features of a formal garden: rectilinear borders, balanced topiary shapes, and a trellised screen covered in clipped ivy, which both provides verticality and marks the boundary of a garden 'room'. Tulips are a major feature of the Sunken Garden in April and May, wonderfully enlivening the scene with their tapestry of colours.

Lime trees are deciduous but do not hang on to their leaves in winter, as beech does, making them not very suitable for hedging. They play a distinguished role, however, in the framework of many gardens, either when pleached to form a see-through but substantial boundary or as an avenue to draw visitors up the driveway to the house. The lime trees used are either the small-leaved lime (*Tilia cordata*) or the common lime (*T.* × *europaea*). The main drawback of the latter is its propensity to produce shoots at the base, but they are both otherwise magnificent, both in leaf and in winter when the young shoots glow orange in sunlight.

At Hidcote, hornbeam (which is more tolerant of a clay soil than beech) was Lawrence Johnston's choice for the rectilinear hedge on stilts in the Stilt Garden. Hidcote is, incidentally, a garden where evergreen hedging is used extensively, and in different ways, to define the garden rooms: yew, especially the monumental yew arch into the Pool Garden, as well as dwarf box in the Fuchsia Garden (see pages 12 and 14).

Mapperton is an Italianate garden of the 1920s laid out in a stepped Dorset valley, which runs north–south. It is a felicitous mix of warm local Ham stone and brick walls, clipped topiary, water and statuary. This picture shows part of the upper garden, Fountain Court.

The two major drawbacks to garden owners of hedging – of whatever kind – are that it needs annual, sometimes twice-annual, trimming and that, being composed of growing plants, it loses its sharp definition in the growing season before it is clipped. Hedges take time to achieve their full height but, once that is achieved, they are a constant charge on the time of any gardener.

Not so hard landscaping, which, if properly constructed, requires little maintenance for many years – hence its appeal down the years to

the rich, the self-confident and the busy. In some of the most satisfactory gardens, the materials used for walling, paths and paving, pergolas, arches, formal pools, terraces, patios and the like have been locally sourced, in order to blend in with any vernacular architecture. Rodmarton Manor in Gloucestershire is a good example of this (see page 109).

Sir Edwin Lutyens was a master of the use of local materials. In many people's opinion, his and Gertrude Jekyll's most felicitous and

ABOVE Sir Edwin Lutyens was famous for both his sympathetic use of local materials and his creative approach to dealing with changes of level. He designed many semi-circular flights of steps, for example at Great Dixter. This is Hestercombe in Somerset, where he worked from 1903. These steps, being 'dry', are easily colonized by self-seeding wall plants such as *Erigeron karvinskianus*.

RIGHT The Great Plat at Hestercombe, with the pergola in the background, allowing glimpses of the Vale of Taunton, and the walk terminated by semi-circular steps. The main building material is the local Ham stone. The pergola exhibits another signature Lutyens device: alternate round and square pillars composed of Morte slates laid horizontally. The planting bears the Jekyll stamp, with masses of evergreen begonias.

adventurous collaboration was at Hestercombe in Somerset (from 1903). Here Lutyens used stone paving slabs as well as tiles set on edge to pave large areas and provide semi-circular steps, and a circular pool; the variety ensures that so much hard landscaping does not become wearisome to the eye. The pergola, which frames the view of Taunton Vale, has alternate round and square pillars, all made with thin slates laid horizontally. (The formal gardens were restored in 1973, and are now under the care of the Hestercombe Gardens Trust.)

On a much smaller, more intimate, scale is York Gate at Adel, just outside Leeds. Here, too, local stone, cobblestones and gravel were employed to make interesting and satisfying patterns which, together with sculptures and other garden ornaments, serve to draw the visitor onwards down the paths.

The most ornate of hard features in formal gardens are to be found in those gardens influenced by the Italianate style, for example Renishaw Hall, Derbyshire, Buscot Park and Iford Manor, the last two designed by Harold Peto, an early twentieth-century architect who lived at Iford Manor. At this garden on a terraced slope above the River Frome, he built an Italian-inspired loggia and installed many statues and architectural fragments, some of

OPPOSITE Local granite setts and grit, with a millstone to interrupt the path in the Iris Walk at York Gate, Adel, in Yorkshire. This is a beautifully designed, carefully laid-out garden of 'rooms', made in an old orchard, using a variety of local materials. It is full of first-rate detailing like this. The wicker baskets are for deadheaded flowers.

ABOVE The pavement maze at the entrance to York Gate.

FOLLOWING PAGES The Loggia Garden at Iford Manor in Wiltshire, with its stone pillars and large terracotta pots, standing on gravel and enclosed by box hedging. The most ornate and heavy hard features are often to be found in gardens in the Italian style.

ABOVE Part of Harold Peto's 328-foot/100-metre-long stone pergola at West Dean in West Sussex.

OPPOSITE A summer scene at The Grove, designed by David Hicks, with pleached horse chestnuts almost surrounding the swimming pool garden but allowing a view out into the landscape. The swimming pool is lined with black tiles, so that it looks more like an ornamental pond. In the far distance can just be glimpsed an 'eyecatcher' gap in the trees.

which he had picked up on travels to Europe (see page 29). The garden is highly structured, but also well planted. Peto also designed the remarkable 328-foot/100-metre-long pergola at West Dean in Sussex. Italianate gardens – with pergolas, pillars, loggias and classical statuary to the fore, but few flowers – were immensely popular with upper-class patrons in the last years of the Victorian age and the early decades of the twentieth century, perhaps because so many of them took their holidays in Italy. Sir George Sitwell, who made Renishaw, had an estate in Tuscany.

In many formal gardens over the years, the design has been influenced by the house architect and where that happens, there is a unity of purpose which can be winning. A good example is Ascott, where George Devey designed both the house and garden buildings such as the Tea House at the east end of the Madeira Walk and the Skating Hut overlooking the Lily Pond. Lutyens designed several houses and also their gardens, notably Munstead Wood in Surrey and Folly Farm in Berkshire. He also remodelled the house and garden at Great Dixter.

It should not be forgotten that utilitarian garden buildings – that is, anything for use rather than strictly for ornament – often help create the

right atmosphere and mood in the formal garden, being either square or rectilinear in shape. Great Dixter's handsome, traditional outhouses provide shelter and scale to the Sunken Garden, which they partly enclose, as well as creating one solid side to the Exotic Garden (formerly the Rose Garden).

One modern formal garden which clearly includes many facets of the style is The Grove in Oxfordshire, made by the late David Hicks, a garden and interior designer. Here he used spare, clean lines and good quality materials to create a coherent, satisfactory design, in a garden no more than 2 acres/0.8 hectares in extent. He cleverly used hedges, and openings in them, to create vistas into the countryside beyond, giving the garden a much greater sense of space than it truly possessed. (Borrowing the landscape is an idea which has been around at least since 1738 with William Kent's Rousham, of course.) The swimming pool is rectilinear, echoing the lines of the pleached horse chestnuts which all but surround it. In a more intimate space near the house, he used clipped shrubs of several types in different containers to add their own element of green architecture to the brick and stone behind.

The list of English gardens that are essentially formal is almost endless. The formal style has been a wonderfully rich and fruitful one in England, in places severely architectural, in others much more plant-based, but always offering the gardener stability and serenity, as well as balance and congruity. Moreover, with modern hedge-clipping machinery able to replace the human labour of old, it remains a surprisingly viable style, even in the present day.

OTHER GARDENS WITH IMPORTANT FORMAL ELEMENTS

Folly Farm, Berkshire
Old Rectory, Burghfield, Berkshire
Cliveden, Buckinghamshire
The Manor, Hemingford Grey
Cambridgeshire
Peckover House, Cambridgeshire
Lyme Park, Cheshire
Cotehele, Cornwall
Mount Edgcumbe, Cornwall
Trevarno Gardens, Cornwall
Holker Hall, Cumbria
Calke Abbey, Derbyshire
Hardwick Hall, Derbyshire
Castle Drogo, Devon
Tapeley Park, Devon
Audley End, Essex
Misarden Park Gardens, Gloucestershire
Hinton Ampner, Hampshire
How Caple Court, Herefordshire
Leeds Castle, Kent
Penshurst Place, Kent
Blickling Hall, Norfolk
Houghton Hall, Norfolk
Canons Ashby, Northamptonshire
Castle Ashby, Northamptonshire
Cottesbrooke Hall, Northamptonshire
Kirby Hall, Northamptonshire
Cragside House, Northumberland
Seaton Delaval Hall, Northumberland
Ashdown House, Oxfordshire
Greys Court, Oxfordshire
Barrington Court Garden, Somerset
Montacute House, Somerset
Somerleyton Hall, Suffolk
Ham House, Surrey
Loseley Park, Surrey
The Courts Garden, Wiltshire
Hanbury Hall, Worcestershire
Harewood House, Yorkshire

2

FLORAL
EXUBERANCE

The most casual observer could not fail to notice that the English garden is wonderfully colourful and exuberant, especially, but by no means exclusively, in the spring and summer time. This is due to a number of benign factors, most notably England's geographical position, climate and soils. It is also thanks to the commitment by a great number of individuals, whom one might hesitate to call a brotherhood or community but who certainly have a passion in common. The urge to grow flowers may be on the slow decline, a victim of burgeoning competition from other leisure pursuits, but it is still a potent national force, which helps shape the way our country looks.

England is at a longitude of 1 degree 30 minutes to 6 degrees, and a latitude of 50 degrees to nearly 56 degrees. The southernmost point, Land's End, is at the same latitude as Prague but, because England is an island, the winters are much less severe than those in the Czech Republic. It is surrounded on three sides by water, and part of the southern and western coasts are influenced by the Gulf Stream. Even away from the coast, the climate is temperate, with mild, wet winters and cool summers being the norm, although, since the beginning of the 1990s, there has been a noticeable trend towards rather hotter summers and drier winters. Around the coasts, February is the coldest month, while, inland, January and February are the coldest. The average minimum winter temperatures in England are –10°C/14°F in inland areas, with –5°C/23°F on the east coast and in the south and west of England. Rainfall ranged in 2004 from 2000 mm/80 inches in the wettest part of Cumbria to 950 mm/37 inches in Plymouth, 764 mm/30 inches in Birmingham, 639 mm/25 inches in York, and 593 mm/24 inches in London. The driest part is East Anglia, with Essex receiving an annual average of 573 mm/23 inches. The greatest number of sunshine hours occur on the south coast of England, the annual average there being around 1,750 hours, whereas in the mountains of northern England the average is less than 1,000 hours.

The soils in England are many and varied, in both constituents and acidity. They have a pH ranging from 4.5 to 8, with the majority of gardens falling between 5.5 and 7.5, that is, acid to slightly alkaline. As for soil structure, there are sandy soils, loams, silts, peats, chalks and clays, and combinations of those, such as sandy loam or limestone brash, which is stony, alkaline clay. Soil is as much a factor in determining the range of

OPPOSITE A sophisticated planting of bearded irises and lamb's ears (*Stachys byzantina*), with simple arches to lend verticality, in a private Gloucestershire garden.

BELOW Orange cannas and yellow and white dahlias bedded out for the summer at Great Dixter in East Sussex.

A cottage garden pergola, giving a sense of direction in an unpretentious country situation. There are tall blue delphiniums on the right, blue *Nepeta* 'Six Hills Giant' spilling over the path, and both blue and white forms of *Viola cornuta* at the base of the pergola on the left. The rose on the pergola is 'Violette', the one on the right in the foreground 'Comte de Chambord'. Roses are an important feature of any pergola, because their heads so often conveniently hang down. The garden was designed by Wendy Lauderdale.

plants grown as climate, but there are very few places indeed where something beautiful cannot be encouraged to thrive.

The combination of geographical position, generally temperate climate and a wide range of soils means that the great majority of plants native to the temperate world or high altitudes in subtropical areas (any indeed which have the capacity to withstand temperatures down to –10°C/14°F in winter) can be grown outside successfully somewhere in this country. There are exceptions to this, especially in mountainous areas, or those greatly exposed to wind or wet, where the choice of plants to use is more limited, but that is generally the case. In our cities, towns and suburbs, non-natural factors, such as heat escape, shade and shelter from buildings, encourage even tenderer plants to flourish. In general, though, subtropical plants cannot be trusted to survive all year round outside in England except in the Isles of Scilly and parts of Cornwall and Devon, and the centres of southern cities, such as London.

English gardeners, especially those living in the north of England or at high altitudes, learned centuries ago that creating microclimates helped the survival of plants which could not withstand below-zero temperatures in the open ground. Walls, fences, hedges and shelterbelts have been enduring and important elements of garden design for many centuries (see Chapter 1) not least because they are all garden features which promote warmer, stiller conditions. Moreover, gardeners have employed a number of devices for preserving tender plants, in particular digging up those with storage organs (dahlias, cannas and the like) and removing them to shelter for the winter. Growing tender plants in containers has also given the gardener the chance to move them under cover before the frosts.

As a result of factors both inside and outside our control, English gardeners are, therefore, able to look to a huge swathe of the world for plants to grow. Since the eighteenth century, both professional and amateur plant hunters have explored the temperate world for exotic additions to English gardens. Nowadays, everyone has the opportunity to enjoy these, since the country is thickly dotted with retail garden centres, served by a range of wholesale nurseries, and there are also specialist retail nurseries, where plants are often grown on site. It is easy enough, these days, to buy plants from Europe as well.

Our history shows a continuous adventurous desire to improve on that which has been introduced; both professional nurserymen and amateur gardeners have bred new plants, especially annual and perennial flowers. Many genera – roses, rhododendrons, petunias, pelargoniums and fuchsias to pluck a few almost at random – have been markedly altered over the years by hybridizers. The characteristics which have preoccupied them

ABOVE Evergreen azaleas in full flight below conifers and maples in the Punchbowl in the Valley Gardens, Windsor Great Park, Surrey in May. Sir Eric Savill made this garden, full of rare trees and shrubs, in undulating woodland when he ran out of space in the adjacent Savill Garden.

RIGHT Exuberant high-summer annuals informally planted in an Oxfordshire cottage garden: yellow marigolds (*Tagetes*), rudbeckia, sunflowers (*Helianthus*) and gladioli, with orange dahlias and pink *Verbena bonariensis* in the foreground.

most have been floriferousness, uniformity and compactness amongst annuals, and disease resistance, range of flower shape, hardiness and continuity of flowering amongst perennials and flowering shrubs.

The evidence for the richness of our floricultural heritage is there for all to see in the annually published *RHS Plant Finder*, which includes nearly 75,000 species and cultivated varieties (cultivars) on sale in participating nurseries. Although almost comprehensive, this gazetteer does not include some very small nurseries, nor plants handed down for generations in private gardens which for some reason have fallen out of commerce and so do not appear in nursery lists. The number of plants that are actually being grown in gardens is probably even larger. Knowledge of the needs and wants of all these plants, many of which have been in gardens for centuries, are known to somebody somewhere.

Flowers, as you would expect, have been the mainstay of a number of garden styles, both historical and contemporary, in particular the nineteenth-century passion for tender bedding-out, which survives in some public parks and private gardens to this day, as well as the fashion for subtropical gardening and the cottage garden style (see Chapter 4). It is the particular choice and placing of flowering plants which lends these garden styles their distinctive character and allows us to distinguish one from another. (Of course, when talking about floristic styles it is

Spring bedding, consisting almost entirely of tulips, in Regent's Park in London in spring. This style of gardening was first popular in the middle of the nineteenth century. It means competely changing the planting twice a year.

important to emphasize the fluidity and relentless dynamic of plant growth, which makes categorization more difficult than it would be with architectural features.)

The practice of bedding-out tender plants in parks and gardens arose in the early decades of the nineteenth century as a response to the desire to grow increasing numbers of tender plant species being introduced then from South Africa and North America. These plants – such as pelargoniums, petunias, verbenas, salvias and calceolarias – were and are wonderfully bright and colourful, and certainly more so than the perennials then grown in gardens. The fashion for planting them in discrete borders grew quickly, at a time when gardening labour was cheap and glasshouses were becoming commonplace. The idea grew

swiftly that they should be massed in single, clean colours and those colours should strongly contrast with each other.

If you planted your beds from scratch for the summer, frost-free months, it followed that you had to do something else with them from October to May. Thus developed, in the 1850s and 1860s, the practice of bedding-out in spring too. Spring bedding was dependent on a number of biennial genera which could be grown to a reasonable size to plant out in October, along with copious quantities of brightly colourful spring-flowering bulbs, such as tulips.[1] Notable in these schemes were, and are, wallflowers (*Cheiranthus*), forget-me-nots (*Myosotis*) and *Bellis perennis*. Bedding-out was popular among the entire garden-owning classes, which expanded rapidly in the nineteenth century with the building of suburbs on the edge of towns and cities.

ABOVE Bedding begonias with variegated 'spider plants' (*Tradescantia*) used as 'dot' plants in summer in Regent's Park. This summer bedding tradition has survived intact here since Victorian times.

FOLLOWING PAGES Spring bedding plants – hyacinths, tulips, wallflowers, *Bellis* and violas – in the Pond Garden at Hampton Court Palace in Surrey. (The Banqueting House is in the background.) The summer display includes heliotropes, pelargoniums, petunias and marigolds. The pleached limes in the foreground were planted as a windbreak in 1704.

The Victorians raised bedding-out almost to an art form, when they planted and clipped ground-covering tender plants, such as *Alternanthera*, to make a smooth carpet. If echeverias, sempervivums and sedums were used, it was possible to pick out initials and patterns in living plants. However, within a few decades, carpet-bedding came in for criticism from eminent commentators, in particular William Robinson, author of the highly influential *The English Flower Garden* (1883), who was never a man to hold back an opinion.

Despite his disapproval, carpet-bedding and bedding-out have survived to this day, albeit in simplified form, in public gardens and parks, where such colourful artificiality is consciously crowd-pleasing. And none the worse for that. Apart from its undeniable public attraction, bedding-out is still popular also in private gardens, where gardeners like to propagate plants from seed or small plugs each spring, and where containers are a feature, since bedding-out plants seem tailor-made for pot gardening.

Two of the most impressive Victorian-style bedding displays are to be found at Waddesdon (see page 30) and at Brodsworth Hall in Yorkshire. Here, in the garden of an 1860s Italianate mansion, English Heritage has reinstated bedding-out, in the authentic Victorian manner, in the Formal Garden, which retains the original shapes of the beds and includes some fascinating figure-of-eight dwarf box hedging. This bedding is brilliantly colourful in spring and summer, with masses of tulips, hyacinths, bellis and polyanthus in spring and nineteenth-century pelargoniums and standard fuchsias (amongst other plants) in summer. The colours are well co-ordinated so that, though they are bright (and a welcome contrast to all the clipped evergreens near by), they are not unsettling.

From the 1860s, so-called 'subtropical' bedding also became popular. In truth, all summer bedding was subtropical, in the sense that most of the plants used came from subtropical regions, but this term really refers to taller plants than those used for bedding-out, and those with large, impressive, exotic leaves: Chusan palms, *Ricinus communis*, cordylines, cannas and bananas, for example. For some, the colours of bedding were too much to endure, and foliage constituted a more restful, but equally intriguing, alternative.

In towns and cities, this kind of planting (sometimes called 'exotic', as a useful shorthand, although it often also includes hardy plants with impressive, tropical-looking leaves, such as *Fatsia*) is now common and, even in the country, warmer winters have encouraged an adventurous spirit at, for example, Cotswold Wildlife Park and Gardens, Oxfordshire, Athelhampton, Dorset, and Bourton House Garden, Gloucestershire. Christopher Lloyd at Great Dixter, East Sussex, was in the vanguard when he pulled up all the roses in the Lutyens-designed Rose Garden and replaced them with cannas, dahlias, tender verbenas and bananas. At East Ruston Old Vicarage, Norfolk, the Exotic Garden is thrillingly bright in colour in summer, and the preponderance of plants with large leaves

ABOVE A collection of exotics by the front door at Great Dixter, including the red-flowered, bronze-leaved *Canna* 'General Eisenhower', begonias and the pinkish white spikes of *Francoa*.

RIGHT A lively variation on the early nineteenth-century auricula theatre theme at Bryan's Ground in Herefordshire. Auriculas are set off well by hand-thrown terracotta pots.

makes for a pleasing jungly aspect. Much of the subtropical planting is replaced each year.

Increased travel abroad, especially since the 1960s to southern Europe, where container growing has long been popular, as well as the shrinking of garden space, has led English gardeners to think much harder about the use of pots and other containers for growing plants, both tender and hardy. Containers can, after all,

Crocus tommasinianus and snowdrops have seeded themselves down the sloping lawn in this Hampshire garden. For the bulbs to flourish, the leaves must be left for six weeks after flowering. The 'banks' of this 'river' are mown before that.

be used as small, discrete flower beds. There can be few gardens in the entire country that have been left untouched by this trend, and they are a marked feature of many open gardens in summer.

One of the best known is Bourton House, Gloucestershire, where warm-coloured terracotta pots of various sizes are used to particularly artistic effect, containing as they do tulips or polyanthus in the spring, followed by confident subtropical plantings in summer. These pots are in places clustered in groups most fetchingly. There are also handsome, fat-bellied urns in front of the south front of the house, and lead cisterns elsewhere with carefully arranged plantings of a variety of tender plants (see page 252). At Cotswold Wildlife Park and Gardens, there are exotic plantings and hanging baskets and container plantings in plenty. Rather more restrained, but also impressive for the care taken over them and the overall effect, are the containers to be found close to the house at the Old Rectory, Sudborough, Northamptonshire, as well as those at Brook Cottage, Alkerton,

Oxfordshire, The Old Rectory, Burghfield, Berkshire, and Tintinhull, Somerset. It is an axiom that those who can order their borders well usually have successful pots and containers too; they require a level of horticultural excellence, as well as inventive flair, to work well and create an impact.

Everything mentioned so far has been temporary, of course, with any scheme requiring to be changed twice a year. However, certain genera of plants seem to lend themselves to permanent mass planting, and gardeners take advantage of this. This is particularly true of spring-flowering bulbs, which grow in their thousands together in the wild. One of the finest displays of spring-flowering hoop-petticoat daffodils (*Narcissus bulbocodium*) is to be found at The Savill Garden, Surrey, a veritable alpine meadow in spring. It is in a damp part of the garden and thus goes some way towards mimicking the alpine snow-melt in spring.

Rather more highly bred cultivars of daffodil are to be found planted *en masse* at Bradenham Hall in Norfolk. Here, growing in grass under

An alpine meadow of the hoop-petticoat daffodil (*Narcissus bulbocodium*) in The Savill Garden at Windsor Great Park in Surrey.

LEFT Narcissi in dewy grass at the restored Saxon mill of Docton Mill in Devon.

ABOVE *Scilla bifolia*, narcissi and pale *Anemone nemorosa* growing in open woodland at Knightshayes in Devon.

FOLLOWING PAGES Narcissi and Japanese cherry trees flowering in spring at Bramdean House in Hampshire. The building is an apple house.

flowering Japanese cherries, magnolias and other choice and rare trees in the arboretum, are naturalized daffodils, ninety separate cultivars in groups or drifts, showing how much more effective this can be than planting them in a mixture.

There are some gardens where herbaceous perennials are planted for massed effect. Such a planting works best with a genus which has been extensively hybridized so that there is a good colour range: a successful example which comes immediately to mind is the Picton Garden at Old Court Nurseries, Colwall, in Worcestershire, where Michaelmas daisies (*Aster*) are grown.

If there is one enduring image of the English garden seared on the retinas of every garden visitor, however, it must be that of the herbaceous border. This is actually shorthand for 'hardy herbaceous perennial border', since perennials are the main components. As an element of garden design, it has a long history, being just about identical with the seventeenth-century 'mixed border', although with a greater range of plants in it. The oldest extant borders using almost exclusively herbaceous perennials are probably the fine, broad, double borders at Arley Hall in Cheshire, laid out by 1846. Contrary to popular belief, the passion for bedding-out, with its solid and contrasting blocks of colour, never banished the mixed border completely from gardens: it simply pushed it further from the house. In

ABOVE A beautifully modulated June colour scheme at Wollerton Old Hall in Shropshire.

RIGHT The longest-established herbaceous borders in the country, these are at Arley Hall in Cheshire: they date from before 1846. In the foreground are the blue stars of *Campanula lactiflora* 'Pritchard's Variety' and the spikes of *Eremurus stenophyllus*. Note also the yew buttresses and the far pavilion flanked by chess-piece topiary. These borders are designed to give colour from June until September and they 'hot up' as the season progresses.

addition, by the 1870s, herbaceous borders were enjoying a resurgence of interest, largely because of the influence of Gertrude Jekyll.

It is generally agreed that Miss Jekyll brought the herbaceous border to a high standard of interest and beauty, thanks to her combination of artistic sense and horticultural knowledge. She wrote prolifically about it. Most of her garden designs contained summer borders, and she developed the art of planting them in accordance with colour theory that she had learned when studying art as a young woman. This is what she wrote about her summer border at her home, Munstead Wood in Surrey:

> The planting of the border is designed to show a distinct scheme of colour arrangement. At the . . . near or western end, there are flowers of pure blue, grey-blue, white, palest yellow and palest pink; each colour partly in distinct masses and partly intergrouped. The colouring then passes through stronger yellow to orange and red. By the time the middle space of the border is reached, the colour is strong and gorgeous, but, as it is in good harmonies, it is never garish. Then the colour strength recedes in an inverse sequence through orange and deep yellow to pale yellow, white and palest pink; again with blue-grey foliage. But at this, the eastern end, instead of the pure blues we have purples and lilacs.

Looked at from a little way forward, for a wide space of grass allows this point of view, the whole border can be seen as one picture, the cool colouring at the ends enhancing the brilliant warmth of the middle. Then, passing along the wide path next to the border, the value of the colour arrangement is still more strongly felt. Each portion now becomes a picture in itself, and every one is of such a colouring that it best prepares the eye, in accordance with natural law, for what is to follow. Standing for a few moments before the endmost region of grey and blue, and saturating the eye to its utmost capacity with these colours, it passes with extraordinary avidity to the succeeding yellows. These intermingle in a pleasant harmony with the reds and scarlets, blood-reds and clarets, and then lead again to yellows. Now the eye has again become saturated, this time with the rich colouring, and has therefore, by the law of complementary colour, acquired a strong appetite for the greys and purples. These therefore assume an appearance of brilliancy that they would not have had without the preparation provided by their recently received complementary colour. [2]

The main border at The Priory at Kemerton, Worcestershire, was planted up after the Second World War by Peter Healing, who planned it after

BELOW 'Now the eye has again become saturated, this time with the rich colouring, and has therefore, by the law of complementary colour, acquired a strong appetite for the greys and purples. These therefore assume an appearance of brilliancy that they would not have had without the preparation provided by their recently received complementary colour,' wrote Gertrude Jekyll.[3] A view of the hottest part of the classic Jekyll border created at The Priory, Kemerton, in Worcestershire. Even the vegetable ruby chard beet has been enlisted to the cause.

OPPOSITE Bosvigo in Cornwall is a very skilfully planned garden, where summer- and autumn-flowering herbaceous perennials are a major feature (not so common in a county known best for its woodland gardens). There are differing planting schemes, including a Pink and Grey Garden and this scintillating Hot Border, the hot colours deepened by dark foliage. The yellow flower in the foreground is *Rudbeckia fulgida* var. *sullivantii* 'Goldsturm', and behind it, echoed by more across the path, is *Crocosmia* 'Star of the East'. At the back is red *Dahlia* 'Bishop of Llandaff' and yellow *Helianthus* 'Triomphe de Gand'.

RIGHT The main herbaceous border at Waterperry Gardens in Oxfordshire. With pink asters, yellow *Solidago* and *Rudbeckia*, it looks its best in early autumn.

FAR RIGHT Double herbaceous borders at Cothay Manor in Somerset, with *Echinacea pallida* in the foreground. This links up with the pink monarda, broken up by *Physostegia virginiana* 'Alba', and echoing the mallow (*Lavatera* x *clementii* 'Barnsley') in the container in the middle.

BELOW RIGHT A satisfying vertical emphasis planting at The Garden House at Buckland Monachorum, Devon, with grasses and *Kniphofia* in the foreground, behind which are *Lobelia*, *Macleaya* x *kewensis* and *Buddleja davidii*.

BELOW FAR RIGHT A symphony of blues and violets at Wollerton Old Hall in Shropshire. This formal garden, made over the last twenty years, complements the fine half-timbered sixteenth-century house. Prominent are delphiniums, ground-covering geraniums and arching sprays of *Veronicastrum*.

reading Gertrude Jekyll's chapter on colour in *The English Flower Garden* by William Robinson while serving in the army in Germany at the end of the war. At a time when hot colours were generally out of fashion, he and his wife made a remarkable border (300 feet/90 metres long by 18 feet/6 metres wide), with a background of yew hedge, in a classic Jekyllian way, starting with cool colours which gradually heated up into a bonfire of crocosmias, dahlias, kniphofia, achillea and rudbeckia and then cooled off.

Many, many gardeners followed Miss Jekyll's example, or attempted to. From time to time her ideas have gone out of fashion because of the amount of maintenance required to do these borders properly, the colour sophistication needed or a desire for only pastel colours, but they have gained ground in the last twenty years, when bright colours have become more fashionable and warmer summers have made them more successful.

In the 1970s and 1980s, the written works of Gertrude Jekyll were reprinted and found a new, appreciative audience very keen to get away

The Rose Garden at Upton Grey in Hampshire, faithfully restored to Gertrude Jekyll's original plans of 1909. The roses, as specified by Miss Jekyll, are 'Mme Laurette Messimy' (China 1887) and 'Mme Lombard' (Tea 1878), with pink peony 'Sarah Bernhardt' fading to white, and *Lilium regale* about to flower on the central plinth. Ros Wallinger, who began the restoration after 1984, has written a book about it (see the Select Bibliography on page 378).

from the disadvantages and narrow-mindedness of low-maintenance, ground-cover gardening, popular at the time. Her ideas were adapted to smaller gardens in a dozen books written by garden designers; and some heroic historical research and reconstruction have been done at actual Jekyll/Lutyens gardens – for example, at Hestercombe Gardens in Somerset and The Manor House, Upton Grey in Hampshire, which the owners reconstructed after 1984 as it would have been in 1909.[4]

Pale harmonious colours have always found favour with gardeners, who sometimes find hotter or clashing colours difficult to deal with, and many a lovely garden depends heavily on them. Margery Fish stamped her imprimatur on their attractions ('We all have our preferences. Mine are for the pastel shades, for with them it is possible to have a riot without disagreement'[5]) and many gardeners, especially timid ones, feel happier with them. When

LEFT The Long Border at Great Dixter in late summer. Self-seeders like *Verbascum* are encouraged and some perennials, like *Helenium* 'Moerheim Beauty' (bottom right-hand corner) are deadheaded after the first flowers, and flower again.

ABOVE Penelope Hobhouse, garden designer and erstwhile chatelaine of both Hadspen and Tintinhull, has made this garden in Dorset since 1993. The walled garden behind the house is exuberantly colourful, full of interesting plants which spill out on to the gravel paths. The standard trees in the background are the false acacia (*Robinia pseudoacacia*).

visiting gardens became popular and possible after the Second World War, people discovered that the National Trust seemed to have a liking for them as well.

It is perhaps rather remarkable that the herbaceous border has survived to the present day, considering how much care those made by Miss Jekyll and other gardeners needed. Because they are intended to look substantial and colourful for only three or four months, they require the 'dropping-in' of plants during the season to augment the flowering: lilies and other summer-flowering bulbs, clematis trailing through. Such attention to detail can still be seen in some gardens today, such as Arley Hall, and Great Dixter, where the Long Border is also 'refreshed' with annuals sown late and planted in summer, as well as summer-flowering bulbs. At East Ruston Old Vicarage, the owners refer to their borders as the Long Borders, in preference to 'herbaceous borders', because they put other elements, such as shrubs, climbers and annuals, in them.

ABOVE In the private garden of a converted barn in Oxfordshire, the borders are predominantly herbaceous but also include shrubs, such as roses, and subshrubs, such as lavender and purple sage. This sort of combination of plants is to be seen in many, many gardens in England.

RIGHT These mirror-image borders are at Bramdean House in Hampshire, and include *Nepeta* 'Six Hills Giant' at the front with carmine *Geranium psilostemon* and yellow *Thalictrum flavum*.

Without this refreshment, herbaceous borders only look *au point* for a limited period; nevertheless in many a country garden when they are flowering well they look magnificent. Every garden visitor must have their own favourites: the double border at Westwell Manor in Oxfordshire, perhaps, or the mirror-image ones at Bramdean House in Hampshire; those at Forde Abbey in Dorset, with their yew columns, the broad pure herbaceous borders going down to the waterside at Newby Hall, Yorkshire, or those at the two best gardens in Northamptonshire, Coton Manor and Cottesbrooke Hall. Broughton Castle in Oxfordshire and Kiftsgate Court in Gloucestershire also have borders with exhilarating colour schemes. In addition, there are the much-admired herbaceous borders at Rodmarton Manor, Gloucestershire, which flank both sides of a stone path in the Long Garden, are interrupted by a circular pool and clipped yews, and terminate in a vernacular stone summerhouse. And, at Nymans in Sussex, classically height-graded perennials, with taller shrubs

ABOVE This is Sleightholme Dale Lodge in Yorkshire, a terraced garden on a steep slope, close to the North York Moors. This border is not schemed, but it is wonderfully vibrant and colourful, as seen here in July, and full of unusual, well-grown plants.

FAR RIGHT Double herbaceous borders at Rodmarton Manor in Gloucestershire, with *Salvia turkestanica*, *Aruncus dioicus* (the creamy plumes on the left) and *Thalictrum flavum* (the yellow flowers on the right) prominent. These borders are broken up by yew buttresses and a circular pond, and there is a summerhouse at the end. The quality of the landscaping is exceptional and adds much to the pleasure to be had in this country garden, behind an exceptionally beautiful Arts and Crafts house which dates from 1906.

BELOW RIGHT This mixed border at Broughton Castle in Oxfordshire is predominantly pink, with roses 'Fantin-Latour' on the left, 'Albertine' on the wall and pink 'Marguerite Hilling' on the right, and clouds of *Crambe cordifolia* (top left), *Alchemilla mollis* (bottom right) and pink *Geranium endressii* spreading on to the path. A seat under the 'window' affords a glimpse of the Ladies' Garden beyond (see page 19).

FOLLOWING PAGES Herterton House is a highly structured garden, made by the present owners, set in a wild Northumbrian landscape. It consists of a number of compartments, all different, bounded by hedges and with topiary incidents. This is the Flower Garden, the underlying structure of which is based on Mondrian's paintings. The colour scheming is very careful: cool close to the house but becoming hotter further away. The owners have built the tall gazebo, which looks both into the garden and into the wider countryside.

behind, grow each side of a narrow path in the walled garden. All these gardens are, as the gazetteers put it, 'worth a detour'.

Planting in garden borders is often not now done in strict accordance with Jekyll's precepts, especially with regard to types of plant – shrubs and roses being a feature of many borders these days – but her emphasis on planting drifts, rather than blocks, and planting some taller plants towards the front, with smaller ones drifting towards the back, is still an ideal we think worth pursuing.

Gertrude Jekyll is also at least in part responsible for the idea of the one-colour-themed border or garden, an idea taken up enthusiastically by Vita Sackville-West in her White Garden, and by many other gardeners. Of course, Gertrude Jekyll never advocated that the flowers be entirely of one colour (if that were possible, since in any event texture affects

BELOW The Red Border at Hadspen in Somerset, designed by Nori and Sandra Pope. They advocated planting in 'a developing monochrome' – that is, in a single colour. The flowers here include *Geum* 'Mrs J. Bradshaw', *Tropaeolum majus*, *Rosa* 'Lilli Marlene', *Dahlia* 'Bishop of Llandaff', *Arctotis* x *hybrida* 'Flame' and *Lychnis chalcedonica*, with agapanthus, *Phormium tenax* and *Tropaeolum majus* providing foliage.

OPPOSITE The White Garden at Sissinghurst in Kent, with the central gazebo smothered in *Rosa mulliganii*. This shows what variety there is amongst white flowers – there are blue-white ones and some yellow-white – and also the importance of texture and foliage.

how we perceive colour), arguing instead that they should include green, glaucous, pale blue and pink; the artistry, she said, was in keeping the main white theme while weaving minor variations on it, as in pale-mauve-flowered hostas, and indeed green and silver-variegated green leaves as foils, and to relieve the eye from too concentrated a visual experience. In the large country house garden, separate enclosures for separate groups of colours are common, and often very successful: the colour-themed borders – yellow, blue and mauve – in the 4-acre/1.5-hectare walled garden at Parham Park in West Sussex, for instance, and the White Garden and Purple Border at Wartnaby Gardens, Leicestershire.

In recent years, some gardeners have been highly adventurous in their planting schemes, using a wide palette of colours and being very conscious of the value of green, both as a colour in its own right and as a way of uniting or buffering different schemes. The term 'colourist' has come to be used for gardeners who strive to use colour, of both flower and foliage, in a bold and experimental way. Most influential have been Nori and Sandra Pope, who ran the walled garden and woodland at Hadspen in Somerset from 1987 to 2005, and wrote about their ideas on colour.[67] Much sophisticated experimentation took place in the old Georgian 2-acre/0.8-hectare kitchen garden with its wonderful, steeply curved, 700-foot/213-metre-long red brick wall, whose apex faces south.

ABOVE A yellow border at Clare College, Cambridge, which yet contains some blue as well. The yellows are composed of the daisy-flowered, all-summer-flowering *Buphthalmum salicifolium* as well as the tall evening primrose (*Oenothera biennis*) and the compact marigold *Tagetes* 'Lemon Queen'.

The borders beneath this wall were composed of herbaceous perennials[8] and shrub roses, and changed colour as the wall wound round. There was, for example, a Chartreuse/Violet Border, a Plum Grey Border and a Double Yellow Border.

The Popes' view, as expressed in their books, is that substantial contrasts should be used very sparingly in a garden picture, and that harmony should really be the major key, as it were. (They tend to use musical metaphors and it's catching.) That does not necessarily mean pastel colours, however. 'As a system of creating dramatic tension, increasing perception and manipulating mood change, we advocate planting in a developing monochrome'[9] (monochrome meaning single colour). 'Less is More', they said, and by using monochrome plantings they could closely control the colour shift, the saturation of colour and the tonal change from dark to light. 'Using a single colour also makes it possible to focus on foliage and on flower shapes, on the rhythm and structure of the planting and, of course, on the full impact of what the colour offers emotionally.'[10]

And that is what they did. For seven months a year. In order to achieve that, they resorted to legitimate gardeners' stratagems, such as pinching

ABOVE One of the Popes' bravura plantings at Hadspen in Somerset. This was the Double Yellow Border. Amongst the bright yellow incidents are *Euphorbia polychroma* (left foreground), *Paeonia lutea* var. *ludlowii* (right foreground), the golden-leaved *Lonicera nitida* 'Baggesen's Gold' and the yellow-variegated pampas grass *Cortaderia sellowana* 'Aureolineata' (syn. 'Gold Band') (left middle ground). The tall plant on the left is a foxglove tree (*Paulownia tomentosa*), which has been stooled – that is, cut back very hard so that the leaves are much bigger than usual.

RIGHT Yellow and blue planting of impressive quality in the Walled Garden at Packwood House in Warwickshire, with behind it the sixteenth-century timber-framed house. The very large daisy flowers are *Inula*, the smaller ones *Anthemis*, and height is provided by pink *Filipendula* and the pink plumes of *Maclaya cordata*. These bright flower borders are a considerable contrast to the yew topiary garden close by (see page 52).

LEFT ABOVE *Verbascum* 'Helen Johnson', *Monarda* 'Beauty of Cobham' and pink *Nicotiana* x *sanderae* 'Domino Salmon Pink' at Hadspen. The warm apricot of verbascum 'warms up' its companions.

LEFT BELOW Flat-headed *Achillea* 'Terracotta' provides contrast of form and colour with crimson-lake *Allium sphaerocephalon* in a thrilling midsummer planting at Scampston Hall in Yorkshire.

ABOVE Purple-leaved sedum, crocosmia and *Scutellaria incana*, together with the foliage plant *Helichrysum petiolare* 'Limelight', in Carol Klein's garden at Glebe Cottage Plants, Devon.

back some stems of herbaceous perennials, including phloxes, in April, to stagger the flowering.

However adventurous and innovative a gardener is, the season of the year dictates colour scheming to quite a large extent, of course: for example, spring means fresh greens, whites, yellows, deep blues predominantly (hence the usefulness as a counterweight of red tulips), while early summer means violet-blues, deep pinks, whites and purples; high summer is orange, purple, cream and apricot and late summer and early autumn carmine pinks, mauves, bronzes and straw-yellows. Within these basic categories, the ingenuity of the gardener has devised many variations but, essentially, these remain immutable. That is why the Popes were so very clever in devising schemes lasting for seven months, based on the same colours. The greatest choice is to be found in plants which flower between June and September and, up and down the country, creative gardeners grapple with the huge host of plants available to them for that season.

ABOVE A pink planting by the talented colourist and garden designer Rupert Golby includes *Verbena* 'Sissinghurst', the darker pink *Verbena* 'Kemerton' together with *Diascia vigilis* and the pink bells of *Penstemon* 'Evelyn'. The slate-blue seedheads of poppies add another element.

RIGHT Sweet peas, on simple beanpole tripods, in the walled garden at West Green House in Hampshire.

Another clever colourist is Marylyn Abbott, who took over the garden at West Green House in Hampshire in 1993. This very handsome eighteenth-century house has a small park with a lake, a number of neo-classical architectural features by Quinlan Terry and a large eighteenth-century walled garden, divided into a number of gardens, some of them thrillingly planted, especially with masses of tulips in the spring. Again harmonies in colour are more evident than contrasts. 'The borders are never static, with a total redesign and planting every five years . . . they bring together combinations of oil, purple and ruby, the colours of steel, then earth shades in separate plantings.'[11] Marylyn Abbott has written about her gardens (she also has one in Australia) and her ideas about colour planting.[12]

Of course, these gardeners are not only concerned with flower colour. Foliage and texture as well as plant habit are also very important to them. They know that pleasing and deliberately planned associations, rather than indiscriminate jumbles of disparate elements, make for a much more satisfying garden picture. It is one reason why amateur gardeners visit open gardens, to learn how such associations are made.

Reflecting on the early decades of the twentieth century, as shown in contemporary *Country Life* articles and photographs, Tim Richardson wrote: 'Perhaps because of the opportunities it presented for individuality and originality, the herbaceous border became, and was to remain, the national horticultural obsession . . . Then, as now, the herbaceous border was a horticultural laboratory in which any combination of plants could be attempted, and it remains the pre-eminent showcase for the gardener's skill.'[13] Quite.

This is what you can grow if you have frosts only once in a blue moon. The yellow-green heads of *Aeonium canariense*, the red flowers of *Lampranthus spectabilis* 'Tresco Fire' and the lighter *L.s.* 'Tresco Peach' give the Middle Terrace at Tresco Abbey on the Isles of Scilly a thoroughly foreign and subtropical look.

More permanent plantings of tender plants are also essayed in English gardens, especially in parts of the country where frosts are a real rarity, such as Abbotsbury Sub-Tropical Gardens in Dorset, Overbecks overlooking Salcombe in Devon and Tresco Abbey in the Scilly Isles. Being all close to the sea, they have remarkably mild and temperate microclimates.[14] These gardens are mainly laid out in an informal manner, and are jungly in parts, but also very strongly colourful when the plants are in flower. Since the sun shines especially brightly in summer in these districts, those colours zing where elsewhere they might blind.

Lack of water in summer, or a fear of future droughts as the climate changes, has also led people such as Beth Chatto of Beth Chatto Gardens, Elmstead Market, Essex, and Christopher Holliday consciously to seek out drought-tolerant plants – in Christopher Holliday's case, those with emphatic, 'sharp' foliage, which make a vigorous statement without flowers (see pages 187–9).[15] Many of these come from southern Europe and the near East, where hot, dry summers are the norm.

A double yellow snowdrop, *Galanthus nivalis* 'Lady Elphinstone', much prized by enthusiasts, who are often known as galanthophiles. A plantsman's delight, all right.

Mediterranean-style gardens may also be found at Denmans, West Sussex, and East Ruston Old Vicarage, Norfolk.

What is interesting is that, for a long time, it has been very important to English people that they rise to the challenge of growing such an enormous variety of plants. The term 'plantsman' has positive overtones for us; we use it, admiringly, for the many individuals, both men and women, who study how to grow plants, many of them rare and/or difficult, successfully. We English are proud of being able to do that. For centuries there has been a very sturdy and enduring tradition of plantsmanship in this country, when the layout of the garden has been subservient, even incidental, to the plants grown in it. There is a strong vein of botanical enquiry running through English gardening, and there will always be people for whom the plants themselves are the guiding light, and for whom the most important thing is to give them the conditions in which they will most thrive (even if that means ugly bulb frames and aluminium glasshouses) and where they will be best viewed and studied. As the landscape architect Sylvia Crowe wrote in *Garden Design* (1958): 'There are two attitudes to plants in gardens. One is that the purpose of a garden is to grow plants, the other is that plants are one of the materials to be used in the creation of a garden.'[16]

There are particular genera, or groups of genera, which seem particularly to attract plantsmen. Snowdrops, hostas, dahlias, ferns and every kind of alpine are all popular candidates – the more challenging, the better. However, there are also plantsmen with wider interests, especially those with woodland gardens who can encompass an interest not only in rhododendrons but in camellias and magnolias as well. Some go for trees as a whole.

It should be emphasized that very often, although not invariably, plantsmen's gardens are lovely places to visit, even if the visitor spends

(see pages 163–4)

ABOVE Stimulating colour planting for July in the Summer Garden at The Old Rectory, Duntisbourne Rouse, Gloucestershire, a garden made by the garden designer and writer Mary Keen. Like Carol Klein, she has both a good eye and strong plant knowledge, by no means a common combination. The box sentinels around the planted 'copper' are *Buxus sempervirens* 'Graham Blandy'.

OPPOSITE The tulip 'Carnaval de Nice' flowering in front of variegated white honesty (*Lunaria annua* 'Alba Variegata') and a deep red *Paeonia delavayi*, in the same garden.

most of their time with their eyes on the ground, trying to decipher labels.

And there have been, and are today, people who combine both plantsmanship and skill in garden design and plant associations. Lawrence Johnston, the creator of Hidcote was one, Vita Sackville-West at Sissinghurst another. In the present day, there is of course Beth Chatto; also Mary Keen, a garden designer and author with an excellent knowledge of plants, at the Old Rectory, Duntisbourne Rouse, Gloucestershire, Carol Klein, a nurserywoman in the Chatto tradition at Glebe Cottage Plants, Devon, Carol Skinner at Eastgrove Cottage Garden (see pages 163–4), and Vanessa Cook, who has laid out a lovely country garden, well suited to its context, next to her nursery at Stillingfleet Lodge, Yorkshire. Such gardeners must truly have been blessed by the Good Fairy at their baptisms.

OTHER FLOWERY GARDENS

(including plantsmen's gardens)
Toddington Manor, Bedfordshire
Mariners, Berkshire
Abbots Ripton Hall, Cambridgeshire
Anglesey Abbey, Cambridgeshire
The Crossing House, Cambridgeshire
Docwra's Manor, Cambridgeshire
Hardwicke House, Cambridgeshire
21 Lode Road, Cambridgeshire
Peckover House, Cambridgeshire
Lyme Park, Cheshire
Caerhays Castle, Cornwall
Copt Howe, Cumbria
Dalemain, Cumbria
Halecat, Cumbria
Dove Cottage, Derbyshire
Hardwick Hall, Derbyshire
Coleton Fishacre, Devon
Marwood Hill, Devon
Overbecks, Devon
Cranborne Manor, Dorset
Glen Chantry, Essex
Eastleach House, Gloucestershire
Brandy Mount House, Hampshire
Spinners, Hampshire
Abbey Dore Gardens, Herefordshire
Stockton Bury Gardens, Herefordshire
Blickling Hall, Norfolk
Bradenham Hall, Norfolk
Houghton Hall, Norfolk
Cottesbrooke Hall, Northamptonshire
Bide-a-Wee Cottage, Northumberland
Cragside House, Northumberland
Wallington, Northumberland
Kingston Bagpuize House, Oxfordshire
Pettifers, Oxfordshire
The Dower House, Morville, Shropshire
Pashley Manor, Sussex
The Courts, Wiltshire
Burton Agnes Hall, Yorkshire

3

THE
LANDSCAPE
TRADITION

There is one style of garden in England whose importance, both historical and aesthetic, is so great that examples of it have survived intact for over two hundred years. The 'landscape garden', developed as a discrete style from the second decade of the eighteenth century, reigned almost unopposed amongst the landed wealthy for more than eighty years. So strong and defined were the principles behind the style, and so coherent was it as an idea, that there are still close to a hundred examples of it that are open to the public at one time or another in the course of the year.

The 'landscape' style was a reaction against the severely geometric formality of seventeenth-century Baroque gardens, influenced as they had been by Dutch, French and Italian gardens (see pages 22–9). Although that formality was breaking down somewhat, in the outer reaches of gardens at least, by 1700, the 'landscape garden' nevertheless represented a considerable change in direction. A reaction against the tyranny of the straight line can be traced to thoughtful gardeners such as William Temple as early as the end of the seventeenth century. There was also a growing chorus of criticism of the artificiality of knots and parterres, especially by the intelligentsia such as John Evelyn and, later, Alexander Pope and Joseph Addison; these men provided the intellectual underpinning for the style. Pope, the poet and commentator, for example, had three rules for his garden in Twickenham: it should contain 'the Contrast, the Management of Surprises and the Concealment of Bounds'. To these people, a garden should be designed to promote reflection and to stir emotions in the beholder.

These commentators persuaded early eighteenth-century educated gentlemen to strive towards achieving Arcadia in their estates (Arcadia being a Greek mythical land of pastoral quiet and content). Giving prominence to the idea that Nature should triumph over Art seemed the way to achieve this.[1] (It is a rich irony that it was the ultra-sophisticated who wished to 'get back to nature', but 'twas ever thus.) The fashionable garden became one that strove to resemble a Claude Lorrain or Poussin idealized landscape (this was the age of the Grand Tour, after all) with plenty of Classically inspired temples and monuments as 'eyecatchers' to make the garden tour an interesting and edifying experience. This was 'naturalism', where Nature was clean, tidy and tamed.

Throughout the first half of the eighteenth century, landowners, often with the help of professionals, felt their way towards a different

OPPOSITE The statue of Apollo, with his back to the Long Walk at Rousham House, Oxfordshire.

BELOW It is hard to overestimate the importance of the restoration of Stowe Landscape Gardens in Buckinghamshire from the 1980s. The process has been so complex and far-reaching that it has provided an enormous boost to the restoration of gardens, not just eighteenth-century landscape ones. This is the Rotunda of 1721, with the figure of Venus recently restored to it.

style, supported by philosophical ideas and classical learning. The landscape garden, once developed, had certain features: a serpentine lake (often made out of an earlier rectilinear canal), plantations of trees, often curved in shape, and drives and walks which meandered through the property, so that the garden could no longer be seen at once, or from any one standpoint, but revealed itself at particular, and usually specially chosen, places. A variety of garden pavilions, obelisks and statuary were carefully placed to close vistas, or to add interest to the walk and prompt reflection. In some places these inclined towards the Gothic rather than Classical, especially as the century wore on. To achieve all this, especially in a flat landscape, often meant earth-sculpting (which they would not have called it in those days), thousands of tons of earth being moved, in some cases, to contour the land and create mounds or lakes. The radical departure from earlier

An accident of history froze the Elizabethan garden at Lyveden New Bield in Northamptonshire in time in 1605. Much of the moat and sculpted landforms, such as this spiral prospect mound, have been uncovered in recent years by the National Trust. With its roofless Banqueting House, this is a garden of great atmosphere as well as historical significance.

styles resided in the fact that, apart from the house itself, there were no longer any straight lines in the garden.

These gardens were solid works of engineering, requiring detailed surveys and plans, and they were very, very expensive. This was a style for the country squire and aristocrat with both the self-confidence and the broad acres to achieve it, and the clout to move houses or villages out of the way if necessary. How dedicated garden owners must have been to the dictates of fashion to allow their knot gardens, parterres and *allées* to be swept away, and replaced by smooth, grazed grass, expanses of water and sinuous paths! It is extraordinary to think that a large number of country landowners allowed themselves to be persuaded that the garden should become like an idealized classical landscape.

The invention of the ha-ha (a sunken ditch between pasture and lawn usually in front of the house, retained by stone or brick, and effectively

stock-proof) meant that the area immediately adjacent to the house could blend seamlessly into this landscape, full of sheep safely grazing, without those sheep making a nuisance of themselves near the house. The ha-ha – so called because that was most people's instinctive reaction when they came across one unawares – was first noted in d'Argenville's *Theory and Practice of Gardening* (translated from French and published in England in 1712), and it is likely that the first one to be constructed in England was made at Levens in 1695.

Visiting such a garden was the equivalent of, these days, sitting down to watch a film, such as *Play it Again, Sam*, *West Side Story* or *Kiss Me Kate*, full of references that the viewer is meant to 'get'. These references and allusions were not difficult – indeed they may even have seemed commonplace to the educated gentry, reared on Homer, Virgil and Ovid in particular; however, in the intervening 250 years they have become largely impenetrable to us, which means that the delight we gain from walking in an eighteenth-century landscaped park is now restricted to its aesthetic value and perhaps also its 'naturalism', to which we tend to respond positively. That said, anyone visiting Stowe, Buckinghamshire, or Stourhead, Wiltshire, say, should find much more enjoyment from a visit if they take time to read the guidebooks carefully.

For those landowners with the money and ambition to 'improve' their property, this style was a bold statement of present prosperity and future intent. Surrendering to the idea of the landscape garden had to be total; there could be no half-measures. But although the style was a huge change from what went before, it would be a mistake to think that the garden became formless, in the sense of being without design. Far from it. It was more that the form was created by hills and valleys, clumps of trees, winding paths, light and shade and architectural incidents. Moreover, contrary to popular belief, 'Capability' Brown did not always remove all features of the earlier garden: he sometimes left linear elements such as avenues of trees, like the double avenue of elms at Wimpole Hall, Cambridgeshire. And there were more flowers in the landscape garden than has been generally appreciated. On the outer edges of tree clumps, for example, were very often flowering shrubs – lilacs, roses, honeysuckle and so on. They were not grouped, being rather usually planted as single specimens, but they brought a touch of colour to what was otherwise an extremely green scene.

Those large gardens which withstood the pressure of fashion were few and far between. The fact that some did was the result of geographical or intellectual remoteness, or an accident of history. Most notable amongst these is Lyveden New Bield in Northamptonshire, which was frozen in time in 1605 on its owner's death, and lay hidden beneath a riot of brambles and ash seedlings until renovated late in the twentieth century by the National Trust. Other survivals of earlier styles include Westbury Court, Gloucestershire, Levens Hall, Cumbria,

Boughton House, Northamptonshire, Bramham Park, Yorkshire, and Melbourne Hall, Derbyshire.

The task of turning English garden and countryside into 'landscape' was entrusted to a small band of professionals, whose reputations gained ground the more gardens that they worked on (although it should not be underestimated how many gardens were laid out by their owners with no professional involved at all). Their fame spread by word of mouth amongst a small but wealthy elite. Most famous, of course, was Lancelot 'Capability' Brown. He was pre-dated by the (at the time) equally famous Charles Bridgeman and William Kent, and followed by Humphry Repton.

Charles Bridgeman became Royal Gardener in 1728 but also worked in a number of non-royal gardens, sweeping away parterres, and putting in ha-has and lakes. He worked at Rousham House in Oxfordshire before William Kent, and laid out the remarkable turf amphitheatre at Claremont in Surrey from about 1715 (one of the first landscape gardens to be

Bramham Park in Yorkshire is a rare survival of the French style. It was designed probably by the owner, Robert Benson, in the early years of the eighteenth century. Very little changed in this garden after 1763. This is the Four Faces Urn from which radiate three tall *allées* of beech. The one on the right leads to canalized water, called the 'T-pond', designed so that the eye skims over the water to a far temple, the Temple of Lead Lads. There are 2 miles/3.2 kilometres of beech hedges in the main gardens; in places they are 6 metres/25 feet tall and 2 metres/6 feet wide. The trees close by have their lower branches removed so that they do not interfere with the hedges.

restored in the twentieth century, from 1975), as well as a round pond (the Round Bason) which William Kent then turned into a lake, adding a temple on the informal island in the middle of it. He was also the first to be called in at Stowe, creating the ha-ha there, which bounds the entire garden. His work is often seen as transitional between the French style and the full-blown landscape one.

William Kent was a painter, stage designer and architect who had spent time in Italy. His influence was crucial; it was of him that Horace Walpole famously said that 'he leapt the fence and saw that all nature was a garden'. He began work for Lord Burlington at Chiswick House, London, which was a Classical house in a basically formal garden, with two *pattes d'oie*, and Classical buildings. Kent turned the formal canal into a serpentine lake, and put in a ha-ha, grotto, cascade and meandering paths through the groves of trees.

He was keen to get away from the canalization of water. In his gardens, water usually became serpentine, as it tends to be in nature. He understood the importance in a garden tour of light and shade and he brought the countryside into the garden (*à la* Pope's 'Concealment of Bounds'). He was a devotee of loose clumps of trees, for framing views and as eyecatchers. Perhaps his training as a stage designer made him a natural garden dramatist; certainly when walking through a Kentian landscape such as Rousham I find it full of a quiet drama.

Rousham has a charm perhaps above all other early eighteenth-century landscapes for me, since it is still in a very rural situation, is in private hands, and has not changed since 1741. Smaller than Stowe or Stourhead and

less grand, it nevertheless has its share of statuary and architectural gems, especially the arcaded Praeneste, which looks down on the meandering and perfectly charming River Cherwell. Bridgeman began work on the garden between 1725 and 1734, and included a turf amphitheatre, but the main work that survives is that of William Kent (of 1737–41). It is his finest garden. There are still pools, cascades, winding rivulets and secret woodland walks, and many lovely views into countryside beyond the garden, especially the 'eye-catcher' mill to be seen across the river and road.

Rousham is almost intimate in scale; Stowe, on the other hand, is enormous. It is the landscape garden *par excellence*, true to the ideals of the style: Bridgeman, Kent and Brown worked there at various times. Moreover, the garden buildings were the work of some of the finest contemporary architects, including Sir John Vanbrugh and Robert Adam.

Bridgeman was called in to advise at Stowe Landscape Gardens by the owner Sir Richard Temple (later Viscount Cobham) in 1713, to make a new garden, and he created a five-sided ha-ha, as well as pools, serpentine

OPPOSITE The epitome of English rural tranquillity: the River Cherwell at the bottom of the Rousham garden in Oxfordshire.

ABOVE Strikingly modern in look, although dating from the late 1730s, the rill winds through the woodland towards William Kent's Temple of Echo above the river. Rousham is a sublimely peaceful and even understated garden, almost intimate in scale in comparison to the other great eighteenth-century gardens, and the best place to see William Kent's craft, since it has remained unchanged since 1741.

ABOVE William Kent's talent for theatre design can be seen at Rousham. This is a garden of light and shade, and of shades of green.

RIGHT The seven-arched Praeneste at Rousham by William Kent, who worked there from 1737 to 1741. In Kent's time there were seats for people to sit on as they looked across the winding River Cherwell and beyond into the wider countryside. Clipped evergreens are a major feature of this garden, and have been since its inception. Rousham is an example of a garden still faithful to its creator's vision. Horace Walpole called it 'the most engaging of all Kent's work. It is Kentissimo.'

walks and an ambitious set of *allées* into woodland. Kent was next, in the 1720s and 1730s, changing Bridgeman's Octagonal Pool into a lake and creating the Elysian Fields (this was an English Arcadia, after all). In 1738, a magnificent Palladian Bridge, modelled on the one at Wilton, was erected over the eastern end of the Octagonal Pool. He also designed the Temple of British Worthies and the Temple of Ancient Virtue. In the 1740s, while he was head gardener there, 'Capability' Brown created the Grecian Valley, without any garden buildings but with plenty of shaping of the land form and planting of belts of trees. At the same time James Gibbs designed a Gothic Temple and a Classical Queen's Temple. This is a wonderful garden to choose for a reflective walk, in which you catch glimpses of the buildings as you go. Even if the classical allusions pass you by, it is still a very beautiful place. Stowe's restoration, undertaken by Dominic Cole and Land Use Consultants, was not only a huge credit to those involved but an example which others have followed.

Every eighteenth-century landscaper has been eclipsed by the reputation of Lancelot 'Capability' Brown, whose work, mainly in the second half of the eighteenth century (he died in 1783), was prodigious. William Cowper, the poet, called him the 'omnipresent magician'. It is said he worked on 170 landscapes. Neo-Classical temples were by his time less fashionable, and Georgian architecture, which had clean, spare lines and excellent proportions, pre-eminent. His landscapes demonstrated those same

OPPOSITE The Palladian Bridge at Stowe Landscape Gardens in Buckinghamshire was erected in 1738 and is a copy of the one at Wilton House in Wiltshire. It spans the eastern end of the Octagon Lake.

LEFT William Kent's Temple of British Worthies (all Whigs!) at Stowe. In the foreground is Sir Thomas Gresham, founder of the Royal Exchange. Among the others honoured are Shakespeare, Milton and Elizabeth I. Stowe is famous for its garden monuments and buildings – dozens of them – carefully disposed about the park. They obey the principle laid down by William Shenstone in 1764: 'When a building or other object has been viewed from its proper point, the foot should never travel to it by the same path, which the eye has travelled over before. Lose the object, and draw nigh, obliquely.'[2]

FOLLOWING PAGES Vanbrugh's 1710 grand bridge at Blenheim in Oxfordshire originally spanned a marshy stream, the River Glyme. Fifty years later, 'Capability' Brown dammed the stream to make a lake and succeeded in balancing up the bridge. The straight lines of trees were planted by Henry Wise, the most fashionable and influential of late seventeenth-century gardeners.

virtues. He planted trees in their thousands, in clumps and belts or as specimens, and sometimes transplanted tall trees. Since the trees were native, this was often more successful than you might imagine.

Among Brown's most famous commissions were Chatsworth, Derbyshire, Blenheim Palace, Oxfordshire, Audley End, Essex, Petworth House, West Sussex, Holkham Hall, Norfolk, and Bowood House, Wiltshire. In the park at Petworth, in the 1750s, Brown altered the formal garden made by George London, and made two beautiful lakes, the larger Upper Pond (a serpentine lake made out of fishponds) and the smaller Lower Pond, as well as thinning existing clumps of trees and planting clumps of oak, beech, sweet chestnut and sycamore trees in the surrounding deer park. He put in a Doric temple and Ionic rotunda as eyecatchers, and made a ha-ha. It is a very pleasing prospect indeed, which charmed J.M.W. Turner sufficiently to paint several pictures there.

Painswick Rococo Garden, Gloucestershire, is on a smaller scale than many (in comparison to Stowe or Stourhead, that is) and with buildings that are less grandiose. It is described as a Rococo garden, because it is elegant and light-hearted, but scholars differ on how useful a description

this is for eighteenth-century gardens. What is indisputable is that the garden buildings are not Classical in influence but Gothic, and on a smaller scale. By the early 1980s it was in a very bad state. Fortunately, hanging in the house there was a picture of the garden of 1748, by Thomas Robins, and, although it was not known whether it was a true representation of the garden, after some preliminary investigation by garden archaeologists, the owner began to restore the garden, from 1984, according to the picture. As work proceeded, it became obvious that the picture was faithful and an elegant, intriguing garden has been revealed.

Painswick is in a steep wooded valley, with paths running through it to the various garden buildings such as the Red House and the Exedra. The garden is also noted for its snowdrops, many of which are *Galanthus* 'Atkinsii', named after a Mr Atkins who lived in the village of Painswick.

Stourhead is one of the gardens that had an amateur creator: Henry Hoare was a banker who, soon after inheriting the estate in 1741, set to work to dam the River Stour to make a lake and build around it Classically inspired buildings such as the Temple of Flora, the Pantheon and the Temple of Apollo. He also planted many trees, as did his grandson

OPPOSITE The Red House at Painswick Rococo Garden in Gloucestershire. In this context, 'rococo' means flamboyant and light-hearted, and the term is used for a style of garden developed roughly between 1720 and 1760. At Painswick, it also meant serpentine paths juxtaposed with formal vistas, and colourful follies, in different styles, disposed around the garden circuit.

ABOVE LEFT The Exedra, a small Gothic building at Painswick Rococo Garden, which was restored in the 1980s, with a steel core inside the timber frame to ensure that it lasts longer than the original did. 'Exedra' can mean one of a number of things, but here it is used for a semi-circular garden pavilion. Between the Exedra and the lake is a re-created geometric kitchen garden.

ABOVE RIGHT The Temple of Apollo (1744) at Stourhead in Wiltshire, inspired by the landscape artist Claude Lorrain and laid out between 1741 and 1780 by the banker Henry Hoare II.

FOLLOWING PAGES The Pantheon (1754) viewed from across the lake at Stourhead. This garden is meant to be circumnavigated by following the path around the lake. As the visitor progresses, new views – of buildings, trees and water – open up, making the excursion stimulating and restful by turns.

The clean-lined Moon Pond, with its two crescent-shaped side ponds, made by John Aislabie at Studley Royal in North Yorkshire, a garden laid out between 1722 and 1742. In the pond is a statue of Neptune, a common choice for such a position.

Richard, many of them exotic (including the tulip tree, *Liriodendron tulipifera*, only introduced into England in 1688) and many of which are now very large trees indeed. As with Painshill, for example, what is so stimulating about Stourhead is that, if you walk around the lake in an anti-clockwise direction, you catch glimpses of classical buildings or incidents and when close, your eye is caught by some other feature. These monuments (by Henry Flitcroft) include Classical temples such as the Temples of Flora and of Apollo and the Pantheon, and also a Gothic rustic cottage, and a grotto. Walpole called the view from the Temple of Apollo 'one of the most picturesque scenes in the world' and certainly it is agreed that the inspiration comes from the landscape paintings of Claude Lorrain and Poussin.

In the last years of the nineteenth century, Hoare's descendants planted a mass of rhododendrons and azaleas close by the lake, as well as many exotic trees, rather undermining the purity of the landscape and the subfusc nature of wood, water and green grass. However, they have undoubtedly contributed to the enduring popularity of this garden with visitors.

At Studley Royal, in North Yorkshire, John Aislabie developed the garden in the main between 1722 and 1742, when he retired to his estate after being disgraced (when Chancellor of the Exchequer) in the South Sea Bubble money scandal and briefly imprisoned. He set about creating a semi-formal water garden in the heavily wooded valley of the River Skell. As well as canals, and a cascade, he made a very beautiful, clean-lined, circular Moon Pond with two crescent-shaped ponds, one on each side, separated by grass. In the centre of the pond he placed a statue of Neptune and to one side of the Moon Pond a Classical Temple of

Painshill Park in Surrey, looking towards the ten-sided Gothic Temple, restored in 1985. It has ogee arches, quatrefoil windows and a painted fan-vaulted plaster ceiling. It is timber, rendered to look like stone. Much of the park can be seen through its apertures. Through these, the visitor catches his first glimpse of the Turkish Tent and Gothic Tower. On the right-hand side of the lake in the picture is the Grotto, not seen by the visitor until he is quite close to it. A circuit of this garden (the making of which ruined its owner, Charles Hamilton) is full of pleasant surprises and engenders varying moods.

Piety. On the steep hillsides above he built both a banqueting house and an octagonal tower, eyecatchers and viewing platforms. His son, William, acquired a more spectacular eyecatcher still when he extended the estate in 1767 to include the twelfth-century ruined Fountains Abbey.

Painshill Park, Surrey, was the work of Charles Hamilton, its owner, from 1738 until he ran out of money as a result and had to sell up in 1773. He, like Kent, had travelled on the Continent and been much affected by the experience. He was inspired not only by Claude Lorrain and Poussin but also by the 'Picturesque' scenes of Salvator Rosa. Also, like William Kent, he possessed a useful theatrical streak. The garden is laid out above, and through, the valley of the River Mole. Parallel with the river he dug out a long serpentine lake, with a scatter of islands in it. On the bank of this lake is a 'ruined' abbey folly and, overlooking it, a wooden Gothic Temple. This was the ornamental pleasure ground.

Further away, the garden is a more obvious landscape with clumps of trees and cheerful glades, but with still more garden buildings such as a lively Turkish Tent in white and blue, and a lowering Gothic Tower, reached by ascending an Alpine Valley, which is bordered by stands of exotic trees. Unlike some other landscape improvers of the time, Hamilton heartily welcomed the influx of North American trees and shrubs. Some buildings have been lost: in particular a Temple of Bacchus as well as the five-arched bridge which spanned the lake near its end, and a Hermitage, which in Hamilton's time (briefly) contained a real hermit. The landscape was

The Turkish Tent, the most flamboyant of the follies at Painshill. It was originally floored with brick and made of coarse painted cloth with papier mâché cornice and ornaments. The restored tent is of rather sturdier construction.

laid out with such great aplomb that Horace Walpole wrote: 'He has really made a fine place out of a most cursed hill.'

More than any other eighteenth-century landscape garden I know, except possibly Stourhead, this one has the power to teach us what these men were about. As you walk the circuit you are frequently confronted with a changing view, or new, often surprising, distant prospect, of a building or feature, in a variety of architectural styles. For example, after standing on the elevated Bastion looking down over a steeply sloping vineyard (producing wine again after a hundred years), you walk into a tree-and-shrub bounded green space, or amphitheatre. Only when you look sideways do you see the Gothic Temple and, as you approach it, you glimpse through its glassless windows the lake and the Turkish Tent on the hill the other side of it. Later, on the return, you discover that the Grotto, on a promontory in the lake, over which you earlier walked unknowingly, comes majestically into view. The effect is created by the use of different buildings as well as changes in level, landform and planting. The entire experience is stimulating, even uplifting, and completely absorbing.

Moreover, the quality of the restoration is truly impressive. With immense foresight and public spiritedness, the local Elmbridge Borough Council had bought up 158 acres/64 hectares of the original estate by 1980, including most of the woods and pleasure grounds as well as the lake. A trust was formed in 1981 and a masterplan devised, and the restoration, which is ongoing, began in 1984.

Towards the end of the eighteenth century, there was an increasing feeling for what came to be known as the Picturesque – that is, landscapes which imitated fierce nature with crags, cliffs, irregular paths, rushing torrents and cascades, rather than orderly, tamed, softly rolling Arcadia. The great publicists of this style were the Revd William Gilpin and Uvedale Price. Grottoes tended to replace classical statuary, and exotic trees became much more popular. (The Douglas fir, *Pseudotsuga menziesii*, was imported into this country in 1827, although the wellingtonia, *Sequoiadendron giganteum*, did not arrive until 1853.) Scotney Castle in Kent, designed by William Sawrey Gilpin, Gilpin's nephew, is an example of a Picturesque garden, developed in the 1830s at the same time as Salvin's neo-Tudor house was built.

The last of the great eighteenth-century designers was Humphry Repton (1752–1818), who brought to the party a renewed emphasis on formality about the house, by reintroducing terraces, with a relaxation of formality as the garden merged into the landscape. This tenet has remained a firm guide for English gardeners in every age since, especially those living in country houses. His plantings tended to be denser than Brown's and the eyecatchers were not Classical, usually, but rather idealized rustic, such as *cottages ornées*.[3] Repton seems to have been much more influenced by the wishes of his patrons than Brown, and the result

ABOVE Thomas Daniell's Oriental-inspired bridge with a pair of cast-iron Brahmin bulls in the garden at Sezincote in Gloucestershire. This is one of the great nabobs' houses, designed by Samuel Pepys Cockerell for his brother Charles from 1805. There are a number of Mughal features in the garden. Daniell was a well-known artist of Indian scenes. This garden benefited from Humphry Repton's advice.

OPPOSITE A suitable garden for a house built in the Mughal style. This fountain at Sezincote, below the bridge shown above, has a serpent twisting around a tree trunk. The vine in the foreground is the Japanese *Vitis coignetiae*.

was often an adventurous eclecticism. At Sezincote, in Gloucestershire, for example, he helped design an Mughal-influenced garden with Thomas Daniell, the artist, who had spent much time in the East. Daniell produced statues of elephants and sacred bulls, as well as Mughal arches, a lotus-shaped pool next to a temple to the Hindu sun god Souriya, and a pool with a three-headed snake fountain. As a result of work here, Repton was asked by the Prince of Wales to design the Pavilion at Brighton, although in the end it was John Nash's design that was realized. Repton was brilliant at designing approaches to houses, for example the drive which suddenly reveals the house at Sheringham Park, Norfolk.

Beauty and utility were his watchwords. He is most famous these days for his leatherbound 'Red Books', in which he painted 'before' and 'after' scenes in watercolour, the latter being revealed by removing the 'before' flap. He produced four hundred or so of these and the two hundred left are now most prized possessions of families for whom he worked. He could site a lake, or a clump of trees, as well as Brown but his earth-moving was on a much less grandiose scale. At Ashridge in Hertfordshire he made a plan for no fewer than fifteen separate gardens, at least partly in response,

one imagines, to the deluge of exotic plants coming in from North America and the East. Repton was working mainly through the time of the Napoleonic wars, which may be the reason why his commissions were less expansive and extravagant than Brown's, although tastes were changing anyway. For example, he designed the first 'rosery' – that is, a formal rose garden. It is interesting to note that Repton said that gardens were works of art rather than Nature. In less than a century, the pendulum had begun to swing back.

In the twentieth century some landscape gardens were altered or truncated by later developments, such as golf courses or bypasses, but, in the latter half of the century, the weather also affected them adversely.

The look of many eighteenth-century landscape gardens was sensationally and disastrously altered first by the loss of elms in the late 1960s to Dutch elm disease, which destroyed, for example, avenues at Blenheim Palace planted by Henry Wise. Then there was the dramatic Great Storm of 16–17 October 1987, as a result of which 15 million trees were felled or shattered, in a line east from Hampshire to Norfolk. The trees were still in leaf, which made the toll much heavier than it would have been otherwise. Many of the losses turned out to be over-mature trees, especially beeches, planted by 'improvers' in the eighteenth century. The effects of the storm of 25 January 1990 were more widespread, since the area affected included Wales and the Midlands as well as the west and south of England, but since it happened in the winter it succeeded in bringing down only (only?) 3 million trees. There has been judicious and sensitive planting in most of these gardens since. The Great Storm prompted the establishment of a database maintained by English Heritage, 'The Register of Parks and Gardens of Special Historic Interest in England'. Suitable parks and gardens are graded. Most are Grade II but 30 per cent are Grade II* (such as Mapperton, Dorset) and 10 per cent are Grade I (such as Painshill) and considered of international importance. Local councils take account of the register when considering planning applciations and, in the case of an historic landscape, are obliged to consult the Garden History Society.

The late twentieth century saw substantial renovation work at some of these gardens, notably Claremont Landscape Garden, Painswick Rococo Garden and, of course, Stowe. Hestercombe, better known as the finest of the Lutyens/Jekyll collaborations (see pages 63–5), also has an eighteenth-century landscape, which was restored in the 1990s. The cost has been tremendous, because of the nature of the garden buildings, which have often needed to be very sensitively restored. It is fortunate that these historic restorations coincided with the foundation of the National Lottery, which has provided many of the funds. A whole crowd of garden history experts have emerged in order to research these gardens and ensure their faithful restoration and imaginative conservation. They are thus in better condition than they have been for two centuries, and also now usually fulfil the visions of their founders.

What landscape gardens offer the twenty-first-century visitor, besides solitude and a good place to take a dog for a walk, is a chance to see – and this is especially true of the early eighteenth-century landscapes, such as Claremont, Rousham, Stourhead and Stowe – as clearly as we do in painting, sculpture and some of the other arts an intellectual mood at the dawn of the Enlightenment, uncompromised or blurred by later alterations or accretions.

OTHER LANDSCAPE GARDENS

Wrest Park, Bedfordshire
Cliveden, Buckinghamshire
Wimpole Hall, Cambridgeshire
Tatton Park, Cheshire
Chatsworth, Derbyshire
Sherborne Castle, Dorset
Cadland Gardens, Hampshire
Highclere Castle, Hampshire
Burghley House, Lincolnshire
Kenwood, London
Syon Park, London
Holkham Hall, Norfolk
Castle Ashby, Northamptonshire
The Alnwick Garden, Northumberland
The Harcourt Arboretum, Oxfordshire
Hawkstone Park, Shropshire
Prior Park, Somerset
Shugborough, Staffordshire
Trentham Gardens, Staffordshire
Euston Hall, Suffolk
Heveningham Hall, Suffolk
Ickworth Park, Suffolk
Sheffield Park Garden, Sussex
Gibside, Tyne & Wear
Charlecote Park, Warwickshire
Farnborough Hall, Warwickshire
Warwick Castle, Warwickshire
Corsham Court, Wiltshire
Longleat, Wiltshire
Wilton, Wiltshire
Croome Park, Worcestershire
Duncombe Park, Yorkshire
Harewood House, Yorkshire
Rievaulx Terrace, Yorkshire
Ripley Castle, Yorkshire
Scampston Hall, Yorkshire
Sledmere House, Yorkshire

4

THE COUNTRY GARDEN

The 'country garden' is a convenient label for a certain very attractive and appealing garden style particularly associated with the twentieth and twenty-first centuries. The country garden is not necessarily in the countryside, of course, since, more than most styles, it is a matter of atmosphere, but that is where you will find most gardens of this type, if only because it is a style which requires some space. It can, for convenience and (I hope) illumination, be divided into a number of sub-genres. As well as the country house garden, there is the English Vernacular garden, the cottage garden, the informal garden and the woodland garden.

The English Vernacular is really a continuation of the Gardenesque style, a name coined by John Claudius Loudon in 1832, when the explosion in building of villas and family houses in the suburbs prompted him to advocate a style of gardening which was aimed at neither large country house dwellers nor urbanites but, instead, the burgeoning property-owning middle classes. The main features of the Gardenesque were island beds, ponds, fountains, arch-covered gravel walks, bowers and borders, with plants planted rather sparsely in them, for their individual quality, beauty and botanical interest rather than for their overall effect.[1] Twice-yearly bedding was *de rigueur*. Lawns were extensive, since Mr Budding had invented the mechanical lawn mower, so horses and scythes could both now be put out to grass. This style was neat and orderly, always an attractive feature to gardeners, and most importantly it could be scaled down to the small garden.

The English Vernacular's distinguishing feature is that it is not 'designed' but often grows organically and is definitely made by the owner without recourse to professional advice. In the 1960s and 1970s, conifers and heathers, for example, were widely used for ground cover, together with variegated and coloured foliage plants, tightly clipped shrubs, and half-hardy plants used as bedding. The style has proved not particularly low on maintenance, since lawns are an important element and their care is time consuming. The English Vernacular can be most attractive when done with conviction and energy. There are a great number of gardens in this style, in suburbs and villages in particular, and some open their gates in the summer to visitors, most usually as one of a group in a village or town. They are unpretentious, have no aspirations to being works of art, but give enormous pleasure to their owners, and

OPPOSITE These are unpretentious, yet elegant wicker wigwams, in beds on a neat brick platform designed by Arne Maynard. The plants include *Verbascum* 'Helen Johnson', *Salvia* 'Mainacht' and lavender yet to flower in this private garden.

BELOW Subtropical bedding at Ascott in Buckinghamshire.

Miss Gertrude Jekyll would surely have approved: a thatched Dorset cottage, with climbing roses around the windows and hollyhocks down the garden path.

visitors too. If they have a fault, it is that they do not always allow sufficiently for their context, especially in the countryside.

The cottage garden style also seems to have lasting appeal for gardeners everywhere, but it is rather different. The style dates from the second half of the nineteenth century, and was initially especially, although not exclusively, suited to, and embraced by, those who lived in rather smaller houses than country houses.

Gertrude Jekyll, in *Wood and Garden*, published in 1899, wrote:

> I have learnt much from the little cottage gardens that help make our English waysides the prettiest in the temperate world. One can hardly go into the smallest cottage garden without learning or observing something new. It may be some two plants growing beautifully together by some happy chance, or a pretty mixed tangle of creepers, or

something that one always thought must have a south wall doing better on an east one.[2]

It may seem remarkable, at first sight, that the great Miss Jekyll could learn something from rural cottagers, but she certainly found plentiful examples of simple wisdom and sense when she clattered past their garden hedges, which flanked the lanes of Surrey, in her pony and trap. Particularly appealing to her was the mix of flowery profusion and practical thrift, of useful herbs growing alongside scented roses, of down-to-earth cabbages under apple boughs.

Vita Sackville-West wrote of the cottage garden in 1958 that it was 'all a flurry of flowers and a paved perplexity of paths, probably the loveliest type of small garden this country has ever evolved'.[3] She made a 'cottage garden' outside the South Cottage at Sissinghurst, the building in the garden where she and her husband, Sir Harold Nicolson, slept, but it was

ABOVE The simple billowing hedge echoes the undulations of the thatch over the windows of this Gloucestershire cottage – a precursor of the 'modern' fashion for cloud topiary.

FOLLOWING PAGES A sophisticated 'cottage garden' in Wiltshire, designed by Wendy Lauderdale, with harmonizing pastel colours, composed of *Rosa* 'Madame Isaac Pereire', *Campanula persicifolia* and its white form 'Alba', and the tall-growing ornamental seakale (*Crambe cordifolia*).

The South Cottage garden at Sissinghurst, Kent, designed by Vita Sackville-West, has always been planted in 'sunset colours'. It was called a 'cottage garden' but as Tony Lord puts it, 'it was as much a cottage garden as Marie-Antoinette was a milkmaid'.

a more complex, colour-themed garden than the cottagers in the village would have managed, and used a wider palette of plants, mostly in what she called 'sunset colours'. This colour theme has survived to this day, under National Trust management.

Along with Gertrude Jekyll and Vita Sackville-West, perhaps the most influential writer for post-war would-be cottage gardeners was Margery Fish, who lived at East Lambrook Manor in Somerset between 1937 and 1969. She spent her gardening life tirelessly seeking out and planting those plants once common in cottage gardens, especially double-flowered forms of old favourites, such as the double or 'hens and chickens' daisy, *Bellis prolifera*. In 1961, she wrote:

> Nowhere in the world is there anything like the English cottage garden. In every village and hamlet in the land there are these little gardens, always gay and never garish, and so obviously loved. There are not so many now, alas, as those cottages of cob or brick, with their thatched roofs and tiny crooked windows, are disappearing . . . but the flowers remain, flowers that have come to be known as 'cottage flowers' because of their simple, steadfast qualities.[4]

Perhaps her greatest contributions to the modern cottage garden style were the way she grew plants in close proximity to each other and knew them intimately. As she wrote, 'Plants are friendly creatures and enjoy each

One of the most influential exponents of the cottage garden style, Margery Fish lived here at East Lambrook Manor in Somerset between 1937 and 1969. The garden has been kept up admirably by every successive owner. The style is relaxed and profuse, even slightly wild, but the presence of a sophisticated shrub like *Cornus controversa* 'Variegata' (right background) is a giveaway.

other's company. The close-packed plants in a cottage garden grow well and look happy.' She was a great advocate of ground-cover plants such as herbaceous geraniums for that reason.

It is not surprising that gardeners should respond so positively to the idea of the cottage garden, since it is less than two hundred years since most of the population of England lived in the countryside, and folk memories last a long time. The mass move to the towns during the Industrial Revolution was so swift, and often so painful, that nostalgia for the 'old life', with its seemingly unchanging and traditional values, was sure to remain a potent force. A good indicator of this is the popularity of Myles Birkett Foster and Helen Allingham, both competent watercolourists who painted sturdy cottagers and their families in front of picturesquely tumbledown cottages, the garden in front a profusion of larkspur, roses, honeysuckle and other traditional flowers, the paths and hedges simply geometric. These images have sunk deep into the collective psyche. In all this, therefore, there is a good dose of old-fashioned hankering after a golden past. So it is not surprising if it suits so many to make a 'cottage garden'. I have done so myself and refuse to be defensive about it, since it offers the opportunity to grow any number of lovely plants in a comfortable, relaxed and nature-sensitive environment. (And to get away with the odd infelicitous grouping, come to that.)

Ever since the Second World War, there has been an accelerating reverse exodus from the city to the countryside on the part of prosperous people, at the very least for weekends, but often permanently, and the style which garden writers like Gertrude Jekyll, Vita Sackville-West and

Margery Fish championed has remained very popular. What has emerged is a simple, but by no means artless, kind of gardening, where thrift and self-sufficiency, so vital for survival in past agricultural depressions, are still admired virtues, resulting in the use of natural fertilizers, and the making of compost and leafmould, as well as the disposition of simple and rustic garden structures, such as pole pergolas and rough-hewn garden seats.

The modern cottage garden is based more firmly on flowers than the original cottage gardens would have been, however. There is a mixture in the flower beds of small shrubs, old roses, small-flowered clematis, perennials (especially irises), herbs, bulbs and hardy and tender annuals with, close by and often ornamentally arranged, rows of vegetables and a fruit bush or two. The traditional cottage garden perennials, rescued by those sophisticated lady gardeners mentioned above, include border auriculas (bear's ears), garden pinks (*Dianthus*), 'Jack-in-the-green' primroses (*Primula*), sweet peas (*Lathyrus*), centaurea, goat's rue (*Galega officinalis*), mezereon (*Daphne mezereum*), lupins, Granny's bonnets (*Aquilegia*), delphiniums and larkspur (*Consolida*), honesty (*Lunaria annua*) and bachelor's buttons (*Ranunculus acris* 'Flore Pleno'), as well as lavender, lilac and philadelphus and a bunch of hardy annuals, such as Shirley poppies. They are now joined by the great tribes of herbaceous geraniums, bergenias, euphorbias, hellebores and hostas, which agricultural labourers in the nineteenth century would not have grown, but which 'feel right' to modern cottage gardeners. Mood is all important in the cottage garden. And, as well as once-flowering old roses, modern cottage gardeners can rely on the myriad Modern Shrub roses, which engender the same sensations but which, usefully, also usually repeat flower.

These days cottage gardens are not entirely confined to country gardens; far from it, since this easy-on-the-eye, seemingly unpretentious style appeals to some city dwellers as well, especially those whose roots are in the country. Most importantly, considering their preponderance now, the cottage garden is well suited to small gardens, since any simple topiary figure or hedge can be scaled down to fit a space. However, the cottage garden looks its best when surrounding a house, however small, in a vernacular architectural style. Any slightly haphazard feature of the architecture is well complemented by the slightly haphazard planting, without too clear or sharp lines, where plants can mingle and self-seed.

A very good example of the modern cottage garden is Eastgrove Cottage in Worcestershire. The atmosphere of the garden is undoubtedly helped by its delightful rural situation, down a country lane, as well as the presence of the seventeenth-century half-timbered yeoman's house, but the owner, Carol Skinner, is a skilled gardener and the pleasingly generous informality of the flower beds under fruit trees is hard won. At Eastgrove, the simple geometry of the traditional cottage garden has

RIGHT The very model of a modern 'cottage garden': Eastgrove Cottage in Worcestershire. Note the apple trees, the plentiful shrubs and perennials in the borders, and the rural aspect.

FOLLOWING PAGES A paved terrace, carpeted with thyme, leads out to a modern ha-ha at Rofford Manor in Oxfordshire. There is no chance of walking down it without treading on scented thyme. This garden, designed by Michael Balston, has decorative structural elements with a practical purpose, such as the wooden pyramids for clematis.

admittedly been replaced by generous curves, although the hedges are straight. There are a number of almost discrete areas, but the garden can still be seen mainly in one go, as a cottage garden often is. Carol has made all the structures, including two wooden greenhouses (she and her husband run a small nursery), propagating frames, a rose tunnel and a rock garden retaining wall, and have laid the herringbone brick paths.

The planting is 'comfortable' with the 'lumpy, dumpy' house, according to the owner. She dislikes 'pretentiousness', and is sensitive to the fact that the garden is positioned on the edge of fields and a dingle. There is no jarring coloured foliage here to jangle sensibilities. But it would be wrong to say that the approach is *laissez-faire*. Far from it. The borders are very carefully, and frequently, tended.

Where the cottage garden ends and the country house garden starts can sometimes be a moot point. It is partly a matter of acreage, partly a matter of the architecture of the house and surrounding hard structures, partly a matter of planting design. (It should be mentioned here that in many a country house garden, there will be one part of it called the Cottage Garden; indeed, even such a grand garden as Chatsworth has one.) Country house gardens, or those open to visitors at least, tend to be of a size which requires the division of the space into compartments or rooms and to have substantial hedges or walls to surround those rooms. These separate spaces will probably all have titles: the Spring Garden, the Summer Garden, the Herb Garden and the Potager perhaps. The further that the space is from the house, the more informal the structure and the planting. There will often be masses of bulbs naturalized in grass, and, if you are lucky, semi-natural woodland as well.

Country house gardens are extremely well represented amongst those which open to the public; indeed, they probably constitute the majority. An impressive example is Helmingham Hall in Suffolk, where the beauty of the parkland setting and the moated Elizabethan house (incomparable as they are) is matched by the exceptional quality of the garden. It is not given to many people to start out with such advantages, but the owners have made very good use of them. There has been a garden at Helmingham since early medieval times, but the present owners – in particular Xa Tollemache, the garden designer, who learned her craft here – have been very busy.

In 1982, Xa Tollemache created a knot, herb and rose garden, one that would be in keeping with the historic house. She had some advice from

The beauty of the setting is matched by the exceptional quality of the gardens at Helmingham Hall in Suffolk. These are the double herbaceous borders in the Walled Garden, in early June, with Oriental poppies and alliums in the right foreground, backed by *Aruncus dioicus*, and *Crambe cordifolia* prominent on the left-hand side. Between the borders and the house is a parterre and moat.

the Marchioness of Salisbury, who had recently, successfully, put in a knot garden close to the Old Palace at Hatfield (see page 18). The knots are 'open', and filled with plants introduced into the country before 1750. One knot is in the shape of the 'fret', the central motif of the Tollemache crest; the other contains the initials of the owners' names. Close by is the rose garden, full of June-flowering shrub roses, such as 'Madame Plantier', 'Ispahan', 'Madame Hardy' and 'Tour de Malakoff', but also now, to prolong the season of interest for garden visitors, some of David Austin's English Roses, as well as late summer perennials. Xa Tollemache has earned the gratitude of rosarians everywhere by designing, and marketing, an ingenious rose support to show them off to best advantage and prevent damage from rain and mud splashes.

The Walled Garden, a place of ancient peace, is a mix of fruit and flower, with ironwork arched tunnels supporting sweet peas in early summer and heavy, dewdrop-shaped gourds later on. The herbaceous borders are laid out as a cross; the flowers in these are designed to blend in colour with old roses in early summer, but become more fiery in late summer. Annuals fill any gaps. And, around the walls, there are a number of different borders – Grass, Shrub, Colour Themes, Potager – with clipped yew buttresses planted at intervals, to allow the eye to travel more slowly along the borders.

The word that best suits Helmingham is 'congruous': the scale and proportion of the structural elements are satisfying, the generosity of flower and scent beguiling, and the sense of timelessness pervasive. Moreover, as in all the best gardens, there is a strong visual connection between house and garden; despite the moats which physically separate the garden from the hall, the latter is everywhere in view.

There are many country house gardens which consist of a number of eclectic elements. One such is Highgrove in Gloucestershire, where HRH The Prince of Wales has consulted many of the great and the good – Lady Salisbury, Rosemary Verey, Sir Roy Strong and Julian and Isabel

Roses on one of the terraces at Gresgarth Hall in Lancashire, close to the Artle Beck, which flows through the garden. This large country garden, the home of the Italian-born garden designer Arabella Lennox-Boyd, has terraced formality around the house, as well as a lake (just visible in the top right-hand corner) and bog garden, a nuttery and orchard, a kitchen garden, a series of colour-themed gardens and borders, a wild garden, a rhododendron hillside, a serpentine walk and a bluebell wood. Indeed, everything that the gardener, and the garden visitor, could possibly ever want. The Arkle Beck, which provides a constant sound of water, is spanned by the Chinese bridge and separates the formal garden from the richly planted woodland.

Bannerman – as well as his own inclinations in the making of the garden. At Highgrove, it is possible to discern the physical expression of Prince Charles's avowed public interests and commitments: organic and sustainable farming (translated to the garden), his interest in design and ornament, and his commitment to patronage. His garden is run on organic lines, with meadows on either side of the drive, but with highly formal gardens, as well as mysterious woodland. Another eclectic garden is Gresgarth Hall in Lancashire, the home of the garden designer

OPPOSITE Goodnestone Park in Kent is a garden, around a house of 1704, which retains features from many eras: an eighteenth-century park, Victorian terraces, interwar woodland, rock garden and pool, 1960s flower and kitchen gardens within an ancient walled garden, and a very recent Millennium parterre, 'golden arboretum' and contemporary gravel garden. It is a fine advertisement for the benefits of continuity in the hands of one family. This is the marvellous walled garden, which consists of three enclosures: an 'old rose' garden, a summer garden and a kitchen garden at the far end. The parish church just beyond the walls is a remarkable ready-made eyecatcher. These borders are predominantly filled with roses, with Irish yews as punctuation marks.

LEFT A border entirely composed of peonies in the walled garden at Goodnestone Park in early June.

LEFT *Rhododendron arboreum* in the gardens at Heligan in Cornwall. These gardens became neglected during the First World War, but were triumphantly restored by Tim Smit (subsequently of Eden Project fame) in the 1990s. Some of the enormous rhododendrons in the Victorian pleasure grounds were grown from seed collected by Sir Joseph Hooker himself.

RIGHT A wonderful, mature specimen of *Magnolia campbellii*, growing with rhododendrons at Lanhydrock in Cornwall. This garden, part woodland, part formal, was laid out for the first Baron Robartes from 1857. It is now looked after by the National Trust.

FOLLOWING PAGES Trebah is one of the great Cornish woodland gardens. Its position, running down a ravine to the Helford River (which can be glimpsed in this picture) ensures drama in plenty, but this is also a plant lover's subtropical paradise. This garden has been heroically and sensitively rescued from neglect by the present owners from 1981. It was laid out originally as a 26-acre/10-hectare pleasure ground by Charles Fox after 1831. His brother, Arthur, created next-door Glendurgan.

beloved of country house gardeners, Arabella Lennox-Boyd. A third is Goodnestone Park in Kent, the family home of the garden writer George Plumptre.

It is hard to pin down exactly the origins of the informal garden, which comprise a substantial number of country gardens these days. By 'informal' I mean where geometry, except perhaps very close to the house, is not a leading component in the garden; instead, the garden consists of winding paths, irregular flower beds and an absence of clipped hedging. It has its origins in the eighteenth-century Landscape style, and was given impetus by William Robinson in his writings, in particular *The English Flower Garden*, where he publicly tilted at the ultra-formalists such as Blomfield and Nesfield. The woodland garden is a species of 'informal garden', as is the English Vernacular style.

No one in 1800, when the first Himalayan rhododendrons arrived in this country, could possibly have predicted that in the next century or so a sizeable number of large country gardens, situated on acid soil in rolling wooded countryside or in deep valleys in the south and west of England (as well as other western parts of the British Isles), would be filled with the plant riches of the Far East and

ABOVE Trewithen is another great Cornish garden, where many marvellous plants have originated, including *Ceanothus arboreus* 'Trewithen Blue'. This garden is noted for its handsome house and Great Lawn, bounded by enormous rhododendrons. As can be seen, they do very well in the mild Cornish climate.

OPPOSITE High Beeches in West Sussex in autumn. This garden, originally created by Colonel Loder from 1906, is informally laid out with glades of woodland exotics, such as rhododendrons, dogwoods (*Cornus*) and magnolias. It also has a wildflower meadow and the only site of naturalized willow gentian (*Gentiana asclepiadea*) in Britain. This garden is full of rare, mature plants but it is the naturalistic atmosphere – created by winding ways amongst the trees and shrubs – which is so beguiling.

the eastern United States. But so it has turned out. At Caerhays, Heligan, Lanhydrock, Trebah, Trengwainton, and Trewithen in Cornwall, as well as at Leonardslee, Borde Hill, High Beeches and Wakehurst Place in Sussex (to select just a few which are open frequently to the public), wealthy Victorian gentlemen with time on their hands, energy and a deep desire to do things properly, experimented with the cultivation of imported exotic plants, most particularly species of the vast rhododendron tribe. These had been collected in upland regions and so had a fighting chance of surviving winters in warm and wet districts of the south and west, where there was also the acid soil they required. Rhododendrons jostled for space and their owners' affections with other acid-loving plants from the same parts of the temperate world, principally camellias and magnolias, although enkianthus, embothrium, kalmia, michelia and pieris also found a place.

The enduring legacy of those well-to-do plant enthusiasts can still be seen in Cornwall, where a number of the best gardens have survived intact in private hands or been given to the care of the National Trust. Set very often on favoured slopes above river estuaries or the sea, and sheltered from Atlantic blasts by belts of trees, they are remarkable for many things, not least the way they have bred an acceptance that exotic flowering plants are appropriate companions for native trees in an English rural landscape. They are also remarkable for the size of the plants, thanks to the latter's age and natural longevity and to the kindness of the Cornish climate. You will find magnolias, such as the best-loved *M. campbellii*, growing 60 feet/18 metres tall, their pink flowers become fluttering birds somewhere in the sky above, while the tree rhododendron *R. arboreum* often grows taller than it does in Nepal.

The 1990 gales brutally, but perhaps on balance beneficently, felled a lot of old trees and overcrowded plantings in many Cornish gardens and, in recent years, the owners have benefited from the breeding work being done elsewhere in the temperate world (especially the United States and New Zealand): now they have many new *Rhododendron yakushimanum* and *R. vireya* hybrids to play with, as well as camellias with scented flowers or dwarf habit, and magnolias which flower when young and in a wide range of colours. Yellow-flowered magnolias such as 'Elizabeth' would surely have caused a sensation with the Cornish grandees if E.H. Wilson or George Forrest had sent them back from western China. There are also evident attempts to rejuvenate and develop plantings. The spectre at the feast is *Phytophthora ramorum*, the misleadingly named 'sudden oak death' (better known now in this country as 'ramorum dieback'), which causes leaf blight and shoot death in rhododendrons; these act as an innoculum for infection passing to the overstorey of native trees, such as beech and oak. Or that is the fear. Owners of these gardens can only hold their breath and wait for the scientists to pronounce authoritatively one way or the other.

The great charm of most woodland gardens is that, although there are paths winding

through them, there is no obvious indication of a controlling design except close to the house. And the exotic Asiatic shrubs and rare trees are often planted amongst native trees, in what was often already woodland, with bluebells and snowdrops flowering underneath in the spring. Colour clashes seem rarely glaring because of the amount of green foliage, which acts as a substantial buffer.

Amongst the greats in Cornwall are Caerhays, which runs to 60 acres/25 hectares, Heligan (which is a woodland garden as much as it is a highly productive restored Victorian kitchen garden), Glendurgan, which like Heligan has a Himalayan-type ravine, and Trewithen, which also has a most attractive formal walled garden, where you will see flowering in May the beautiful azure flowers of *Ceanothus* 'Trewithen Blue'.

In Hampshire there is Exbury Gardens, on the Berkshire/Surrey border the Savill and Valley Gardens in Windsor Great Park, and in Sussex some very fine woodland gardens at Leonardslee, Borde Hill, High Beeches, Wakehurst Place and Sheffield Park. All these gardens have bounced back, so to speak, from damage caused by storms. Most of them are also in lovely countryside – by the sea or a river estuary in Cornwall or on the edge of the Downs in Sussex – of which the visitor catches glimpses on the garden tour.

In these woodland gardens, the most colourful plantings often belong to the azalea group of rhododendrons. The variety of flower colour, yet consistency in habit and size, in azaleas seems to make them ideal for mass grouping in large, acid-soil gardens. There are impressive plantings in the Savill and Valley Gardens and at Exbury Gardens in Hampshire. At Castle Howard, in Yorkshire, there is a planting of the fifty forms of dwarf hybrid 'Kurume' azaleas (which are named after the place on the island of Kyushu where they were raised), and from where E.H. Wilson collected them in 1918. There is also a spectacular display of these in the Punchbowl in the Valley Gardens, Windsor Great Park (see page 76). Planted in their thousands, in groups of up to 200 plants of a single variety, they are, as Jane Brown puts it, 'one of the astounding sights of the English spring; from April to throughout May, this bowl of colours merges from apple-blossom pink into deeper pinks, mauves, whites and

ABOVE Autumn in the Acer Glade at the National Arboretum at Westonbirt in Gloucestershire.

RIGHT Like High Beeches in West Sussex, the nearby woodland garden at Sheffield Park was also badly affected by the Great Storm of 1987, but has recovered well and is particularly noted for the quality of the autumn colour. The tupelo (*Nyssa sylvatica*) is a speciality. The garden was laid out by 'Capability' Brown in 1776, and Humphry Repton also worked here.

creams into rich deep reds, carmines and orange-scarlet flowers, seen though the tracery of larch and silver firs.'5

As well as woodland gardens, there are a number of arboreta in England which are open to visitors, and prove a tremendous draw, especially in the spring and autumn. They differ from woodland gardens in that they feature a variety of specimen trees and shrubs, not always disposed particularly for the overall picture, and in that regard they are often the arboreal equivalent of the plantsman's garden. The most famous and beautiful is the National Arboretum at Westonbirt in Gloucestershire, which was laid out (by Robert Holford originally in 1829, and by subsequent generations) with care, so that a number of lovely pictures have been made, especially in autumn in the Acer Glade. It is now run by the Forestry Commission. In the same county is another fine aboretum at Batsford Park.

In Surrey, in a beautiful steep valley, Dr Wilfrid Fox developed an arboretum on 110 acres/44 hectares at Winkworth, near Godalming, from 1937 until 1952, when he handed it on to the National Trust. It is a lovely spot with very good views over the wooded Surrey countryside, and there are exceptionally fine collections of sorbus, for example, and magnolia.

LEFT The hedges are clipped in such a way as to echo the 'ridge and furrow' conformation in the pasture beyond the Barn Garden at Home Farm in Oxfordshire, designed by Dan Pearson. The geranium-red flowers of *Rosa moyesii* may be seen in the background, together with the grass *Stipa gigantea* and a crescent of *Eremurus* 'Moneymaker' (yellow) and 'Cleopatra' (burnt orange).

ABOVE At Home Farm Dan Pearson developed a distinctive naturalistic look. This is the thyme carpet running up to the front terrace, with the pond in the background. 'The garden itself is an impression of nature; it uses a different palette of plants but attempts to make them appear as if they had arrived and colonized the place,' he wrote.[6]

The plantsman's arboretum *par excellence* must surely be the one created from 1953 by Sir Harold Hillier, close to the tree and shrub nursery he founded in Hampshire. It has been managed by Hampshire County Council since 1977. It is reputed to be the largest collection of hardy trees and shrubs in the world, containing as it does about 12,000 different species and cultivars in 180 acres/79 hectares. No fewer than eleven National Collections are held here, including oak and witch hazel. Although it was laid out to show off individual plants, it is a very pleasant place in which to walk, and there is an excellent and extensive Winter Garden.

An example of a more modern, informal, country garden style is a garden designed by Dan Pearson over the space of a decade, called Home Farm, Oxfordshire. Although this garden is not open to visitors, or indeed still in the same hands, we are lucky Dan Pearson wrote about it and also made a television series.[7] Here he developed the naturalistic, slightly wild country garden idea, happily settled in its rural context with a thyme lawn carpet, stilt limes and a wavy hedge on one boundary giving views of the countryside beyond, yet using a wide and relaxed choice of plants, in particular generous quantities of

At Denmans in West Sussex, a stretch of gravel runs through the garden, imitating a dried-up riverbed. Annuals and biennials, such as *Verbascum*, are allowed to self-seed. Also in the picture are eryngiums ('Miss Willmott's Ghost') and the iris-like *Sisyrinchium striatum*. This garden was created by Joyce Robinson from 1946 and developed by the garden designer John Brookes, who lives there now.

herbaceous perennials, hardy grasses and masses of expensive eremurus. The colour combinations are very far from being haphazard or random but are often startling and invigorating, and always assured. It is all very considered and deliberate, for, as he wrote, 'control is essential even in a garden that is aping the soft informality of nature'.[8] There are echoes of the surrounding countryside: the grasses are meant to imitate the nearby fields; the clipped yews are like emerging hills and the boundary hedges are shaped to connect with the 'ridge and furrow' of the adjacent pasture.

Gravel is sometimes a good indicator of a country as opposed to a true cottage garden, since cottagers would not have been able to afford it. It is a sympathetic medium (or rather more so than many paving materials), especially if it has been quarried locally. At Denmans, Sussex, the informal garden is remarkable for the gravel which flows like a river through it, with plants spilling luxuriantly on to it, which also ebb and flow. The garden was initially laid out by Joyce Robinson from 1946, but developed still further by another influential designer from the

Shirley poppies (*Papaver rhoeas* 'Mother of Pearl') and love-in-a-mist (*Nigella damascena* 'Miss Jekyll White') in the Gravel Garden made out of the car park at the Beth Chatto Gardens in Essex.

generation before Dan Pearson, John Brookes (who runs his garden design practice from Clock House there). Great care has been taken with the planting: their grouping, their form and texture, their repetition and their editing, for though highly sensitive to nature, and natural communities, he believes in a garden 'thinning nature out'. He is also a fan of woody plants, and of the possibilities of leaf shape and texture. In the walled garden, Mediterranean plants, such as myrtle (*Luma apiculata*), luxuriate in the long hours of Sussex sunshine.

At the Beth Chatto Gardens near Colchester in Essex, gravel has been used as a complete medium to protect an enormous range of drought-resistant plants. It is important to know that Beth Chatto has a deep knowledge of the ecology of plants, and was a pioneer of naturalistic planting in the 1970s and 1980s, before it became widely fashionable. This interest informed her decision to transform the old, compacted, grass visitors' car park in 1991 – on very poor, free-draining soil – into the Gravel Garden. She wrote: 'For some years I had dreamt of making my Gravel Garden, *with plants adapted to the prevailing conditions* [my italics],

Beth Chatto has a great interest in plant ecology and the plants in her Gravel Garden are mainly Mediterranean species which revel in the dry climate and sharply draining soil. Prominent in this picture are the globes of *Allium cristophii*, spikes of yellow *Eremurus stenophyllus* and yellow mullein (*Verbascum bombyciferum*).

instead of watching mown grass turn biscuit-brown for weeks every summer. I hoped to see which plants would survive without hosepipe irrigation and was prepared to lose some of the many new introductions not yet sufficiently tested for summer drought or winter cold and damp.'[9] The story which she tells in her book about the determination she felt not to water the young plants, even though she lives in the very driest part of the country, has proved inspirational to this gardener and, no doubt, to many others too.

First the compacted soil was broken up; then it was ploughed and rolled, and masses of organic matter was incorporated into the top two spits (spade depths). As at Denmans, the gravel evokes a river. 'I had in mind a dried-up riverbed as I made a gently sinuous walkway through the length of my piece of land, breaking up the long curving borders thus planned with several spur exits and entrances, and leaving space in the central walkway for large island beds for the gravel to swirl around.'[10] She planted a wide variety of southern European subshrubs, such as cistus, as well as perennials like euphorbias, bulbs such as alliums and South African tulbaghias and, to give height, junipers and wind-blown grasses such as stipas. The following year, she mulched the surface of the beds with a locally quarried ½ inch/12.5 mm gravel, to a depth of 1 to 2 inches/25 to 50 mm, depending on the size of the plants. Because many seedheads are left in the winter, this garden looks lovely at every season of the year. And she never weakened and watered it, even at the height of two extremely dry, hot summers after it was planted.

OTHER COUNTRY GARDENS

Cholmondeley Castle, Cheshire
Dunham Massey, Cheshire
Jodrell Bank Arboretum, Cheshire
Penjerrick, Cornwall
Trewidden, Cornwall
Brockhole, Cumbria
Holker Hall, Cumbria
Hutton-in-the-Forest, Cumbria
Sizergh Castle, Cumbria
Blackpool Gardens, Devon
Castle Hill, Devon
Killerton, Devon
Tapeley Park, Devon
Chiffchaffs, Dorset
Cranborne Manor Garden, Dorset
Forde Abbey, Dorset
Minterne, Dorset
Glen Chantry, Essex
Saling Hall, Essex
Stancombe Park, Gloucestershire
Rotherfield Park, Hampshire
Hergest Croft Gardens, Herefordshire
Emmetts Garden, Kent
Bressingham Gardens, Norfolk
Lexham Hall, Norfolk
Sandringham House, Norfolk
Coton Manor, Northamptonshire
Cottesbrooke Hall, Northamptonshire
Belsay Hall Gardens, Northumberland
Cragside House, Northumberland
Howick Hall, Northumberland
Dorothy Clive Gardens, Shropshire
Dunster Castle, Somerset
Greencombe, Somerset
Munstead Wood, Surrey
Standen, Sussex
Thorp Perrow Arboretum, Yorkshire

GARDENING WITH NATURE

At the beginning of this chapter, there is no escaping the obligation to define terms, since 'the natural garden' has a variety of meanings. It rarely, if ever, is used to refer to a garden where there are only native plants, since most people would agree that that does not really constitute a garden. However, it often means one where native plants are included (or some of the better-behaved ones at least), where manufactured chemicals are used sparingly if at all, and where strenuous and informed efforts are made to encourage wildlife. It can mean a garden where design considerations are subordinate to the proclivities of plants (not much hard landscape, for example) and where the intention is to grow plants in plant communities, such as can be observed in the wild. This is sometimes much easier said than done, not only because natural plant communities have disappeared from many places, mostly because of man's activities over thousands of years, but also because certain plants will become dominant if intervention is minimal. Although that is natural, it is not necessarily desirable in a garden. The most successful practitioners of 'natural gardening' are, ironically, not non-interventionists but those who are very careful in their interventions.

Making a garden with at least a nod in the direction of nature has long been a preoccupation with gardeners. How could it be otherwise? After all, flouting the rules rarely leads to long-term success; that much has been empirically tested. Even when the influx of foreign and exotic plants was at its height in the nineteenth century, gardeners were quick to learn that, in order to succeed, they had to take care to provide the kind of conditions – of soil and climate, in particular – that those plants were used to in the wild. By experimentation and experience they learned what would grow where. Famously, for example, they discovered that Japanese camellias were hardy enough to leave the kind of glasshouse protection thought necessary when they first arrived,[1] yet would not thrive in alkaline soils. Successful gardeners have always been those who combined a lively spirit of enquiry with a sober respect for natural laws.

In recent years, widespread concern about the loss of our own native flowers and their habitats – caused, in the main, by efficient, intensive agricultural operations as well as widespread house and road building – has affected the attitudes of gardeners profoundly. When told by pioneering conservationists, such as the late Dame Miriam Rothschild,

OPPOSITE The Mansion House at Ashton Wold in Northamptonshire, home to the late Dame Miriam Rothschild, scientist and naturalist. The house is almost completely covered in ivy and other climbers, to provide nesting places for birds and food for butterflies.

BELOW Endsleigh in Devon, laid out by Humphry Repton. Here pink campions, buttercups, rhododendrons and conifers merge into the woodland.

5

Annual cornfield flowers known as 'Farmer's Nightmare' in a meadow designed by Arabella Lennox-Boyd. 'Farmer's Nightmare' is a seed mixture created by Miriam Rothschild. The soil has to be rotovated each winter to imitate ploughing. The trees are apples, bird cherries and holm oaks. Buttresses of yew are used to separate meadows (compare with page 41).

that private gardens were the best refuge for many birds, small wild mammals and wild flowers that have been chased out of their original habitats, gardeners have listened and acted. They have planted hedges of native plants, created 'meadows' and introduced plants known for bearing fruit and wildlife-attractive flowers. And they have learned to integrate these features into gardens without, necessarily, any drastic compromise with aesthetics. So concerted has been the campaign to inform by ecologists and environmentalists that the importance of biodiversity and sustainability now seems self-evident, which was not the case even twenty years ago. There are few gardeners who do not have at least some appreciation of what those terms imply.

This has been a sea change in attitude. Apart from a few sage souls, gardeners after the last war were much more preoccupied with how to maintain their gardens to a reasonable standard in a time of fast-dwindling labour resources than they were in preserving wildlife. The use of chemicals, especially herbicides and insecticides, seemed the cheapest and easiest way to replace the work of human hands and it was not yet known what baleful consequences these might have for wild creatures. 'Ground cover' became a shibboleth, and labour-saving design options, such as conifer and heather beds, which need little close care once established, seemed highly desirable. Gardens were often rather barren, with a lot of brown earth exposed, especially in winter, but they were tidy. The gardener remained in control, more or less. Nowadays, the situation is more complex and subtle. Sure, the gardener likes still to be in control, but in a laxer and looser way.

Dame Miriam Rothschild's garden at Ashton Wold in Northamptonshire was an exemplar of the ideas which motivated her

ABOVE A romantic choice of paths through an orchard at Westwell Manor in Oxfordshire.

OPPOSITE A colourful mix of annual 'Farmer's Nightmare' native wild flowers – corn marigold, corn cockle, cornflower and poppy – at Chatsworth in Derbyshire.

FOLLOWING PAGES The 'natural' Cottage Garden, influenced by a trip to Crete, designed by Keith Wiley at The Garden House, Buckland Monachorum in Devon, with the wild carrot (*Daucus carota*), *Lychnis coronaria*, *Verbena bonariensis* and Californian poppies (*Eschscholzia californica*) prominent (see page 214). St Andrew's church is in the background and, beyond, the Cornish hills.

and other conservationists. The house (see page 190) was altered in the 1970s, when the top storey was removed. At the same time, the garden was changed, and she allowed the house to become covered from ground floor to roof in ivy, to please bees and butterflies in the autumn when they flowered. She removed flower beds and replaced them with flowering shrubs, many of them native ones, as well as fruit trees. She sowed wildflower meadows where the lawns had been, and experimented with growing annual wild flowers on the old tennis courts and stable yard. She was a farmer as well, and eventually produced wildflower seed commercially, including the mixture 'Farmer's Nightmare'.

It is hard to overstate the importance of Dame Miriam Rothschild's legacy in changing the attitudes of commentators and, therefore, with time, gardeners. In the last twenty years, many a garden, public and private, has followed her lead and created, or reinstated, its own meadow

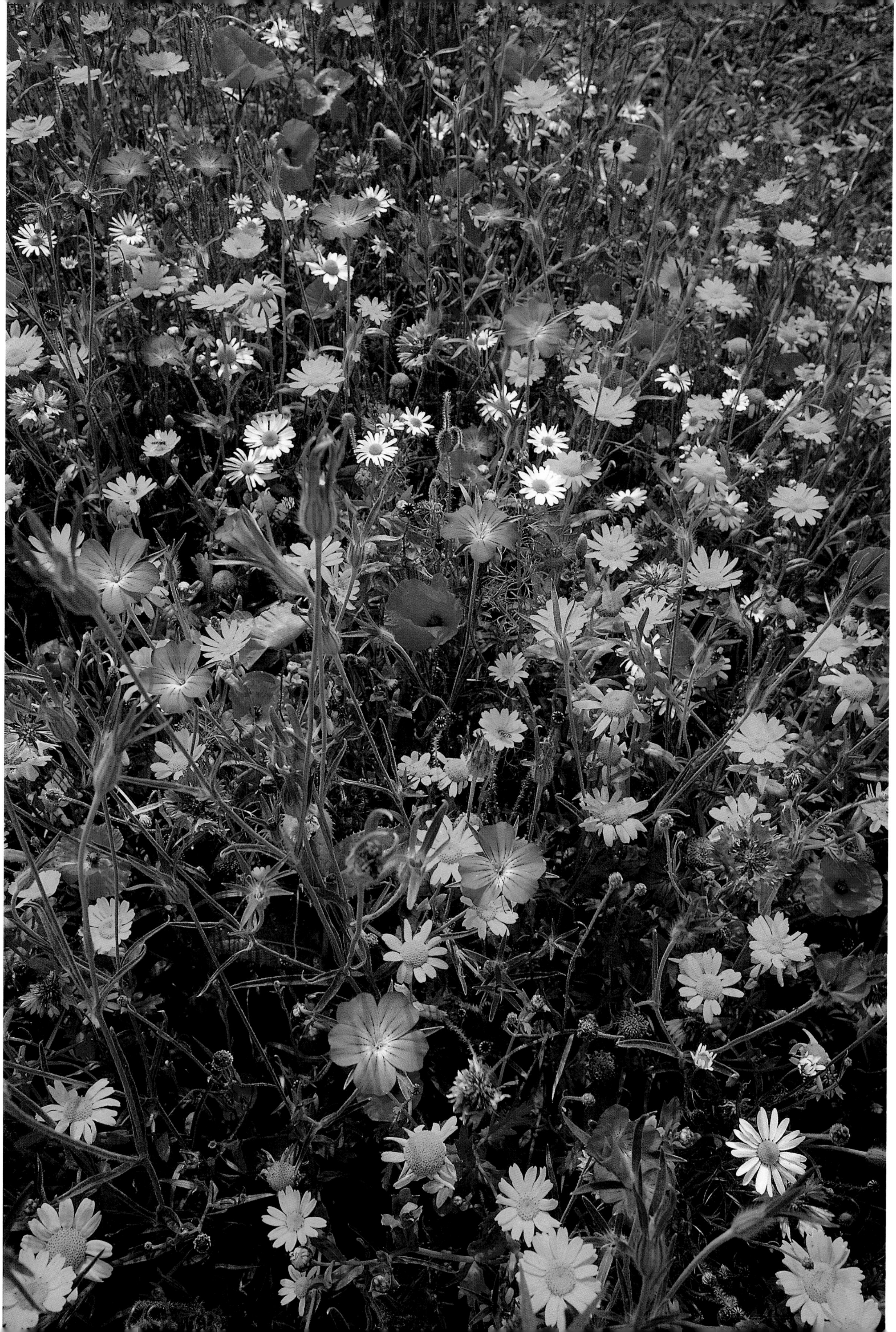

or meadows, in a valiant attempt to encourage native wildlife lost both to farmland and to gardens. It is now possible to see 'flowery meads' in a number of gardens open to visitors, amongst them Sticky Wicket in Dorset, Coton Manor in Northamptonshire, The Garden House at Buckland Monachorum in Devon and Highgrove in Gloucestershire.

Sticky Wicket shows what can be achieved in the hands of knowledgeable people prepared to take the task seriously. This 2½-acre/ 1-hectare garden is divided into distinct areas, all designed to please some aspect of wildlife, but showing also how attractive such a garden can be for humans as well. There is, *inter alia*, a Frog Garden (with ponds and wetland), a Round Garden, formally laid out with flowers for bees and butterflies, a Bird Garden and a White Garden with a number of different habitats in it, not to mention a wildflower meadow and a hay meadow. Pam Lewis, the owner, has written two books on the subject.[2]

In the early days of this country's enthusiasm for wildflower meadows, it was thought necessary, except where the soil was very poor, to strip away the topsoil first, in order that lush, coarse grasses would not

OPPOSITE On both sides of the main drive at Highgrove in Gloucestershire Dame Miriam Rothschild's wildflower seed mixture is sown annually. The mixture includes ox-eye daisies and corn poppies.

ABOVE The native wildflower meadow at Sticky Wicket in Dorset, in May with moon daisies, buttercups, ragged robin and the all-important yellow rattle.

ABOVE Common spotted orchids and yellow rattle at Sticky Wicket in Dorset. Yellow rattle (*Rhinanthus minor*) parasitizes grasses, giving native flowers a better chance to flourish. It is widely used by meadow gardeners.

RIGHT The clever juxtaposition of meadow with the very carefully gardened Long Border at Great Dixter. The flowering tree on the left is the false acacia (*Robinia pseudoacacia*).

overwhelm the more delicate native wild flowers, and indeed in one part of Sticky Wicket this is what has been done. However, when it became widely known that the native annual hay rattle (*Rhinanthus minor*) acquires part of its nutrient requirement by parasitizing the roots of grasses, meadows became much easier to manage. In many instances where hay rattle is present, it has not been necessary to strip the topsoil.

Some of the most famous garden meadows in the country must surely be those at Great Dixter, East Sussex, since they have been a feature of the garden for eighty years or so. Christopher Lloyd's parents, in particular his mother, were influenced by William Robinson's *The Wild Garden*, published in 1870, in which he advocated, amongst other things, growing garden perennials and bulbs in grass, and they incorporated his ideas when they made the Dixter meadows from undisturbed grassland. These days, there are six discrete areas, including a drained moat, the grass around the old horse pond, the grass in old orchards and an experimental 'North American prairie', developed with plants raised from seed and brought back from Minnesota. The meadows are wonderful for the diversity and fascination of the plants in them, in particular orchids, and also bulbs such as the native *Fritillaria meleagris* and *Narcissus pseudonarcissus*. The two areas each side of the path leading to the house porch are spangled with crocus and narcissus in early spring.

Moreover, the presence of a grassy orchard just across the stone-flagged path from one of the most carefully gardened mixed borders in the land is a lesson in what variety can be included in a single garden.

Great Dixter is probably the best garden in England for 'natural' gardeners just starting out to see what can be achieved in time. But because the flowers are not purely native (there are plenty of Dutch crocus and *Gladiolus byzantinus*) it is a bridge between the conventional garden and the purist's wildflower sanctuary. Christopher Lloyd wrote: 'With the Dixter meadows having, above all, an aesthetic purpose, I am free to cut them when it best suits me (and the meadow) and I can add or remove plants at will, introducing non-native plants to good effect.'[3]

The beauty of meadows is that, although they look their best in a country situation – especially if the impression, true or false, can be given that what you see is restitution rather than starting from scratch – it is also possible successfully to make them in gardens in suburbs, towns and cities too. Even a small urban 'meadow' will still foster a variety of native insects which would otherwise struggle to keep a toehold in the city.

The fascination of meadows in gardens to me is how different they can be, depending on soil composition and acidity, and aspect. Native wild flowers can be very fussy as to

where exactly they will grow. What you will find on a chalky south-facing grass bank will, obviously, be very different from an acid bog, but plants growing in a chalk beechwood will also not be the same. There are a number of much-loved British natives which either tolerate the shade of deciduous trees, or grow up and flower before the leaves come in spring – foxgloves, dog's mercury, cowslips, bluebells and wild garlic, to mention just a few; so woodland gardens, composed mainly of exotic rhododendrons, azaleas, magnolias and camellias, but with a good scattering of deciduous native trees, are places where woodland natives can flourish. This kind of planting in 'wild gardens', the furthest reaches of country gardens, has been recommended for more than a hundred years – ever since the days of William Robinson and his seminal *The Wild Garden*, in fact.

The author and designer Noël Kingsbury, in a thought-provoking essay on the politics of the 'natural garden',[4] divided natural garden makers into those influenced by the Enlightenment, who take a quasi-scientific approach, and the 'neo-Romantics', who are critical of the modern world and wish to reconnect with 'traditional' ways of doing things. Whatever the motivation, the results have been similar.

Implicit in the idea of gardening with nature as seen by the neo-Romantics is the notion that no foreign agent should be introduced. Although few gardeners are sufficiently purist to grow only native plants in their garden (if only because they deny themselves the benefit of a huge tranche of plants, indispensable to all but the fanatic), there are many who will not countenance the use of chemical – that is, not naturally occurring – fertilizers or pesticides. These we call, rather lazily but usefully, organic gardeners. At the present time, for example, there are slightly more than 30,000 members of Garden Organic (until recently known as the Henry Doubleday Research Association), but there are millions more gardeners – 90 per cent of us according to a 2006 RHS survey – who scarcely, if ever, use chemicals these days.

It is easy to pick holes in the philosophy of the organic movement, since it is rather contradictory, especially in its qualified acceptance of naturally occurring insecticides, such as derris, when it will not consider manufactured ones, which are often more specific and not harmful to a wide spectrum of beneficial or neutral insects. Nevertheless, the emphasis on feeding your soil, not your plants has had a beneficial effect on fertility and, in the case of many a kitchen garden, productiveness, and the holistic approach, of helping to provide shelter, corridors and food sources for birds, insects and small mammals, has had demonstrable, if not always easily quantifiable, benefits. Organic gardeners have, at the very least, proved that it is possible to achieve a rough balance between friend and foe in the garden, by encouraging beneficial creatures, even if there are some short-term depredations and compromises with which the gardener must come to terms.

A good example of a 'wild' garden, as advocated by William Robinson, is to be found at Abbotswood in Gloucestershire, with native and non-native plants happily intermingling. In spring, there are snakeshead fritillaries, narcissi and scillas, followed by spotted orchids and American skunk cabbage (*Lysichiton americanus*), seen here on the right-hand bank of the stream.

BELOW A wild, exuberant planting of *Verbena bonariensis*, grasses and *Echinacea* in a butterfly expert's garden in Dorset.

OPPOSITE Small tortoiseshell butterflies seek nectar in the flowers of the ice plant *Sedum spectabile* 'Meteor'. Scientists have discovered that many insects are happy to feed on non-native plants. Which is good news for everyone who wants to make a garden using exotic plants.

In the last decades, a number of English garden designers and commentators (I am sure influenced by the Enlightenment) have begun to draw inspiration from post-war German public parks and other projects, and a style dubbed the New Naturalism (also known as the New Wave or New Perennials movement) has evolved. Ironically, it is an idea which has, in essence, been around almost as long as Jekyllism. It can be traced to Professor Karl Foerster (1874–1970), a nurseryman of Bornim near Potsdam, whose 'nature garden' included three distinct German habitats (mountain, heathland and beechwood margin). This garden had a substantial influence on those responsible for public spaces like West Park in Munich and Britzer Park in Berlin. Foerster was the first man really to see the possibilities of grasses as garden plants, and he did a great deal of breeding work on now highly fashionable herbaceous perennial genera such as *Helenium*. For example, 'Mahogany' is one of his. (Ease of maintenance was for Foerster, Richard Hansen, Rosemary Weisse and the other Continental exponents of naturalism a vital consideration; they wanted it to work in public spaces as well, and we

Late-summer perennials soften the strict grid of rectangular beds in a garden designed by Christopher Bradley-Hole. Grasses include *Stipa gigantea*, *Miscanthus* and the shorter, airy *Deschampsia cespitosa*. Herbaceous perennials include *Eupatorium*, fennel, *Helenium* and *Gaura lindheimeri*.

all know that many indigenous plants can turn into weeds if put in the wrong place.)

One of the striking aspects of New Naturalism is its emphasis on trying to replicate the way plants grow in the wild, often called the 'ebb and flow of plant communities'. Very few people have the opportunity to achieve this replication faithfully, since most of our gardens have been tinkered with and enriched over the centuries, but it is possible in many instances to make a brave stab at it.

The garden at Lady Farm in Somerset has been developed since 1991 by its owners, with the help of the horticulturist Mary Payne. Of particular interest to us here is the acre of the garden given over to 'prairie' and 'steppe' gardens; these are large-scale plantings on a south-west slope leading down to two lakes. Ease of maintenance was an important consideration, and indeed these gardens have proved to need little routine care, apart from a strim of the dead seedheads in spring. The work at the beginning, eradicating perennial weeds, was another matter, but few gardeners escape having to battle with those problems initially.

The steppe, the hottest, driest part of the slope, has been planted with warm-season grasses, such as *Stipa gigantea* and *S. tenuissima*, together with Mediterranean sun-lovers such as *Origanum laevigatum* 'Herrenhausen', *Eryngium bourgatii*, *Artemisia alba* 'Canescens' and *Verbascum*.

The prairie, which is on a more moisture-retaining clay, has a good selection of North American prairie plants, most notably those with an autumn display: *Echinacea*, such as *E. purpurea* 'White Swan', *Liatris spicata* (both mauve and white forms), *Rudbeckia fulgida* var.

LEFT The 'steppe' garden at Lady Farm in Somerset, on the driest part of the south-west-facing slope, is at its best from May until July. Although there are some flowers, its impact depends largely on billows of foliage and the spiky flowerheads of tall *Stipa gigantea* and other grasses.

ABOVE A section of the 'prairie' at Lady Farm includes agastache, achillea, *Rudbeckia fulgida* var. *sullivantii* 'Goldsturm', *Calamagrostis* x *acutiflora* 'Karl Foerster', heleniums and *Echinacea purpurea* 'White Swan'. Many of these plants are of North American prairie origin.

sullivantii 'Goldsturm', *Helenium* 'Moerheim Beauty', *Solidago*, *Helianthus* 'Lemon Queen' and the grasses *Calamagrostis* × *acutiflora* 'Karl Foerster', *Miscanthus sinensis* 'Malepartus' and *Panicum virgatum* 'Strictum'. The steppe, not surprisingly, since the conditions are drier, grows less tall than the prairie. But tall as many of the prairie plants are, they are not staked (nor do they need to be), and nothing has been watered since it was first established.

Unlike the traditional planting of groups, in drifts or clumps of uneven numbers, here an essentially quite limited palette of plants is repeated over and over in different-sized groupings. The secret of the success appears to be in the choice of plants. No one is much more vigorous in the circumstances than another, and the colours harmonize quite well, being in the range that we are used to: gold, yellow, white, mauve and purple. Even where the colours contrast, the use of so many members of the daisy family, interspersed liberally with neutral, tall-growing grasses, means that the mixture is visually a happy one.

What the New Naturalists on the Continent realized is that natural communities are orderly, structured and predictable, even if they do not look that way to an untrained eye. Conventional garden practices such as hoeing, digging and soil enriching disrupt all that. If plants of equal or

A Dan Pearson planting in a garden in a Devon combe close to the sea. This relaxed combination of garden plants – tree lupins, black opium poppies, mulleins and white valerian – is designed to chime with the native wild flowers in the surrounding meadows.

nearly equal vigour are put in close competition with each other, as they may be in the wild, no one species will gain overall control. If the planting is layered – that is, it includes trees, shrubs, subshrubs, perennials, grasses and bulbs – a self-sustaining community is possible. The real difficulty practitioners in this country experience is distinguishing and holding the ring between good and bad grasses, since in our wet, mild climate, both annual and rhizomatous weed grasses grow extremely well, and are not obviously distinguishable from ornamental ones when small.

A central figure in the New Naturalism movement at present is Piet Oudolf, the Dutch nurseryman and garden designer; his influence is discussed on page 224. In this country, the guiding gurus have been Noël Kingsbury, especially in his writings, and Keith Wiley, head gardener at The Garden House in Devon from 1978 until 2003 and author of *On the Wild Side: Experiments in the New Naturalism*, published in 2004. Wiley's thesis is that we can learn much from the varying plant communities we see around the temperate world – prairies, grassland, mountains, cliff faces, woodland and woodland floor, bulb and other meadows, and semi-arid landscapes – and (if I have understood him correctly) that not to let that learning inform our gardening and instead to continue with our artificial garden making is frankly perverse.

The Garden House was developed originally by Lionel Fortescue (after whom *Mahonia × media* 'Lionel Fortescue' was named), in the 6.5-acre/2.6-hectare garden, part of it walled, of an old rectory in Devon. He was a very fine plantsman and gardener, and his garden had a high reputation for plants put sympathetically together. He died in 1981, by which time Keith Wiley was head gardener and beginning to extend the garden still further. After visits abroad, he made a Cretan-influenced Cottage Garden (see page 196) and a South African Garden as well as an Acer Glade. The important lesson that he learned from his trips abroad was that a plant community may have two or three dominant species, which occur frequently, but there will be smaller numbers of a far greater range of species as well; and that the density will be much greater than that in the planting in the average garden. This is beneficial in two ways: it lowers maintenance and it is very satisfying visually. This is really the crux of New Naturalism planting. He also recognized that if an area of planting is to flower in synchrony, it cannot be expected to last for very long, so there need to be a number of different areas. (Which incidentally was also Gertrude Jekyll's view, although Hadspen – see page 112 – perhaps proves that a longer synchronistic flowering is possible.)

At the same time as Keith Wiley was working at The Garden House, the owners of East Ruston Old Vicarage (what is it about old vicarages?), 1½ miles/2.5 kilometres from the Norfolk coast, were coming to some of the same conclusions, certainly on the importance of growing plants in habitats which suit them. In this very eclectic garden, which is beautifully kept, and gardened with great brio, there is a Californian Border, where a number of species from the west coast of the United States grow, including caerulean blue ceanothus. Close by, the picturesquely named Desert Wash is laid out to imitate a semi-arid desert such as those found in Arizona, with the rough channels in the surface caused by heavy thunderstorms twice a year. As the guidebook graphically describes it: 'but when it does rain it floods and great rushes of water channel through the landscape tossing rocks and stones asunder, leaving behind dry channels and islands where succulent plants flourish' (see also page 367).

They certainly seem to and, moreover, in the mild Norfolk coastal climate and with very careful soil preparation, even opuntias, agaves and aloes come through the winter unscathed.

Keith Wiley wrote of the New Naturalism style: 'I firmly believe we stand on the edge of perhaps the most exciting period in gardening history for maybe the last hundred years.'[5] He may very well be right. But Alexander Pope said something nearly three hundred years ago which leads me to wonder whether things don't just go round in circles: 'I believe it is no wrong Observation, that Persons of Genius, and those who are most capable of Art, are always fond of Nature, as such are chiefly sensible, that all Art consist in the Imitation and Study of Nature.'

It is hard to overstate the value of English gardens open to the public in the preservation and promotion of wildlife, even where strict organic principles are not adhered to. The presence of a large space, managed sympathetically and protected for many years against the encroachments of housing, roads or riotous outdoor activities, acts as a strong attractant to wildlife of every kind. One of the most satisfactory aspects of garden visiting is how loud the air is with bird song, and how busy the bees on the lavender. Most garden owners only protect their gardens against the depredations of real pests such as badgers and deer, by erecting defences against them; otherwise, they are happy to promote wildlife, even where they do not specifically reinstate meadows or grow *Sedum spectabile* for the butterflies.

On the matter of the preservation of humanity, as well as wildlife, the presence of an important historic garden is often the means of fending off an oppressive clamour for development, especially in our crowded southern counties, and this is one potent reason why gardens are so appealing to us as havens of peace and even sometimes balm for our troubled souls. Turn off a busy, noisy A-road or motorway and follow a brown sign and, if you are lucky, you may soon find yourself enfolded in the immemorial peace of Groombridge Place, say, or Goodnestone Park.

OTHER NATURAL GARDENS

Toddington Manor, Bedfordshire
Englefield House, Berkshire
Mariners, Berkshire
Bluebell Cottage Gardens, Cheshire
Bonython Manor Gardens, Cornwall
Trengwainton Garden, Cornwall
Acorn Bank Garden, Cumbria
Brantwood, Cumbria
Dalemain Gardens, Cumbria
Sizergh Castle, Cumbria
Hopton Hall Gardens, Derbyshire
Feeringbury Manor, Essex
The Gibberd Garden, Essex
Marks Hall, Essex
Olivers, Essex
Colesbourne Park, Gloucestershire
Daylesford House, Gloucestershire
Gilbert White's Garden, Hampshire
Houghton Lodge, Hampshire
Hergest Croft Gardens, Herefordshire
Jenningsbury, Hertfordshire
Ballalheanagh, Isle of Man
Stoneacre, Kent
Doddington Hall, Lincolnshire
Roots and Shoots, London
Althorp House, Northamptonshire
Canons Ashby, Northamptonshire
Coton Manor, Northamptonshire
Evenley Wood Garden, Northamptonshire
Belsay Hall Gardens, Northumberland
Howick Hall, Northumberland
Hodsock Priory, Nottinghamshire
Dudmaston, Shropshire
Wyken Hall, Suffolk
Gravetye Manor, Sussex
Burford House Gardens, Worcestershire
Stillingfleet Lodge, Yorkshire

6

INFLUENCES
FROM
ABROAD

The English garden, in one or another of its forms, has been transported far and wide across the temperate world. There were, and sometimes still are, 'English'-style gardens in, *inter alia*, Russia, Germany, Australia, India, South Africa and the United States. Some were copies of the eighteenth-century landscape garden, such as Tsarkoe Selo and Pavlovsk in Russia, and Wörlitz and Muskau in Germany; others were grand formal affairs, such as Château de la Garoupe in Cap d'Antibes and Villa Taranto on Lake Maggiore. Many more were humbler flower gardens made by homesick colonials trying to recapture, with varying degrees of success, some of the beauty and scents they remembered from their childhoods. When, soon after the First World War, Gertrude Jekyll was asked by the Imperial War Graves Commission (as it then was) for advice on plantings for the many British military cemeteries in northern France and Belgium, she chose English cottage garden flowers to fill the narrow borders in front of the gravestones. It was their homeliness and familiarity which recommended them to her, and it is those qualities which still appeal to the many visitors to these cemeteries today.

The traffic has by no means been all one way. English gardens have not been immune to influences from abroad: far from it. We are not so arrogant, apparently, that we cannot learn from others – as I have shown in earlier chapters and will explore further in this one. In the past, we have drawn on ideas from the French, Dutch, Italian, Persian, Indian, Japanese and Chinese; and, these days, thanks to high standards of illustrated books and the reach of the Internet, we are influenced strongly by the Germans, Dutch and North Americans as well.

The first foreigners to have an impact on English gardens were the Romans, who introduced a great many plants, such as the beech tree, the grape vine and ground elder, into this country. More importantly from our perspective, they also made enclosed, formal gardens (see page 13).

As for garden features, the knot appears to be an Italian invention of the late fifteenth century, which we embraced soon after with alacrity. We saw in Chapter 1 how we made it our own; and how, at the beginning of the seventeenth century, the prevailing French style became important and fashionable in England, influencing the gardens of the great and the good (well, the great anyway). This lasted, initially, for a hundred years. James I's wife, Anne of Denmark, employed a Huguenot gardener but, more importantly, Charles I's wife, Henrietta Maria, was

The extraordinary twisted petals of *Tulipa acuminata*, a tulip introduced from Turkey in the eighteenth century but not now known in the wild, if it ever was. It has been the parent of a number of lily-flowered cultivars.

The Egyptian Court at Biddulph Grange in Staffordshire, with its sentinel stone sphinxes and a 'pyramid' of yew. This garden was laid out by the owner, James Bateman, in the 1840s and brilliantly restored by the National Trust 150 years later.

French, and her gardener, André Mollet, introduced many French garden features to England. At one of the royal residences, Wimbledon Manor, he did away with the knots and replaced them with elaborate embroidered parterres, and removed the orchard, instead creating a maze and hedged groves and putting in a *patte d'oie* of five avenues radiating from a point close to the house. French influence brought many statues, often made of lead, to big gardens, as well as intricate ironwork gates and canals of water. After William and Mary arrived in 1688, a simplified version of the French style, which we now call Dutch, made headway also. Parterres were simplified, and topiary common. The important feature of all these gardens was that they were governed by axial geometry.

As we know, all that had come to an end (see Chapter 3) by the second third of the eighteenth century, but French influence of the elaborate Versailles/le Nôtre variety crept back again, perhaps in a self-consciously nostalgic way, in some gardens in the nineteenth century. Most notable was Waddesdon, where the garden was laid out by a Frenchman, Élie Lainé, in the 1880s, in line with Baron Ferdinand de Rothschild's passion for all things French (see page 30).

During the nineteenth century, a number of other styles, some of them 'period', jostled for the public's attention and approbation, but the Italian garden was certainly a favourite with many big landowners. Sir Charles Barry designed a succession of Italianate terraces at Shrubland Park in Suffolk (in the 1850s) as well as Trentham Gardens in Staffordshire (from 1833). Elements of this style included statuary (of course), elaborately balustraded stone terraces, broad walkways and formal water gardens. At the turn of the century there was Harold Peto (see pages 29 and 67) and also Sir George Sitwell at his own garden at Renishaw in Derbyshire, who was closely influenced by his knowledge of Italian and Renaissance gardens. And William Waldorf Astor (later Viscount Astor), after acquiring Cliveden, Buckinghamshire, in 1893, laid out a garden on a beautiful site overlooking the River Thames, with substantial Renaissance Italian elements. These included an arcaded terrace in front of Barry's grand Italianate mansion, with a sixteenth-century balustrade bought from the Villa Borghese, no less. He had acquired a number of other antiquities in his travels in Europe which are to be found either at Cliveden or at Hever Castle in Kent, which he bought in 1903. There he made a 4-acre/1.5-hectare walled garden, with a Classical loggia and the so-called Pompeian Wall as a background to many of his acquisitions. He also built a stone pergola, and grottoes and fountains to echo the Villa d'Este, the great Renaissance garden near Rome. You could say that Astor put the 'g' into grandiose. The last Italianate garden to be laid out was probably Ditchley Park in Oxfordshire in the 1930s, by Sir Geoffrey Jellicoe for Ronald and Nancy Tree (as Nancy Lancaster she gardened in later years at Haseley Court – see page 82).

The Chinese garden, even a Westernized version of it, never enjoyed great popularity in England, although aspects of Chinoiserie were fashionable in the eighteenth century. For example, there are 'Chinese' buildings in a number of landscape gardens, such as Shugborough, Staffordshire (a 1748 Chinese pavilion), and Studley Royal, North Yorkshire. And, most famously, there is William Chambers' Pagoda (1761–2), recently triumphantly restored, at the Royal Botanic Gardens, Kew. From the nineteenth century, we can point to the 1827 Chinese Pagoda Fountain (a copy of the To Ho Pagoda in Canton), painted red and green, at Alton Towers in Staffordshire, designed by Robert Abrahams. Alton Towers is, these days, an entertainment park, usually avoided by garden visitors like the plague, but the extensive gardens are worth seeing, nevertheless.

At Biddulph Grange in Staffordshire there is a garden of startling eclecticism and great interest, laid out in the 1840s and brilliantly restored by the National Trust in the 1990s. As well as a formal Italian terrace and an Egyptian Court (with stone sphinxes to guard it and a pyramid in yew), there is a fascinating Chinese water garden, complete with a richly decorated pagoda, a pool and bridge, whose design was influenced by the willow pattern story, as well as a miniature Great Wall of China. Tunnels and walkways connect the disparate elements of this garden, a veritable *tour d'horizon* of world styles, as conceived by a High Victorian. Made by the owner, James Bateman, a great plantsman and botanist, with the help of his friend, Edward Cooke, who was a marine artist and son-in-law of the renowned nurseryman George Loddiges, the garden was the repository of huge numbers of rare and newly imported plants.

Chinese gardens were far less commonly created than Japanese ones, which became all the rage from the 1890s onwards. The craze was given intellectual underpinning by two influential books by Josiah Conder, entitled *Flowers of Japan and the Art of Floral Arrangement* and *Landscape Gardens in Japan*, published in 1891 and 1893 respectively. These, at last, gave people in England some understanding of the symbolism inherent in true Japanese gardens. Fortuitously, English gardeners also had the opportunity to plant some of the marvellous hardy trees and shrubs which were pouring in from the Far East at the time.

Cliveden, Buckinghamshire, was probably the first place to acquire a water garden in the Japanese style, while Heale Garden, Wiltshire, has an important one, with a thatched tea house and red-painted Japanese bridge. Ramster in Surrey also has elements of a Japanese garden. The most impressive one, however, must be that at Tatton Park, Cheshire, restored in 2000–2001; it has a tea garden, with a kasatei (rest house), a lake with an island, which contains a Shinto shrine, and a representation of Mount Fuji, surrounded by a bamboo fence. The garden was laid out by Japanese gardeners between 1910 and 1913. Undoubtedly, Japanese gardens which were actually laid out by

OPPOSITE A view of the Chinese bridge from the richly decorated pagoda at Biddulph Grange in Staffordshire.

FOLLOWING PAGES The thatched tea house and red-painted Japanese bridge at Heale Garden in Wiltshire. The bridge and tea house were imported from Japan in 1910 and put together by four Japanese gardeners. There is a certain creative licence here: the *Gunnera manicata* is a native of Brazil.

Japanese craftsmen were the most authentic, and also therefore the most successful.

Although never hugely popular, and at times embarrassingly inauthentic, this style has had its loyal adherents ever since, notably in public parks (Holland Park and Royal Botanic Gardens, Kew) as well as in a few domestic gardens, such as Dartington Hall, Devon, with its 'dry stone' garden. There are well-executed Japanese-influenced elements, such as cloud hedges and a Japanese arch, at Saling Hall in Essex.

Other Oriental influences that can be glimpsed in English gardens are Mughal ones, as at Shute House, Dorset, in the work done by Sir Geoffrey Jellicoe, and Sezincote, Gloucestershire (see page 150), and the Persian-influenced Knot Garden at Sudeley Castle, Gloucestershire.

In the last fifteen years, the foreign style which has created the most impact is, without doubt, the New Naturalism. I have outlined briefly something of the history of this in Chapter 5, but here is the place to acknowledge the enormous influence of one man, on both English attitudes to this style and our ability to copy it. That man is the Dutch garden designer and nurseryman, Piet Oudolf. His reputation and influence rest on a show garden he made for the Chelsea Flower Show in 2000 with Arne Maynard, which won the prize for Best in Show; a number of high-profile garden projects he undertook in England, most notably the RHS Gardens at Wisley, Pensthorpe Waterfowl Park in Norfolk (where he made a Millennium Garden), Bury Court in Hampshire, Scampston Hall in Yorkshire and, most recently, with Tom Stuart-Smith, Trentham Gardens in Staffordshire (see page 32); and a trickle of books in which he explains the style, and how it can be achieved.

His long experience as a nurseryman (together with his wife, Anja) means that, more than most garden designers, he understands the ways and needs of the plants that he uses. Indeed, he has selected and named some of the cultivars he uses in his schemes, such as *Stachys officinalis* 'Hummelo', and has certainly succeeded in popularizing others, for example *Cirsium rivulare* 'Atropurpureum'. This is extremely important in the New Naturalism style since, in an ebb-and-flow situation, if too

The Perennial Meadow (left) and Katsura (*Cercidiphyllum japonicum*) Grove (right) at Scampston Hall Walled Garden in Yorkshire, designed by the Dutch designer and nurseryman Piet Oudolf. The Walled Garden consists of a number of rectangular gardens, with paths interestingly offset, all of which have a different atmosphere to them. Although still very young, with hedges and topiary elements not yet grown completely, this is already a thrilling garden, full of thought-provoking and playful ideas. Another inventive planting is the Drift of Grass Garden, where *Molinia caerulea* subsp. *caerulea* (tall flower spikes with masses of tiny dark florets in late summer) is planted in sinuous curves through the close-mown lawn. This is a garden to see from the air, if possible!

vigorous (or conversely too fragile) species and cultivars are employed, they will swamp or be swamped.

Since Oudolf's interest is in echoing the dynamic of nature, his gardens are designed to delight through most of the year. Although the majority of the perennials and grasses flower between July and September, they are not cut down in the winter, in order that their seedheads can be properly appreciated (as well as provide food sources for birds), especially after frosty nights. The plants are often grown in great bold drifts, but far larger than anything Gertrude Jekyll designed, or planted in blocks or curvilinear diagonals (as at Scampston Hall, Yorkshire).

The liberal use of evergreen and deciduous grasses as buffers means that the eye happily accepts daring colour clashes, where they occur. (Oudolf has no time for agonizing about the colour wheel, incidentally.) Grasses are central to his schemes, and a number have found enormous favour in English gardens as a result. Examples include *Deschampsia caespitosa*, *Sesleria nitida*, *Molinia caerulea*, *Stipa gigantea* and *Panicum*

virgatum. North American prairie perennials feature prominently, notably *Rudbeckia, Monarda, Liatris, Eupatorium, Veronicastrum* and *Asclepias.*

Form is also hugely important to him, strong verticals being provided by, for example, *Eupatorium* and *Veronicastrum*, and ground cover by, for example *Salvia* × *sylvestris* 'Rügen' and herbaceous geraniums.

Oudolf uses predominantly perennials, but also bulbs, such as alliums, as well as ferns, small shrubs, which can be pruned hard, like *Indigofera heterantha*, and even self-seeding annuals, such as Shirley poppies (*Papaver*). It is important to realize that he is prepared to countenance more 'wildness' than Gertrude Jekyll. He appears to be conscious of the potential tension between 'natural' and 'garden', seeing his approach as principally concerned with atmosphere, but also influenced by fashion. Although he does not specifically exclude indigenous plants, he is wary of them, since low maintenance is a very important consideration for him, as it is for all practitioners of this style. The criticism of his planting, and indeed that of all the New Naturalists, and it is a valid one, is that

The four-sided viewing mound in Scampston Hall Walled Garden in Yorkshire. It stands in a meadow of wild flowers and bulbs, as well as *Prunus yedoensis* trees.

such a reliance on herbaceous perennials makes these summer gardens, with frankly pretty little to see in the spring.

It would be a mistake, however, to think that Oudolf does not use formal and permanent elements at all. At Scampston Hall, there are, *inter alia,* a grass pyramid, axial lines of clipped hedges and gravel paths, a circular pool and avenues of trees. Even the meadows are confined by mown paths. At Bury Court, Hampshire, there is even a knot garden of clipped box as well as other clipped elements.

Other foreign influences have filtered through over the years and affected the way some of our gardens look. The Modernist movement, which made little impact initially in England in the 1920s, was far more successful in the United States, and a number of landscape architects came out of the universities, imbued with Modernist ideas. Some of these have had quite an influence on English gardens, although it has not always been direct. These include Thomas Church, Dan Kiley, Lawrence Halprin and Garrett Eckbo. Where they designed gardens for private clients, their interest was focused on the people who would be using those gardens. Garrett Eckbo wrote a book published in 1950

Oudolf is not averse to using formal elements, such as this modern take on a knot garden at Bury Court in Hampshire. The rounding of the tops is more common on the Continent, but it may have the advantage of throwing off rain, and perhaps thereby inhibiting the spread of box blight.

called *Landscape for Living*, while Thomas Church's 1955 work is entitled *Gardens are for People*. They could not have made their intentions clearer. They were early pioneering environmentalists, yet experimented with new materials and ways of flow through the garden as well. Church, whose designs became more abstract with time, created some two thousand gardens, is famous for his curvaceous swimming pools, his Californian timber decking (often built out over a hillside), and his use of ground-cover and indigenous Californian plants. His emphasis on 'outdoor living' had a profound impact on other designers. As for Eckbo, his garden was sponsored by ALCOA, and was full of aluminium elements.

Of course, no consideration of foreign influences is complete without at least a nod in the direction of Roberto Burle Marx (1909–94), the Brazilian artist, gardener, botanist, plant hunter and landscape designer who created plantings that were akin to his abstract paintings, in great, free-flowing, colourful patterns, using native ground-covering plants. Some of these he had collected himself for he was an early champion of Brazilian plant conservation.

This is the hornbeam tunnel each side of the Grand Cascade (see page 296) at The Alnwick Garden in Northumberland. The tunnel comprises 850 hornbeams and was designed by the Belgian designers Jacques and Peter Wirtz. Much of The Alnwick Garden, the most ambitious garden to be made for many a long year, is their work.

What all these men did was to enthuse and invigorate the landscape architects in this country after the Second World War, when they were starved of home-grown inspiration. These included Dame Sylvia Crowe, Brenda Colvin, Sir Geoffrey Jellicoe, Russell Page and, latterly, the garden designers John Brookes, David Stevens, Dan Pearson and Christopher Bradley-Hole (see Chapter 11).

The internationalism of modern illustrated publishing means that contemporary garden designers have been well exposed to their American counterparts, such as James van Sweden and Wolfgang Oehme, and the Belgian Jacques Wirtz and his son Peter (their work can now be seen at The Alnwick Garden in Northumberland as well). Other foreign designers presently collaborating with English garden owners include Pascal Cribier, François Goffinet, Isabelle van Groeningen and Brita von Schoenaich, all contributing to a lively exchange of ideas. And, of course, Arabella Lennox-Boyd brings an Italian flair to her garden designs, including her own garden at Gresgarth Hall, Lancashire. The preoccupations of gardeners and garden designers everywhere seem to be converging. They are, at present, absorbed by notions of achieving a light environmental footprint in the garden, in doing the least harm to nature and yet achieving something individual, even individualistic, and permanent.

As well as design styles which have been imported from elsewhere in the world it seems to me important to say something about foreign plants, since it is hard to overstate their influence in shaping the look of our gardens.

Apart from those plants brought by the Romans, information about foreign plants is pretty well non-existent until 1140, when Thomas Becket, of all people, brought back the first fig tree (supposedly) from Italy, whither he had travelled on pilgrimage, and planted it at the Priory of West Tarring in Sussex.

Not long afterwards, the saffron crocus (*C. sativa*) was introduced by a pilgrim returning from the Holy Land, setting off a sadly short-lived commercial operation based at Saffron Walden, Essex. Peaches arrived from southern Europe by the end of the century, certainly in time for a surfeit of them to kill King John in 1216. In that century we also got walnuts (*Juglans regia*), lavender (*Lavandula spica*) and almonds (*Prunus dulcis*), while in the next we acquired rosemary and 'gilliflowers' (*Dianthus*). Knots would not have been possible in the form they took without the introduction of box from Holland, and lavender and rosemary from southern Europe.

In the sixteenth century, we acquired the holm oak (*Quercus ilex*), our only evergreen oak, both the red and the white mulberry (*Morus nigra* and *M. alba*), the tomato (*Lycopersicum lycopersicum*), the tulip (*Tulipa*), and the potato (*Solanum tuberosum*). This century also saw the introduction of laurustinus (*Viburnum tinus*) and phillyrea (*P. angustifolia* and *P. latifolia*), both 'greens' that proved very useful for planting in the Baroque garden. There were now opportunities for adventurous experimentation in both the productive and ornamental gardens.

The horse chestnut (*Aesculus hippocastanum*) and common larch (*Larix europea*) arrived in the next century and, after 1620, there began a steady stream of imported North American plants such as the strawberry (*Fragaria vesca*), sumach (*Rhus typhina*), false acacia (*Robinia pseudoacacia*) and Virginia creeper (*Parthenocissus quinquefolia*).

In the eighteenth century, explorers managed to get as far as South Africa (pelargoniums and *Kniphofia*) and North America, introducing *Magnolia grandiflora* and *Hamamelis virginiana*. There were also the first introductions from China and Japan, such as *Camellia japonica* (1739),

FOLLOWING PAGES

LEFT ABOVE Pelargoniums were introduced from South Africa in the eighteenth century. This is a particularly beautiful and delicate cultivar called 'Ardens'.

LEFT BELOW Kniphofias (often known as red hot pokers) were also introduced in the eighteenth century. They are natives of South Africa, but essential denizens of the English herbaceous border. This is *K. rooperi*.

RIGHT A good example of the dependence of English gardens on foreign plants. This is a view of *Acer palmatum* cultivars and *Pinus* at the National Arboretum at Westonbirt, Gloucestershire. The setting may look reasonably 'natural' but none of the trees used is native.

Magnolia stellata was introduced from Japan in 1877. It is acknowledged to be the best magnolia for small gardens, growing slowly to 10 feet/3 metres tall, and it flowers in the first year after planting. Not surprisingly, it is widely planted.

Aucuba japonica (that obligatory denizen of the Victorian shrubbery) and the repeat-flowering China rose *R. semperflorens*. By the end of the century we had both the zinnia and the dahlia from Central America, so the stage was set for exuberant bedding-out schemes in the Victorian era.

In the nineteenth century, plants came from all over the globe: wisteria (*W. sinensis*), *Camellia reticulata* and *Rosa chinensis* from China, the Douglas fir (*Pseudotsuga menziesii*) and sitka spruce (*Picea sitchensis*) from North America, *Cedrus deodara* and *Rhododendron arboreum* from the Himalayas, and *Petunia axillaris* and *P. integrifolia* (1837) from Brazil. Early in the twentieth century, we acquired *Lilium regale* and the mophead 'hortensia', *Hydrangea macrophylla*.

These are just a few of the important introductions which, when taken as a whole, played a central role in shaping the English garden, and we can see the result in many gardens today, even though the stream of foreign plants has now slowed to a trickle. (There are still plant hunters working in the field and bringing back gardenworthy plants, but they are under greater restraints than their forebears and, though the quality is high, the numbers are definitely lower than they were 100 years ago.)

It is hard to see how garden creators would ever have got the Japanese garden style even approximately right if a large number of Japanese maples (*Acer japonicum* and *A. palmatum*) and azaleas had not been imported. Their scale and colour, as well as their presence in Japanese art, ensured that it was possible to make a fine job of the Japanese Garden at Tatton Park, for example.

Moreover, it is surely improbable that the woodland garden (see pages 175–85) would ever have developed at all without the magnolias, camellias, rhododendrons, azaleas, michelias and pieris which arrived on these shores in the nineteenth century. For example, *Magnolia stellata*, which arrived in 1878 from Japan, and *Rhododendron fortunei*, introduced from China in 1843. The influx of hardy evergreen conifers – the wellingtonia (*Sequoiadendron giganteum*) and Lawson cypress (*Chamaecyparis lawsoniana*) from California, and also the western red cedar (*Thuja plicata*), all in 1853 – was also crucial to the layout and look of large gardens, and that is so even today.

Finally, the large, productive kitchen gardens of the nineteenth and early twentieth centuries were strongly dependent on foreign fruits and vegetables to tempt the palates of country house families: peaches, nectarines, dessert grapes, pineapples, tomatoes, even the workaday potato were all imports that have influenced taste, fashion and culture in this country, right up to the present day.

OTHER GARDENS WITH INFLUENCES FROM ABROAD

Swiss Garden, Bedfordshire
Waddesdon Manor, Buckinghamshire
Henbury Hall, Cheshire
Lamorran House, Cornwall
Pine Lodge Garden, Cornwall
Holker Hall, Cumbria
Dartington Hall, Devon
Killerton, Devon
Abbotsbury Sub-Tropical Gardens, Dorset
Compton Acres, Dorset
Kingston Lacy, Dorset
Melplash Court, Dorset
Marks Hall, Essex
Batsford Arboretum, Gloucestershire
Belmont, Kent
Lullingstone Castle, Kent
The Exotic Garden, Norfolk
Thrigby Hall Wildlife Gardens, Norfolk
'Pure Land' Japanese Garden, Nottinghamshire

ORNAMENT IN THE GARDEN

Ornament is, and always has been, an integral part of many gardens, for it is a powerful tool in the creation of atmosphere, as well as often a visible sign of prosperity and worldly success. Over the centuries, topiary, statuary, sculpture, garden buildings and follies, fountains, urns and even humble benches have been employed by garden makers to create or promote a particular mood, as well as to act as eyecatchers, to close vistas, to prompt reflection of an elevated kind or simply to add interest over and above that provided by the architecture of the house, the hard landscaping or the soft garden planting. Depending on where, or how, they are sited, ornaments can be an invitation to survey the scene or to retreat to secluded privacy. Where time, thought and artistic sense have been deployed, they contribute significantly to the aesthetic quality of gardens.

What is employed as ornament is important, when the gardener is seeking to create the appropriate atmosphere. Is it to be Italianate, rustic, old-world, shiningly contemporary, brashly in-your-face or carefully sympathetic to the vernacular architecture of the house? Whatever the decision, it usually has an enormous impact on the garden.

It is an axiom that gardens, especially large ones, need good circulation to deliver the maximum satisfaction and pleasure from a tour. Those features mentioned above often provide opportunities, even excuses, to stand and stare. They are called, rather inelegantly, punctuation points, and they can create both surprise and the expectation that there will be further surprises.

Eyecatchers have long been popular as devices for slowing a garden visit down to a pace at which the garden can be thoroughly appreciated. The most obvious, and natural, eyecatcher is the view of the landscape beyond the garden, of course, if there is one; this often has most impact when it is framed like a picture, the frame being trees and shrubs, gateways, circular holes in walls or even simple gaps in a boundary hedge. In the eighteenth century, vertical monuments, such as obelisks, were very popular, because they could be used effectively both as distant eyecatchers and for the greater glory of the garden maker.

Eyecatchers come in many forms, and one variation is the vista-closer, which is often, in gardens laid out in the seventeenth and eighteenth centuries, a large urn on a plinth, but can be as simple as a bench backed by a hedge. It is anything which both draws the eye to it and stops it

OPPOSITE Queen Caroline's Monument at Stowe Landscape Gardens in Buckinghamshire, an impressive eyecatcher (as well as an elegant example of currying favour with your sovereign, George III, whose wife Caroline was). There is also a monument to the king himself at Stowe.

BELOW 'What is this life if, full of care/We have no time to stand and stare?' A resin sculpture by Giles Penney in a garden in Sussex.

ORNAMENT IN THE GARDEN

An eyecatcher, known as the Mausoleum, in the 1750s landscape garden by Coplestone Warre Bampfylde at Hestercombe in Somerset. This has recently been restored.

from going any further. At Bramham Park, there is an interesting variation on that: the so-called Four Faces Urn on a plinth seems to close the vista from the T-Pond until the visitor gets near to it, and then he or she discovers that the ride continues on down a slope to the ha-ha, invisible until that point (see page 129). Nowadays, a vista-closer is as likely to be a church across the valley, as at The Garden House, Buckland Monachorum, or even a handsome mature tree in a neighbour's garden. At East Ruston Old Vicarage, one vista is closed by distant Happisburgh lighthouse, another by Happisburgh church. These views, come upon unexpectedly, create a real frisson of excitement, although perhaps I should apologize for spoiling the surprise!

At various times in the history of the English garden, but particularly in the early eighteenth century, ornament was employed where it seemed fitting to push on the 'narrative' of the garden. The largest scale on which this was done was at Stowe, of course, where there are more than twice the number of listed buildings than in any other garden, all put there for a purpose. Amongst them are the Temple of Venus, the Gothic Temple, the Doric Arch, the Corinthian Arch and the Palladio-inspired Palladian Bridge. There is also the Temple of Ancient Virtue on a small hill overlooking William Kent's Elysian Fields, which is domed and colonnaded and contains statues of heroes of the classical world, so important to eighteenth-century educated gentlemen. Until the 1770s,

A simple but effective carving on wood by Janet Boulton, a protégée of Ian Hamilton Finlay. The quotation is from the Greek philosopher Epicurus. A rather problematic exhortation, it seems to me, but this is certainly a handsome and distinctive garden ornament.

when it was removed, there was a nearby Temple of Modern Virtue, built as a ruin. How those gents must have laughed! For the owners, the Temples, with the family motto '*Templa quam dilecta*' (How beautiful are thy temples), temples obviously had a punning, as well as serious, meaning. They were Whigs to their fingertips but fell out of favour with Sir Robert Walpole, the Whig prime minister. So they used the gardens for making a number of political points, which contemporary visitors would not have missed. The statuary carved especially for the curved Temple of British Worthies all represents prominent Whigs, such as Alexander Pope, or famous historical figures such as Elizabeth I, whom Whigs admired (see page 137).

Garden ornaments can be triggers for reflection and inspiration, but also vehicles for symbolism or underlying meaning. In the contemporary garden, these are once more important to gardeners, who are struggling just as hard as eighteenth-century intellectuals to make sense of religion and philosophy, not to mention the strife of a war-torn world; the kind of meaning, in fact, which could not, or cannot, be divined or expressed by simply the layout and composition of the garden itself.

The best contemporary exponent of this was undoubtedly the late Scottish poet and landscape artist Ian Hamilton Finlay, and the English garden is the poorer for there being so little of his work in England (his garden, Little Sparta, is alas, outside the scope of this book, as it is to be

found in the Pentland Hills in Lanarkshire), but we are lucky that he did some work at Stockwood Park in Bedfordshire, on the southern outskirts of Luton, owned now by Luton Borough Council. Of the eighteenth-century estate, only a stable block, the walled gardens and pleasure grounds survive. The fascination of this garden lies in the part of the park close to the original ha-ha, called (in a witty reference to eighteenth-century landscape gardens) 'The Improvement Garden', where he placed six sculptural works, alluding to the classical landscape garden. Most playful is the scatter of flattish stones, which he called 'a flock of sheep', but there is also a brick wall, with beautifully inscribed stone plaques, 'translating' Latin words, called the Errata of Ovid, as well as a plaque to the Muse on an ash tree, a 'fallen' capital, half buried in the ground, and two birches growing out of stone column bases. This garden is, by turns, mystifying and amusing, but always thought-provoking.

Rather zanier, but also with an important underlying symbolism, is the work of Ivan Hicks, a trained arboriculturist who was Edward James's head gardener at West Dean, as well as working on his employer's

OPPOSITE A plaque by Ian Hamilton Finlay affixed to a weeping ash tree in what he called 'The Improvement Garden' at Stockwood Park in Bedfordshire. He put in a number of sculptures with witty references to eighteenth-century classical landscapes, including 'a flock of sheep' composed of rough-hewn stones disposed on the grass near the remains of the eighteenth-century ha-ha.

ABOVE The curved brick wall sculpture at Stockwood Park which Ian Hamilton Finlay named 'The Errata of Ovid'. The other plaques read: 'For DAPHNE read LAUREL'; 'For PHILOMELA read NIGHTINGALE'; 'For CYANE read FOUNTAIN'; 'For ECHO read ECHO'; 'For ATYS read PINE'; 'For NARCISSUS read NARCISSUS'; 'For ADONIS read ANEMONE'.

A stone spiral designed by Ivan Hicks. It is plainly an important symbolic motif for him; there is also one in the Enchanted Forest at Groombridge Place in Kent.

gardens in Mexico, Ireland and Italy, and a man plainly imbued with James's fascination with the surreal. He has done something to bring the surreal to staid old English gardens; in particular he did so at the Garden in Mind at Stansted Park in Sussex, now sadly replaced by a yew maze.

His gardens have a not unpleasant dream-like quality to them. He is influenced by ancient Celtic tree mythology and, although the Garden in Mind is no more, his work can be seen in the 25-acre/10-hectare Enchanted Forest at Groombridge Place, Kent, a traditional broadleaf woodland which has been made a place of wonder (or adventure playground, depending on your point of view) for children. It is reached by raised walkway, by canal boat or by twisting path and contains *inter alia* a Mystic Pool, as well as a Serpents' Lair, inspired by myths about snakes and sacred pools, and a Double Spiral pattern laid out on the woodland floor. There is a Valley of Tree Ferns with more than a hundred large specimens from Australia. There are many 'found' natural objects such as tree roots and even a giant spider's web of twigs suspended between trees. How much children (or even adults) perceive

The bears in the Howdah Court at The Laskett in Herefordshire. These bears were originally part of a tableau designed by Julia Trevelyan Oman for the conservatory at Warwick Castle. They stand on salvaged industrial brick and metal grilles.

of the ideas behind all this may be conjectured, but it certainly makes it fun for them. Hicks calls it escapism in the same vein as Harry Potter and J.R.R. Tolkein.

At The Garden in Mind he combined a highly classical, formal layout with anarchic artifacts, as if to suggest that these elements were at war. There were carefully pruned tree sculptures and 'towers' formed from circles of trees. At another (private) garden which he has designed, he has put in a Plant Prison, where 'criminals' such as tobacco plants and opium poppies are detained. Recently, he has created a Family Wood at Escot Park in Devon, which includes Jurassic Park and upside-down trees. When writing of what he does, he mentions the importance of atmosphere in a garden, as well as a particular interest in using gardens to evoke drama and surprise as well as fantasy and fun. Which is something of an understatement.[1]

This desire to stimulate thought can also be seen clearly at The Laskett, Herefordshire, where ornament is central to the garden's purpose and is used in some places almost as a theatrical prop. The

stone stag in the orchard, for example, has gold-painted antlers, while a monument to a much-loved cat has incorporated in it a ball painted with gold leaf – indeed Sir Roy Strong has written persuasively on the virtues of gold leaf for outside ornamentation. There is also adventurous use of painted Victorian radiator panels, heating grilles and spiral staircases in the garden called Howdah Court, made in the late 1990s. Strong recalls: 'colour in the garden became an increasing preoccupation during the 1990s and by it we meant not that from plants but that which could be applied to the garden's artifacts'.[2] He admits to being influenced, to a certain extent at least, by both Ivan Hicks' work at Groombridge Place, and Derek Jarman's at Prospect Cottage. The result, however, is highly individual.

In a very different way, the garden outside Prospect Cottage at Dungeness, Kent, made by Derek Jarman, the film director, from 1987 is also a prompter of reflections through ornament, not all of them very comfortable ones, I imagine, considering that Jarman was tragically ill when he made it. Derek Jarman 'made' the garden in the most inhospitable possible surroundings: the sun-beaten, salt-wind-fretted

OPPOSITE A garden full of resonances and made in the most inhospitable surroundings; this is the late Derek Jarman's garden at Prospect Cottage, facing the monumental Dungeness Power Station in Kent. Jarman's garden, composed of shingle, salt-tolerant plants such as seakale (*Crambe maritima*) and *objets trouvés*, some of which were combed from the beach and made into sculptural shapes, as here. 'A garden is a treasure hunt, the plants the paperchase.'[3]

ABOVE Like Ivan Hicks, Jarman was influenced by the mystical. The placing of these objects is not random. 'I invest my stones with the power of those at Avebury . . .'[4]

shingle outside his wooden hut, facing the monumental and unquestionably threatening Dungeness power station. Although not a gardener when he began, he discovered that quite a few plants which we grow in gardens, such as seakale (*Crambe maritima*), poppies (*Papaver rhoeas*), helichrysum, santolina and cistus, would survive there and, amongst the plants, he put *objets trouvés* – often metal and wooden flotsam given up by the sea. These were carefully placed, as were stones to make circles and abstract patterns and what he called, when put vertically, 'dragon's teeth'. Like Hicks, he was influenced by the mystical: the stone circles had a symbolic meaning.

Although a surprising number of flowers blow, this is very far from being a conventional garden. 'There are no walls or fences. My garden's boundaries are the horizon,'[5] he wrote. The fact that Jarman was dying when he made this garden has imbued it with a 'fist shaken against fate' defiance, which is unusual, but by no means unheard of, in a garden. Intimations of mortality have sometimes been powerful motive forces for garden makers.

Sir Frederick Gibberd was another who was famous for using salvaged objects as garden ornament. He laid out a 7-acre/3-hectare garden in Essex for himself which is, these days, thanks to the Frederick Gibberd Trust, open to garden visitors. In a clearing in the wood, for example, there are Classical pillars, which he salvaged from Coutts Bank in The Strand in London when he was remodelling the building. This garden has some eighty pieces of sculpture, as well as large ceramic pots and architectural salvage, garden follies and fountains. In one place, he dug a moat,

LEFT The artist Janet Boulton's garden in Oxfordshire. Included in this picture is the carving that is portrayed in close-up on page 241. On the left is a still life entitled *Homage de Juan Gris*, an unusual feature for most gardens, but not this one, which contains allusions to many admired twentieth-century artists.

RIGHT This door does not lead anywhere but, half-hidden, it creates mystery and expectation – particularly useful attributes in a small garden, which this is, in Ludlow in Shropshire, designed by Mirabel Osler.

made a mound out of the spoil and placed on top a castle composed of chopped elm logs, with a drawbridge to get to it, as a plaything for his grandchildren.

Objects and ornaments in English gardens are made of a whole host of materials, of course, and the choice of material undoubtedly evokes particular reactions and assumptions in the beholder. Galvanized steel planters, for example, mean modern, urban, even edgy, while stone (or Haddonstone) fat-bellied Grecian urns suggest period, traditional, even landed. As far as the materials used for containers are concerned, terracotta is particularly versatile and perhaps also the most classless. It can be workaday but handsome, when it is a rhubarb forcing pot, or elaborate and self-confident, if it is a large pot ornamented with Italianate loops and swags.

Just the placing of a few simple pots together makes for a charmingly unified

ORNAMENT IN THE GARDEN

garden picture, as at Bourton House, Gloucestershire. Bourton is also lucky enough to have lead cisterns which, when put against the wall of a building, and planted up, give a powerful sense of permanence to a garden, since these were functional objects common in the seventeenth and eighteenth centuries.

Size matters as far as containers are concerned. Large pots are acceptable in a small garden, provided that the planting is equally bold (see page 371, for example). Small pots at a distance can enhance the feeling of space. They are useful tools for perspective and false perspective.

OPPOSITE A lead cistern becomes more than a container for plants: it is sufficiently interesting and decorative to be an ornament in its own right. This is at Bourton House in Gloucestershire.

BELOW This is a carefully thought-out jumble of pots by garden designer Andy Rees, showing that, in the right hands, unpromising materials can create impressive garden ornaments. This is in his own small garden in Buckinghamshire.

ORNAMENT IN THE GARDEN

RIGHT The Carrara marble *White Wall* by Ben Nicholson at Sutton Place in Surrey. The sculpture was made specially. Reflected in the water, it seems to float. Moreover, the circles, which are concave in the original, become convex in the reflection. I feel its impact would be even greater if the reflected image was not partly masked by water plants.

FOLLOWING PAGES Ornament can be revealing of the gardener's personality. Here, at Gresgarth Hall in Lancashire, a lion couchant adds a touch of levity.

At Sutton Place, Surrey, Sir Geoffrey Jellicoe placed a number of very large antique urns, bought at the famous Mentmore sale, on plinths in the so-called Magritte Garden, close to a narrowing path, made of progressively smaller paving stones, which leads to a wall with no obvious exit. This gives a very disturbing perspective, in conscious homage to the surrealist artist, René Magritte – hence the name the garden has acquired.

Ornaments of every kind can add humour, even wackiness, to a garden. Some gardens are very good at this, especially if the owners are keen to draw in families with children. One garden which has not compromised the idea of a garden, yet is most enjoyable, thanks to its Giant Chessboard, Golden Key Maze and Ivan Hicks-designed Enchanted Forest, is Groombridge Place. Another with giant forms of children's games – snakes and ladders, chess and draughts – is to be found in the Walled Garden at Burton Agnes Hall in Yorkshire.

For a very long time, topiary specimens have been used to promote an atmosphere of light-heartedness or gentle irony in the garden. I have discussed topiary as a constituent of garden structure in Chapter 1; here it is sufficient to point out what good, old-fashioned, innocent jollity it can provide as well: Arabella Lennox-Boyd's couchant lion in her garden at Gresgarth Hall for example; the 'bedroom' garden at Chatsworth, with a 'four-poster bed' of ivy and a privet 'dressing table'; and the ivy-clad figures of the Dowager Queen, Katherine Parr and Lady Jane Grey 'on their way to church' in the garden at Sudeley Castle, Gloucestershire.

A dead cherry tree acquired a new life when painted as a garden ornament in Andrew Lawson's Oxfordshire garden. Note also how carefully the terracotta pots have been disposed, and also the tiny hedge-bound pond. At the back of the garden is a false perspective created by a tapering path. There are a number of sculptures in the garden, the work of his wife, Briony.

Ornament in gardens need not be complex or expensive (although it very often is). It can be as simple as an intriguing colour paint on wood or metal. In Andrew Lawson's garden, Gothic House in Oxfordshire, when a precious cherry tree died, he painted it a wonderful lapis lazuli blue and turned it, thereby, into a work of art. In the process, he added his own contribution to the sculptures in the garden, the work of his wife, Briony. Sad to say, four years later the cherry tree was so attacked by fungi that it had to be removed. It has been replaced by a *Malus transitoria*. Such is life.

Trompe l'oeil is the term for a painting technique which is intended to provide an optical illusion: for example, to trick the eyes into believing that an object is three-dimensional, when in fact it is only two. It is particularly useful in smaller gardens, where

three-dimensional ornament might feel out of scale, even overbearing. It can also be just a bit of fun. Mirrors are used in gardens, especially small ones, and in garden buildings as well, to give a false sense of space.

Garden owners have also often felt the need to introduce beautiful objects to their gardens, as they would in their houses. Just as they wished to patronize (in the best sense of that word) contemporary craftsmen and artists indoors, they saw that it was important to do so outside as well. Garden owners have been important patrons of sculptors and craftsmen right up to the present day. Indeed, in some gardens, the garden layout itself has been dictated by the particular statuary or objects chosen. Sir Frederick Gibberd recalled his wife buying a sculpture: 'She buys immense works by young sculptors and we have the fun of finding sites which enhance both them and the garden. Sometimes the right site does not exist and so I make a garden for it.'[6]

In a number of gardens open to the public, the introduction of beautiful objects has been done selectively and most cleverly, and to the enhancement of the aesthetic pleasure of the onlooker. One example is

OPPOSITE A trick is being played here. This is a *trompe l'oeil* painting by Jessie Jones. I think we must assume that the *Clematis montana* is real. This is the garden of Mirabel Osler, the garden designer and writer, in Ludlow, Shropshire.

ABOVE Count the pots. There are actually only four, because another classic gardener's trick is being played on the unsuspecting visitor to her garden by Mirabel Osler, using a mirror to give a false sense of space.

FOLLOWING PAGES

LEFT ABOVE Roche Court in Wiltshire, is not, strictly speaking, a garden, but rather a sculpture park, in a beautiful parkland setting. This is *Back Flip* by Allen Jones.

LEFT BELOW A circular carved seat by Alison Crowther, also at Roche Court.

RIGHT ABOVE Dame Elisabeth Frink's monumental, but surprisingly benign-looking, bronze *War Horse* at the end of the Canal Pond at Chatsworth in Derbyshire. It was installed in 1992.

RIGHT BELOW Willow figures by Lynn Kirkham beckon you on through the woodland at Stone Lane Gardens in Devon. Although its lifespan is short, dried willow has proved popular in gardens, being comparatively cheap, light and extremely versatile.

BELOW At Highgrove in Gloucestershire, the Prince of Wales has enlisted the help of a number of garden designers and advisers, notably Rosemary Verey, Sir Roy Strong, the Marchioness of Salisbury and Dame Miriam Rothschild. The woodland is in the process of development by Julian and Isabel Bannerman and features a contemporary adaptation of the Victorian stumpery, with weathered tree stumps interplanted with ferns, hostas and foxgloves.

OPPOSITE *Three Fruit*, by Peter Randall Page at The Manor House, Bledlow, in Buckinghamshire. Randall Page has a number of sculptures in gardens open to the public, such as the *Jupiter Stone* at Antony in Cornwall, *Jacob's Pillow* at Dartington Hall in Devon and *Inner Compulsion* at the Millennium Seed Bank at Wakehurst Place in Sussex.

FOLLOWING PAGES
LEFT The sculptures in the ½-acre/0.2-hectare Barbara Hepworth Museum and Sculpture Garden at St Ives, Cornwall, are an integral part of this garden, but so equally are the plants and setting. Indeed, since the garden belonged to Barbara Hepworth and contained her studio (and has been kept as she left it when she died), it is probably easier for the visitor to understand her intent here than anywhere else. The sculptures, though abstract, are influenced by natural shapes and forms.

RIGHT The sculptures are in bronze, stone and wood. Barbara Hepworth lived here from 1949 until her death in 1975. This garden, with its subtropical plantings of arum lilies and palms, as well as *Prunus* 'Amanogawa' cherries and roses, became the permanent setting for her works after her death. Since 1980, it has been managed by the Tate.

the sensitive choice of modern sculpture in both the Formal Garden and the Wilderness at Antony in Cornwall, including, of course, the William Pye cone fountain, mimicking the shape of the yew topiary over the hedge. Another is the placing of two works by Peter Randall Page, and two water features by William Pye, at The Manor House, Bledlow, Buckinghamshire. Peter Randall Page's work also adorns Dartington Hall in Devon, as does a sublime Henry Moore, entitled *Memorial Figure* (1946), a recumbent woman in Hornton ironstone, her curves echoing those of the rolling Devon hills.

The most famous 'sculpture garden', perhaps, and hugely successful because of the presiding genius behind it, is the Barbara Hepworth Museum and Sculpture Garden, Cornwall. Here the sculptress lived for twenty-five years and had a studio in the garden looking out over the half-acre site, quiet and hidden away from the street in busy St Ives by high walls. Her sculptures are abstract, and both enhance and are enhanced by, the exotic, jungly feel of the garden plants and the twisty, narrow paths through the sloping site. Barbara Hepworth, like Henry Moore, wanted to bring out the essence of the natural materials with which she worked, so placing them in a 'natural' setting was most

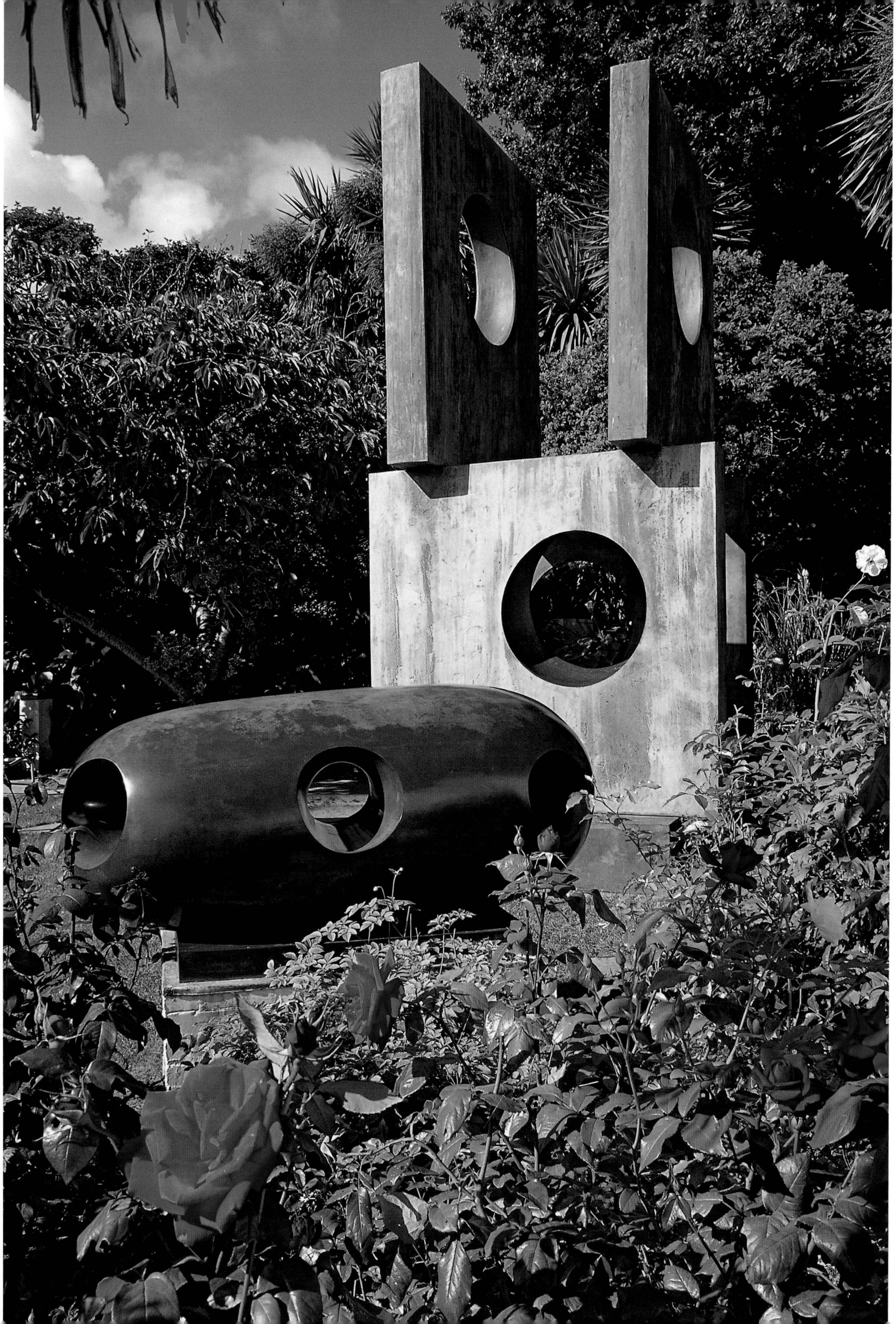

OPPOSITE Swans of willow and dried leaves by Lynn Kirkham in the pond at Stone Lane Gardens in Devon.

LEFT A Mondrian-influenced concrete wall, with associated planters, in the garden at The Manor House at Stevington in Bedfordshire. This is a garden with a strong emphasis on ornament and art, as well as highly structured planting using succulents and spiky xerophytes. It has a 'Rothko' garden with purple foliage, as well as an airy 'Hepworth' one, based on her 1947 geometric drawing of *Green Caves*, with ornamental grasses and herbaceous plants.

satisfactory. The garden was her creation, developed over many years, where she could contemplate her work, past and in progress.

Adventurous gardeners all over the country are installing interesting modern sculptures in their gardens. One such is Kathy Brown, who has built a Mondrian-inspired wall at The Manor House, Stevington, Bedfordshire; while the garden writer Stephen Anderton commissioned from Christopher Bradley-Hole *The Lyceum*, a wall 7½ feet/2.3 metres high and 25 feet/7.6 metres long, with reliefs, running north–south, as a device to show how shadows pass over the planes in the course of the day.

In the last three decades, a number of 'sculpture parks' have been created, for either permanent exhibitions of outdoor sculpture, or a mixture of permanent and temporary. Not always do these work as gardens *qua* gardens, since the emphasis on the art may overshadow, or fight with, the purpose of the garden. As successful as any is probably the Hannah Peschar Sculpture Garden, in a secret valley at the edge of the Surrey hills, where a number of artists, British and international, both well known and new on the scene, have their work sensitively displayed in an informally laid-out wood and water garden. Hannah Peschar is an art dealer, but her husband, Anthony Paul, is a well-known garden designer, so the garden, which he developed over more than twenty years, is a sympathetic setting for the works of art.

Stone Lane Gardens in Devon is an arboretum which contains many beautiful trees, in particular birches and alders, in copses, groves and circles. This garden is so much on the edge of Dartmoor that it feels a part of it. Every year, since 1992, between April and September it turns into the Mythic Garden, an annual sculpture event that shows a variety of contemporary pieces, some of them quite quirky and offbeat. One of the most intriguing aspects of this garden is what the owners themselves think about it: 'The Mythic Garden combines scientific research and selective planting with uncontrived landscaping. Its appealing presentation of art and design has helped to make art lovers into botanists and garden lovers into art enthusiasts.'[7]

OTHER GARDENS WITH ORNAMENT

Tofte Manor, Bedfordshire
Goldney Hall, Bristol
Cliveden, Buckinghamshire
Abbots Ripton Hall, Cambridgeshire
Anglesey Abbey Gardens, Cambridgeshire
Henbury Hall, Cheshire
The Manor House, Chelford, Cheshire
Chideock Manor, Dorset
Feeringbury Manor, Essex
Bourton House, Gloucestershire
Mill Dene, Gloucestershire
Stancombe Park, Gloucestershire
The Little Cottage, Hampshire
Monnington Court, Herefordshire
Great Comp, Kent
Marle Place Gardens, Kent
Clearbeck House, Lancashire
Gresgarth Hall, Lancashire
The Old Zoo Garden, Lancashire
Burghley House, Lincolnshire
Kenwood, London
Cottesbrooke Hall, Northamptonshire
The Old Rectory, Orford, Suffolk
Charlecote Park, Warwickshire
Chisenbury Priory, Wiltshire
The Old Malthouse, Wiltshire
Land Farm, Yorkshire

 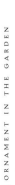

8

WATER, WATER EVERYWHERE

Clear, misty lake on which glides a silent, stately swan; smooth surface to reflect the sky; rushing cascade of water over fearsome rocks; fountain shooting water high into the sky; murky, eel-filled moat; shallow, gurgling brook; musical rill; bubbling millstone – these are all images we have of water in English gardens.

It should be no surprise that water is such an important part of gardens. Its central role in sustaining plant life alone would earn it such a place (as it did in Persian and Islamic gardens in ancient times), but our maritime and riverine heritage makes us well disposed towards water as a powerful life force and yet something which can be tamed, domesticated and bent to our will. Garden owners and designers have expended much ingenuity and thought on how to handle water in the garden. Despite the obvious practical challenges in living close to water, many gardeners will move house in order to gain the privilege. And it is very hard not to envy anyone who inherits it in their garden.

In the Middle Ages, water-filled moats were one way of defending manor houses and castles from attack. They were also a sign of high status. They began to go out of fashion in the fifteenth century but some remained filled, even when defence was no longer a consideration. (To be effective defensively, they had to be at least 13 feet/4 metres wide and 6 feet/2 metres deep.) At Helmingham Hall in Suffolk, for example, the beautiful, red-brick Tudor mansion dating from 1510 is completely surrounded by a moat, making the house look from a distance as if it floats romantically on water. And much of the walled pleasure and kitchen garden is surrounded by a second moat. Other examples include Leeds Castle and Groombridge Place, both in Kent, Eltham Palace in south London, Kentwell Hall in Suffolk, Mannington Hall in Norfolk and Broughton Castle in Oxfordshire. The moat at Groombridge Place was described by Sir Arthur Conan-Doyle (who was a frequent visitor) in his 1875 story 'The Valley of Fear' as a 'beautiful broad moat, as still and luminous as quicksilver'. At Kentwell Hall, as at Helmingham, there are not one but two moats, a main one and a secondary one, a sign apparently of high renown.

Gardeners have also used drained, or dried up, moats to excellent advantage: at Benington Lordship in Hertfordshire, for example, where masses of snowdrops in the grass of the moat are succeeded by the beautiful blue stars of *Scilla bithynica* as well as yellow narcissi; and at

OPPOSITE The medieval moat which bounds the garden and separates it from the park at Broughton Castle in Oxfordshire. It apparently keeps rabbits out of the garden, but not moles, which are good swimmers.

BELOW The lake at Home Farm in Oxfordshire, created after 1999 by Dan Pearson. 'It acts as a mirror to the sky and, as you walk around it, a mirror to the garden as well. Planted entirely with wild plants, it was a deliberate move to integrate wildlife into the garden and the garden into the landscape.'[1]

Great Dixter, in East Sussex, where the water-meadow bulb *Fritillaria meleagris* revels in the damp soil on the banks of the drained moat.

At Lyveden New Bield, Northamptonshire, the square moat around the pleasure grounds was not completed before Sir Thomas Tresham died in 1605. Less than three out of the four sides had been dug out. It has been sensitively conserved, with all the trees which had grown up in it removed, detritus cleared and the silt dredged, but the part which was never dug has been left alone.

Blickling Hall, Norfolk, is notable for a number of beautiful gardens set around the Jacobean mansion. One of the most charming elements is the dried moat which partly encircles the house and once helped defend the earlier medieval one. Sheltered by the moat walls, which also serve to retain the parterre, it is a calm green sward bounded by flower borders. Its charm lies at least partly in its hidden nature: it is only revealed when you are upon it.

In the seventeenth century, largely as a result of Dutch and French influences, water was mainly confined in linear canals, stone- or brick-sided, and not normally planted with water plants. Water's use as a surface to reflect nearby garden buildings was already a priority for garden makers. A famous example is the canal at Westbury Court in Gloucestershire, which the National Trust restored in 1971 (see pages 22–3). Once you have seen the garden pavilion, on its Ionic columns, reflected in the calm canal, it is unlikely you will forget it.[2] Other seventeenth- and early eighteenth-century formal water gardens include Bramham Park, Yorkshire, Wrest Park, Bedfordshire, and Melbourne Hall, Derbyshire.

Most limpid, elegant canals and moats did not survive the revolution in taste in the early eighteenth century, and many were filled in or, more often, changed into serpentine or sinuously curved lakes. At Claremont Landscape Garden, Surrey, Charles Bridgeman made a round pool, called the Round Bason, by 1718, which William Kent enlarged and altered twenty years later; Kent also made a lake out of the canal at Chiswick House. Later, in the 1830s, the moat at Scotney Castle in Kent was widened by William Sawrey Gilpin (nephew of the Revd William Gilpin), when he remodelled the garden in the Picturesque style.

At Blenheim Palace in Oxfordshire, in the 1760s, 'Capability' Brown dammed the small, slow-moving River Glyme to form a lake (see pages 138–9). What is so clever here is that the grandiose stone bridge by Sir John Vanbrugh was built before the damming, yet it is in perfect balance and proportion to the lake on both sides of it. Streams were also dammed to make lakes at Bowood House, Wiltshire (where there is also a rocky landscape consisting of Picturesque cascade, grottoes and hermit's cave designed by Charles Hamilton, the owner and creator of Painshill) and at Audley End in Essex.

One eighteenth-century landscape which should be better known is that at Stanway in Gloucestershire, where (most probably) Charles

Bridgeman designed a water garden, consisting of a 500-foot/150-metre long rectangular, formal canal, on a terraced slope east of the house, into which once debouched what may be the longest cascade in England. Some way up the slope is a fine, pyramid-topped stone banqueting house by Thomas Wright (1750), recently restored, at the base of which there are holes through which the water can pass from the circular pond and narrower cascade above (although it is usually piped).

However, the *pièce de résistance* of this garden must surely be the fountain in the canal, which sends up, from its 2½-inch/6-centimetre-diameter nozzle, a single jet 320 feet/100 metres into the air, and is entirely gravity fed from two reservoirs in the hill above. The water comes via a 12-inch/30-centimetre-diameter polyethylene pipe, which is 1½ miles/2.5 kilometres long. This fountain breaks records by being the tallest gravity-fed one in the world. What is more, it is a recent

ABOVE The Robert Adam bridge in the 'Capability' Brown park at Audley End in Essex. There is also a cascade on the site of an old mill dam and an impressive Victorian parterre of 1830 by Willliam Sawrey Gilpin.

FOLLOWING PAGES The thrilling fountain at Stanway in Gloucestershire, which can send water 320 feet/100 metres into the air, and is thus the tallest gravity-fed fountain in the world. It has been installed by the present owners, who are in the process of restoring the eighteenth-century garden. Behind it is the pyramidal banqueting house by Thomas Wright (1750).

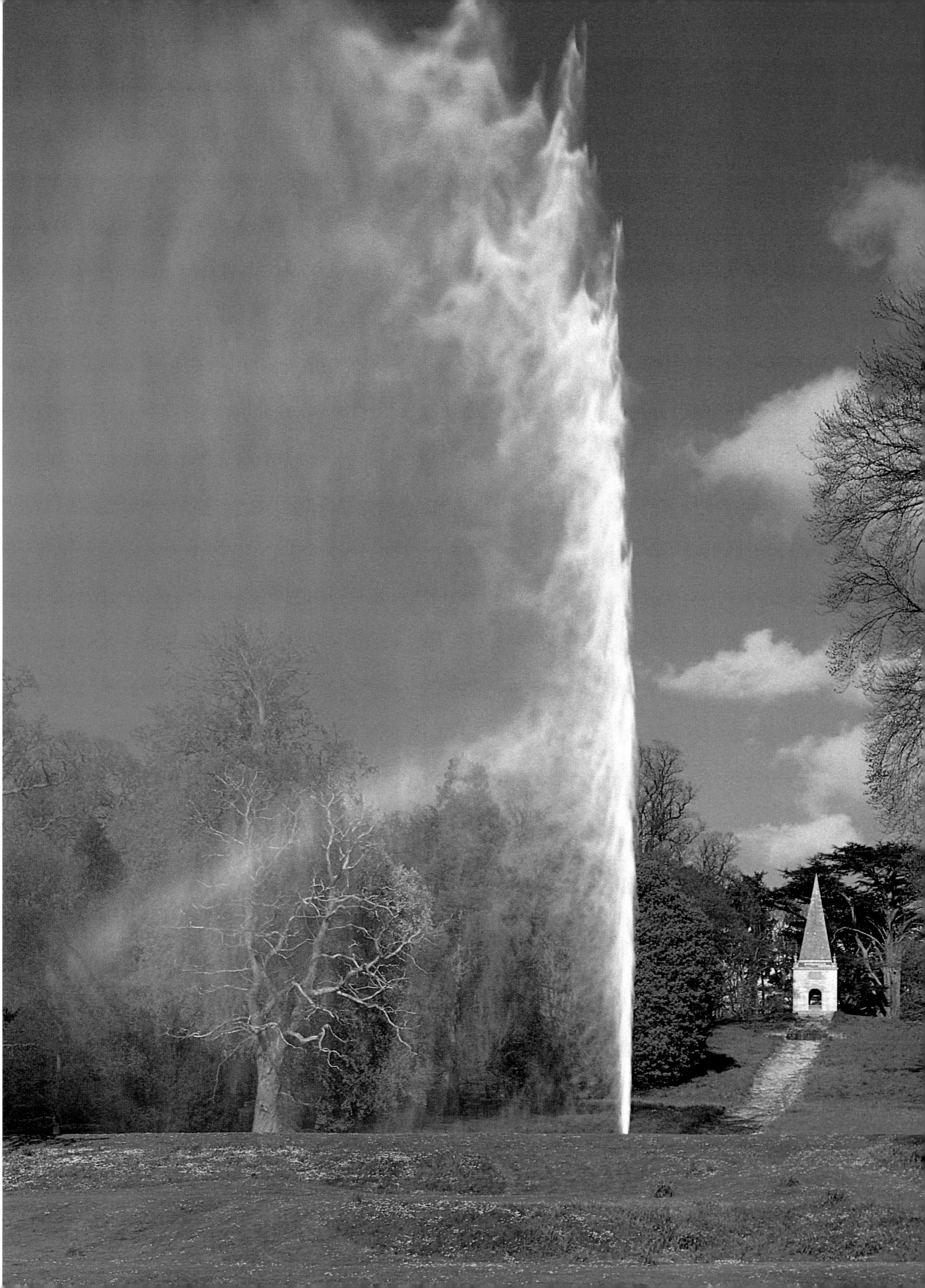

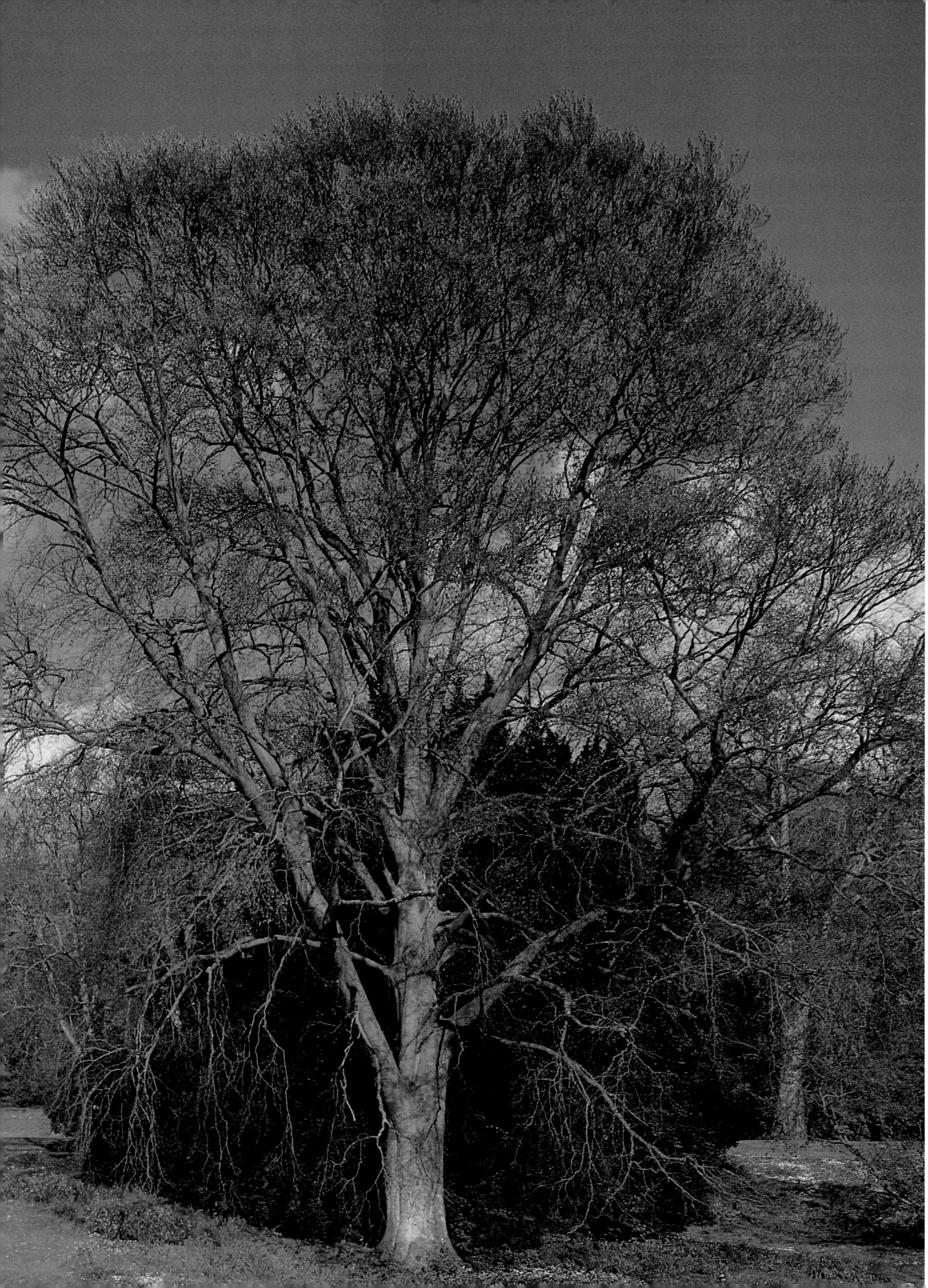

LEFT The Cascade at Chatsworth in Derbyshire, built at the very end of the seventeenth century, remarkably. It has twenty-four sets of steps, varying in size so that the 'music' that the water makes alters as it descends. The Cascade House at the top is by Thomas Archer and dates from 1702.

ABOVE The strikingly modern-looking copper 'willow tree' at Chatsworth dates originally from 1692, although it has been repaired more than once since. Water would spray out, unexpectedly, drenching unsuspecting onlookers. It looks particularly realistic in winter when the surrounding trees are without leaves.

installation, and it seems somehow too ambitious a project for our cramped contemporary imaginations. There is more restoration of the cascade in the offing, so this is definitely a garden to revisit in future years. It is a bravura performance, indeed.

When thinking about the bravura use of water in a garden, most readers, I feel sure, will bring Chatsworth to mind. This garden has been developed and redeveloped over 400 years, and every time, water has been involved. At the very end of the seventeenth century, the monumental Cascade was laid out, with its twenty-four sets of steps, all different in size, to ensure that the 'music' the water made altered as it flowed downhill. The Cascade House at the top, which was designed by Thomas Archer in 1702, had water piped under it, so that jets would, apparently, suddenly start up and soak unwary visitors. The formal Canal Pond was also dug out at the time, and the copper 'willow tree' (which looks strikingly modern) was installed: a fountain from whose 'branches' water sprayed out, again wetting the unsuspecting.

In 1844, Joseph Paxton, Chatsworth's head gardener, oversaw the installation of the Emperor Fountain in the Canal Pond, which shoots a stream of water 160 feet/50 metres into the air and once reached 296

ABOVE The lily pond at Rofford Manor in Oxfordshire, designed by Michael Balston, with water lilies almost covering the pool, to prevent the scene being just too austere.

RIGHT Part of the moat at Blewbury Manor, Oxfordshire. The border is planted up with colours most gardeners consider difficult – apricot and orange. There are day lilies (*Hemerocallis*), red hot pokers (*Kniphofia*) and achilleas prominent. *Alchemilla mollis* and nepeta froth over the paving edge.

feet/90 metres. It was named after the Emperor of Russia, who in the end never visited. At the same time, the great Rock Garden was created, as well as new waterfalls. In 1999, *Revelation*, a water-powered kinetic steel sculpture by Angela Conner (some of whose dry-land works may be seen in the house), was installed. This remarkable range of water features is gravity fed from lakes in Stand Wood, 400 feet/120 metres above the garden. These are in turn fed by streams that run off the Derbyshire moors. Since no power is involved, and the water is not recirculated by pumping, the water features depend on sufficient rainfall to operate fully. Sometimes, in dry summers, the hours when the waterworks are functioning have to be limited.

Formal pools, often sunken and surrounded by vernacular stone walls, are almost an axiom of Arts and Crafts gardens, especially those in the limestone Cotswolds. Snowshill Manor in Gloucestershire consists of a number of small, walled enclosures, connected by steps and terraces designed by the Arts and Crafts-inspired architect, Mackay Hugh Baillie-Scott and the owner, Charles Wade, in the 1920s, making sense

of a steep hillside on the edge of a Cotswold village. One of these enclosures is the Well Court, which consists almost entirely of a rectangular pool. It comes as quite a surprise, which is what the owner and designer intended, I expect.

Water, and its confinement, are also handled very cleverly at Hidcote Manor, Gloucestershire, in particular in the Bathing Pool Garden: a small, enclosed, dark garden with a circular stone basin. What is so intriguing about the pool is that it takes up practically the entire space inside the hedges, making it a suitably stark contrast to the spacious Old Garden close by, as well as the Theatre Lawn, which is empty except for two mature beech trees on a raised platform. Further away from the house is the Stream Garden, which is quite the antithesis of the Bathing Pool Garden: loose, relaxed, arboreal, with a shallow stream and lively bog planting consisting of large, exuberant perennials.

OPPOSITE The Stream Garden at Hidcote Manor in Gloucestershire, with streamside plants, the slightly tender Brazilian *Gunnera manicata* in the foreground, and variegated hostas further away.

ABOVE The rill at Hestercombe in Somerset, with water irises partly masking the beautifully laid stonework. The Great Plat is to be seen on the left, forming a triangle with the pergola beyond (see also pages 64–5).

The last century also saw the making of a number of more natural water gardens. One of these is at Hodnet Hall in Shropshire (begun in 1922) and notable for its 'daisy chain' of pools, which were formed by the damming of a stream that ran through the garden. There are seven of these pools, running along a valley, fringed with trees and edged with handsome waterside plants such as *Gunnera manicata*, perhaps the most outrageously exuberant of bog-loving plants. Black swans lend a wonderfully exotic feel to this garden, while the maples, rowans and birches add another dimension with their rich autumn colour.

Simpler, and in a lower key, but nevertheless beguiling, is the woodland water garden at Vann in Surrey, designed and planted by Gertrude Jekyll in 1911, which has simple, attractive Bargate stone crossings at several points down its length. This garden also has a pond and a stone-lined, narrow canalized stream between yew hedges, thickly planted with marginal plants.

Harold Peto's 1904 'water-garden-in-a-wood' at Buscot Park in Oxfordshire, made on a slope, which was terraced, leading down to the lake and with the eighteenth-century Classical temple in view. It is dramatic, stylish and, frankly, unique.

We have considered earlier a number of Italianate gardens made in England in the late nineteenth and early twentieth centuries. Water was always a most important element. One of the very best is the 'water-garden-in-a-wood' at Buscot Park in Oxfordshire. The house is eighteenth century and neo-Classical in style, and there are a lake and temple on the far shore which date from the same period. In 1904, Harold Peto (of Iford Manor fame) was commissioned to make a water garden to lead down to the lake. He set it so that the view terminates with the temple. The water garden is a narrow canal, which occasionally widens to form a circular or rectangular pool. The slope has been terraced, and the water cascades down it, while statuary stands sentinel. The rill is bordered first by paving,

Mapperton in Dorset was laid out in the 1920s in a Dorset combe. The garden has Italianate water features, including these fishponds, which have been canalized and are flanked by symmetrical yew cones and yew 'niches', and were extended by Victor Montagu in the 1950s. There is an arboretum in the bottom of the valley. This garden runs north–south, so the yew cones cast interesting shadows.

then grass and then clipped box hedges, which follow the line of the water. The visitor crosses the rill every so often at Classical footbridges. There is drama and style in plenty here.

Much of the garden at Mapperton, a sixteenth- and seventeenth-century stone house which stands at the head of a delightful sloping Dorset combe, was laid out in the 1920s in the Italianate fashion. It is on three levels, essentially, the side slopes being terraced, and the Fountain Court has an octagonal pool together with sentinel topiary and ornate Italianate statuary (see pages 62–3). Below that, further down the valley, are canalized seventeenth-century fishponds, flanked by neat, symmetrical yew cones. At the bottom of the valley is an arboretum. It is a most romantic and atmospheric place.

Few really innovative water gardens have been created since the end of the Second World War, but two of the finest are the work of one man,

Sir Geoffrey Jellicoe. At Sutton Place in Surrey he designed, amongst other things, a moat close to the Elizabethan house spanned by clean-edged stepping stones to the Paradise Garden. There were also Miro-influenced stepping stones to a raft in the sunken pond in the Swimming Pool Garden, though no longer. The most famous feature in this garden is the rectangular pond, in which is reflected, most magically, Ben Nicholson's famous Carrara marble *White Wall*, which was especially commissioned for the position (see pages 254–5).

As masterly, it seems to me, although very different, is the garden at Shute House in Dorset, which Jellicoe laid out for Michael and Lady Anne Tree from 1969. The River Nadder flows through the sloping garden and he used this to wonderful advantage, confining it, as it passed through various enclosures, in canals, rills, pools and a straight-sided 'musical cascade', where the water flows over projecting copper 'Vs' set

Shute House in Dorset is one of the greatest water gardens in England, designed by Sir Geoffrey Jellicoe for Michael and Lady Anne Tree from 1969, and carefully maintained, repaired and, with Jellicoe's blessing, improved by the present owners. Jellicoe wrote of Shute that it was 'a garden that breaks through classicism into a landscape created with deeper aspects of human nature'.[3] From the spring and pool at the top of the garden, the River Nadder is treated in two ways: 'romantic' with curving lakes and pools, and 'classical' in the Canal and Rill. This is the Canal, and Jellicoe professed to being influenced when designing it by Westbury Court (see page 22), in particular in the way hedges line the sides.

in concrete, each one slightly different so that the water makes a variety of sounds as it passes over. This cascade makes its elegant way down to three pools with Kashmiri-inspired bubble fountains. The idea of the rill originated in the irrigation channels of Persian paradise and Islamic gardens, and Sir Geoffrey Jellicoe acknowledged their influence on him, as he did the Italian villa gardens that he had studied as a young man.

While on the subject of rills, at West Green House, in Hampshire, the neo-Classical architect Quinlan Terry designed a 'nymphaeum' at the top of the garden from which water runs downhill in a straight-sided rill, spills over steps and then disappears and reappears in two oblong ponds. Recently, Marylyn Abbott has made a 'Paradise Courtyard', inspired by the Persian garden tradition, consisting of circular ponds, connected by straight streams. Crab apple trees (*Malus* 'John Downie') rise out of the centre of the ponds, giving the impression that they are growing in the water although (to spoil the fun for you) in reality they are

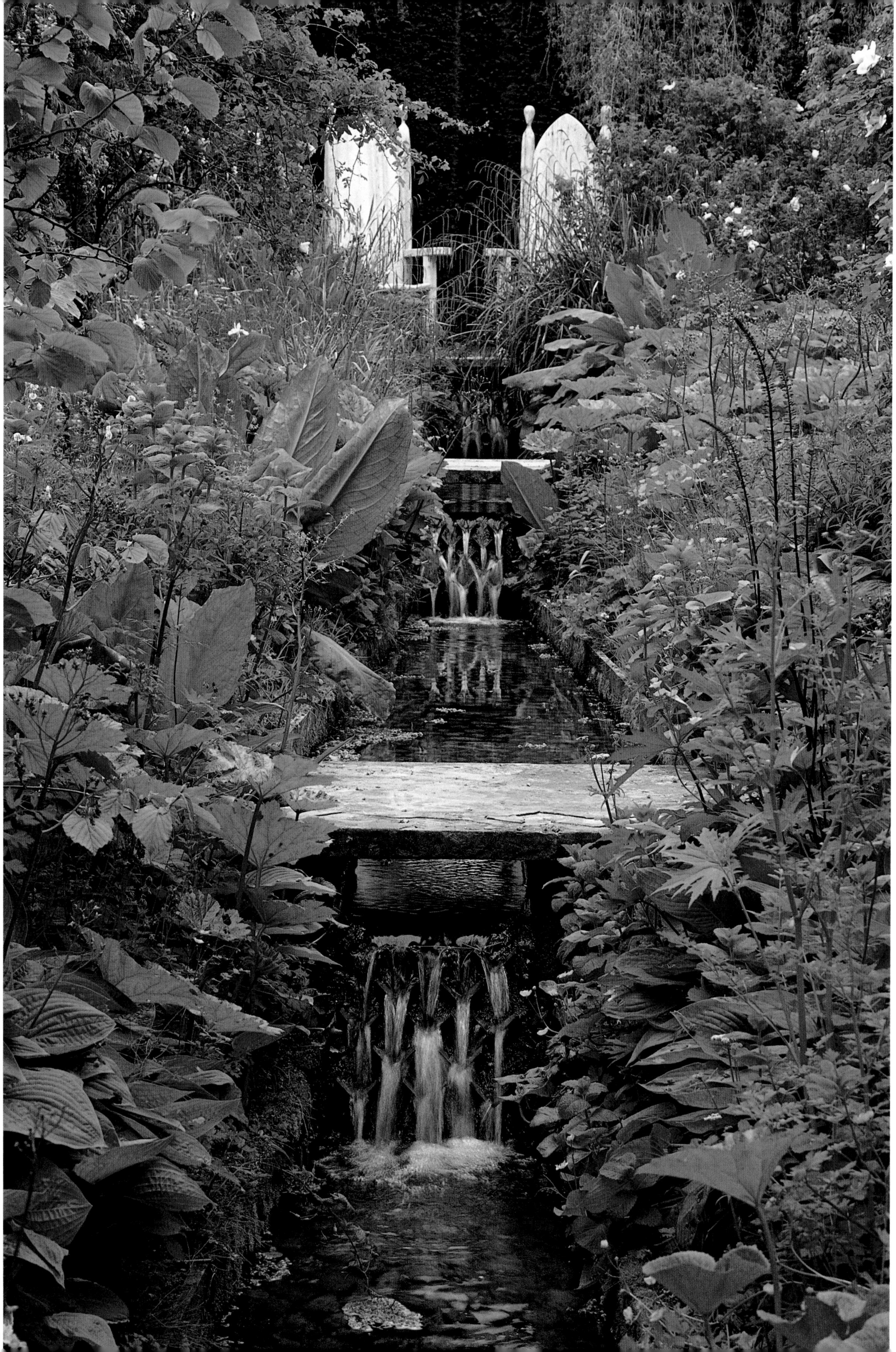

planted in soil, insulated from the water, and indeed need to be regularly watered!

Twentieth-century garden owners cannot always do without their swimming pools, despite a cold and variable climate. At Hidcote Manor, one slightly wonders whether Johnston ever plumbed the murky depths of the Bathing Pool in its enclosure (presumably the hedges acted to temper the wind and provide privacy as well as making an aesthetic statement). Next door, at Kiftsgate Court, there is an elegantly curved swimming pool at the bottom of the garden, in full sun and close to the Mediterranean Garden. In 1999, the present owners laid out a minimalist garden, where once there was a yew hedge-enclosed tennis court. The centrepiece is a black-lined rectangular pool (some gardeners have discovered how much more *sympatico* black is in comparison to the usual caerulean blue), edged in very pale Portland limestone, with stepping stones leading out into the middle to an island of green turf. Rising out

OPPOSITE ABOVE The Paradise Courtyard at West Green House in Hampshire, with its fountains and rills and the crab apple *Malus* 'John Downie' in full flower. There is a teasing trick being played on the onlooker. The roots of the crab apples are insulated from the water.

OPPOSITE BELOW The Nymphaeum by Quinlan Terry at West Green House. Below the two oblong ponds (just visible), the rill splits into two, spilling down both sides of the steps to the Moon Gate in the brick wall of the Walled Garden.

ABOVE Twenty-four gilded bronze *Philodendron* leaves on stainless-steel stems, designed by Simon Allison, rise out of the water in the formal Water Garden at Kiftsgate Court in Gloucestershire. They sway slightly in the wind and drip water gently into the pool.

A water sculpture by Simon Allison in the River Coln, which flows through the garden of the Old Rectory at Quenington, Gloucestershire. The owners, who are art lovers, have made good use of their situation to stage a biennial sculpture show, but some pieces are permanent. The sculpture is entitled *Millrace* and it is fascinating to see how the reflection completes the hoops.

of the pond are a group of gilded bronze *Philodendron* leaves on stainless-steel stems, a work by Simon Allison.

In the contemporary garden, there is such an emphasis on naturalism and the conservation of wildlife and biodiversity that natural-looking lakes and ponds are very much the rage. One such is that designed by Dan Pearson at Home Farm (see page 271), and another the serene and beautiful Longstock Park Water Garden, Hampshire. This exemplifies an ornamental water garden that is a magnet for wildlife. There were ornamental lakes from the 1920s, fed by the chalk-stream River Test, but John Spedan Lewis (of department store fame) developed the garden from 1948, creating many islands, inlets and bridges, and planting unusual trees and interesting water plants. This garden is especially strong on water lilies, with eighty types represented, but there is a rich mix of marginals here, such as Asiatic primulas and irises, as well as native flowers. The really difficult trick to bring off with a water garden (which is probably why there are so few gardens where water is the completely dominant feature) is to allow it to be profuse and lush, but not seriously wild. They triumphantly succeed at Longstock. Moreover, the combination of shelter, food, nesting sites,

OPPOSITE The canal with stepping stones and cascade at Broughton Grange in Oxfordshire, showing the designer Tom Stuart-Smith's sureness of touch with hard landscaping. This view reveals his command of planting as well. Broughton Grange is one of the most imaginative and stimulating gardens made in England in the last ten years (see also pages 358–9 and 374).

LEFT Longstock Park Water Garden in Hampshire, mainly developed by John Spedan Lewis from 1948, although there were lakes here, and the thatched summerhouse, from the 1920s. In the picture may be seen *Rodgersia pinnata* 'Superba' with variegated hostas on the far bank. This garden, like many water gardens, is a home for diverse wildlife.

water and bog is a winner for a really wide range of wild creatures, from kingfishers to woodpeckers, and from dragonflies to water boatmen. And the impressive thing is that this garden was created long before any gardener had heard the word 'biodiversity'.

No description of twentieth-century water features could ignore the hydraulic wonders designed by Jacques and Peter Wirtz at The Alnwick Garden in Northumberland. This is the most ambitious eclectic garden project embarked on by a landowner for many a long year. In what had been a derelict 12-acre/5-hectare walled garden, a Grand Cascade has been made, which runs down the main north–south axis on a slope originally created by William Nesfield in the nineteenth century. The sides retaining the Cascade are shaped into serpentine curves, and made of a local stone (Darney), and there is a series of twenty-one weirs on the way down. There are three central jets, with forty smaller ones and eighty side jets, as well as four jumping jets in the bell mouths. There are four computer-controlled fountain sequences, which change every half-hour. The water falls into the Lower Basin and is then recycled. This bald description of a most complex hydraulic system does insufficient justice to the spectacular nature of this cascade, with parabolic water streams sparkling in the sunlight. It is hard not to laugh in sheer delight when the fountains strike up. It is a magical place for adults and children (who play in the water splashed at the bottom on warm days).

LEFT The Grand Cascade at The Alnwick Garden, Northumberland, designed by Jacques and Peter Wirtz. It is hard not to laugh out loud with sheer delight when the fountain jets start up.

ABOVE One of the William Pye sculptures in the Serpent Garden at Alnwick. This one is called *Torricelli*. There are several shiny steel sculptures from which water falls, rises, tumbles, sprays, bubbles or reflects.

That is by no means all. At the top of the garden is a trapezoidal walled space known as the Ornamental Garden. Strictly geometric, and divided into many squares and diagonals, it has a central square pool from which emanate canalized rills to left and right, terminating in circular ones. Even more memorable is the Serpent Garden, to one side of the Grand Cascade, which has a serpent hedge composed of evergreen holly and

A streamside planting at Trebah in Cornwall, with yellow candelabra primulas in the foreground. There are many rhododendrons and camellias here, but also subtropical plants such as Chusan palms and tree ferns (*Dicksonia antarctica*). After a run of mild winters, tree ferns are finding their way into more inland gardens.

yew enclosing seven unique water sculptures by the *ne plus ultra* of British water sculptors, William Pye. The sheer beauty and inventiveness of these water sculptures is truly breathtaking, although they are placed too close together to make as much impact as they might otherwise do.

So much for water gardens where there is free-standing or flowing water. Bog gardening has a venerable history as well, and is a significant feature in a number of gardens, such as Hidcote Manor, Gloucestershire, Chyverton, Cornwall, Wakehurst Place, West Sussex, Wartnaby Gardens, Leicestershire, Marwood Hill, Devon, Vann, Surrey, and Stone Lane Gardens, Devon. Bog gardens are usually man-made, or at least man-assisted, and consist either of damp areas, often in shade, which have no free-running water, or areas where it disappears for periods of the year. They are by no means confined to regions with peaty soil, as you might imagine from the phrase 'bog garden'. The idea is that they should look natural, although the use of exotic plants which like to have their roots in soil which never dries out ensures that they are much more colourful than they would be if only native plants were used. Plants like the American skunk cabbage (*Lysichiton americanum*), the large-leaved *Darmera peltata*, the ornamental rhubarb (*Rheum*) and the magnificent Brazilian *Gunnera manicata*, not to mention rainbow-coloured irises, such as *I. sibirica* and *I. ensata*, and tall primulas, with all their many named cultivars, ensure that a bog garden is a striking affair, especially in the spring and early summer.

OTHER WATER GARDENS

Wrest Park, Bedfordshire
Scotlands, Berkshire
Cliveden, Buckinghamshire
The Manor House, Bledlow, Buckinghamshire
Durham Massey, Cheshire
Tatton Park, Cheshire
Bonython Manor Gardens, Cornwall
Holker Hall, Cumbria
Sizergh Castle, Cumbria
Renishaw Hall, Derbyshire
Coleton Fishacre Garden, Devon
Docton Mill Gardens, Devon
Marwood Hill, Devon
Athelhampton House Gardens, Dorset
Forde Abbey, Dorset
The Beth Chatto Gardens, Essex
Feeringbury Manor, Essex
The Gibberd Garden, Essex
The Arrow Cottage Garden, Herefordshire
How Caple Court, Herefordshire
Lower Hope, Herefordshire
Westonbury Mill Water Gardens, Herefordshire
Hever Castle, Kent
The Old Zoo Garden, Lancashire
Besthorpe Hall, Norfolk
Corpusty Mill Garden, Norfolk
Fairhaven Woodland & Water Garden, Norfolk
Lake House Water Gardens, Norfolk
Oxburgh Hall, Norfolk
Boughton House, Northamptonshire
Coton Manor, Northamptonshire
Wallington, Northumberland
Dudmaston, Shropshire
Preen Manor, Shropshire
Selehurst, Sussex
Sheffield Park, Sussex
The Courts Garden, Wiltshire
Witley Court, Worcestershire
Burnby Hall Gardens, Yorkshire

9

If there is one genus of plants which can be said to be essential to the English garden, it surely must be the rose. Loved, even revered, by English people, with a love expressed by countless poets, it has long been a potent symbol of nationhood as well as an icon of beauty. It combines, at its best, exquisite symmetrical form, sweet scent and poignant associations. Who could possibly resist that combination? And its flowering is, or certainly was, transient, which for many people adds to its allure. 'They are not long, the days of wine and roses,' wrote Ernest Dowson in *Vitae summa brevis* in 1896, a sentiment which still strikes a deep chord with us.

There are a number of rose species native to England, *Rosa canina,* *R. arvensis* and *R. rubiginosa* (syn. *R. eglanteria*) amongst them. The Romans probably introduced *R. alba*, while the Crusaders brought back *R. damascena* from the Holy Land in the early Middle Ages. (*R. damascena* has been grown in Bulgaria to produce attar of roses for three hundred years.) At much the same time *R. gallica* was introduced from southern Europe via France. *R. gallica officinalis* was the apothecary's rose, and the red rose of Lancaster, while the white rose of York was a semi-double form of *R. alba*. All these roses were single-season flowerers, blooming either in late May or June. Although the mechanism for rose breeding was not properly understood until the nineteenth century, chance hybrids arose before then, as did sports (spontaneous mutations) such as the striped Rosa Mundi from the red rose of Lancaster. Roses' value to people in the Middle Ages was largely medicinal, and they were grown extensively in monastic gardens as a result.

It is thought that the first rose garden *per se* was planted by the Empress Joséphine at the Château de Malmaison, the house outside Paris that she moved into in 1798 while her husband was away at the wars. Her fascination with roses was so intense that she intended (and may have succeeded) in growing all roses then known to the West. These included some new ones from China, and Centifolias (colloquially, cabbage roses) and their sports, the Moss roses, from Holland. The idea of a rose garden became popular amongst those wealthy French who survived the Revolution, and the idea spread to England.

By 1900, breeding had extended the colours of roses beyond pinks, reds, purples and whites to include pale yellow and apricot. But, as far as modern roses are concerned, the real breakthrough came in 1929, when

THE
ENGLISH
ROSE

OPPOSITE A felicitous early summer planting of the striped once-flowering *Rosa gallica* 'Versicolor' (perhaps better known as Rosa Mundi), with *Astrantia major* and the blue *Campanula persicifolia*.

BELOW Roses around an archway at Broughton Castle in Oxfordshire. The roses are 'Sander's White Rambler' and Bonica.

a sport appeared which had orange-red flowers. Now only blue was denied the rose breeders (and still is, just).

Because roses only flowered once in the season, over a period of three to four months overall, it became fashionable to grow them by themselves, often in walled gardens which need not be visited outside the season. Rose gardens were called rosariums or roseries and Humphry Repton designed one, as early as 1800, for the garden at Belton House in Lincolnshire (now gone). They were filled with what we now call 'old roses', which could grow quite tall and spreading, and the beds were usually edged with lavender. In 1818, roses grown as 'standards' arrived from France, and these soon became important features of rose gardens, both to line paths and to act as simple and inexpensive focal points.

It was then that the recurrent Bourbons burst upon the scene. The first Bourbon is thought to have been a chance crossing which occurred on the Île de Bourbon (now Réunion in the Indian Ocean) between a recurrent-flowering China rose, 'Parson's Pink' or 'Old Blush China', and a Damask called 'Autumnalis' (the Four Seasons rose). Later in the century came the Portlands and the Hybrid Perpetuals. Hybrid Perpetuals flowered twice (hence their optimistic name), and were very popular for a long time, despite the fact that they made rather ungainly tall bushes. All these roses, of both Oriental and European origin, and hybrids between the two, are now referred to, very often, as 'Heritage' roses to differentiate them from the modern kinds such as Hybrid Teas and Floribundas.

All through the nineteenth century, roses continued to be grown in separate gardens, where there was space, sometimes on parterres and sometimes away from the rest of the garden. The latter attracted the ridicule of the outspoken William Robinson. Even when he designed rose gardens for others he advocated edging the borders with saxifrages, gentians, veronicas and other ground coverers. He called it 'Mulching with Life'.

Gertrude Jekyll agreed. She had a great influence on country house rose growing in the early twentieth century, with her book *Roses for English Gardens*, published in 1902, in which she expanded greatly the number of situations in the garden where she thought roses were appropriate. Her view was that there should still be garden areas in which roses were predominant, but that they should also be freely mixed with other plants. The idea of letting Ramblers scramble up trees, such as yews and hollies, as well as old fruit trees in orchards comes from this book. It was taken up enthusiastically by Vita Sackville-West at Sissinghurst, who took advantage of the consanguinity between roses and apples, with the April blossom of apples being followed by similar-shaped rose flowers in June. Gertrude Jekyll also advocated catenaries (ropes or chains strung between sturdy tall posts) for Ramblers, and sloping banks and wilder

Folly Farm in Berkshire, a garden created by Sir Edwin Lutyens (note the signature elaborate paving) with modern Floribunda roses in a monoculture, their bright colour cooled somewhat by the water and central bed of lavender.

places as well. As for the rose garden, she advised that it be surrounded by yew hedges and woodland trees as a backcloth.

From 1867 onwards, a race of roses was developed which were definitely not suited to growing in borders along with other plants. Hybrid Tea roses were, and are, compact and rather stiff-legged in growth and, along with the Polyanthas (later Floribundas), were obvious candidates for being grown in separate gardens, especially because of their requirement for lavish quantities of farmyard manure. In effect, although not dug up every year (every three years was usual) they were treated as if they were bedding plants, with each cultivar being grown in a separate bed, to give uniformity of height and habit, and with varying colours. Gardeners were back growing them in discrete gardens again, and that trend has continued in many gardens to this day. This is the case in particular where early rose gardens have been re-created, such as the restored parterre, known as the Queens' Garden, at Sudeley Castle in Gloucestershire (see pages 310–11). This Nesfield parterre of 1859, with its octagonal central pool, is on the site of a Tudor parterre (the Dowager Queen, Katherine Parr, and Lady Jane Grey lived at Sudeley Castle), and is surrounded by monumental double yews planted in 1860, pricked by

small, arched openings. In 1989, Jane Fearnley-Whittingstall designed formal beds of Shrub roses and herbs (as well as hyacinths and other bulbs in early spring) which seem to me happily to evoke the atmosphere of a scented, enclosed Tudor garden. Height is provided by ironwork arbours, topped with crowns, up which rambles the free-flowering pink and apricot 'Phyllis Bide'.

Climbing roses found a place elsewhere from Victorian times, usually clothing house walls, pergolas, arches and trellises, as they still do today, and on wooden open pyramids in the rose gardens themselves (see pages 304–5). Pergolas were an important element of the Arts and Crafts garden in the early decades of the twentieth century, and no other climbing plant seemed more suited to them. This was especially true of Ramblers, which benefited from the freer air circulation in comparison to that against walls, and were therefore less prone to mildew.

For much of the twentieth century, breeders concentrated mostly on developing Hybrid Teas and Floribundas but, especially on the Continent (in Germany and Denmark in particular), they never stopped working on other kinds, such as Shrub roses. Once-flowering Modern Shrub roses such as 'Nevada' (1927) and 'Frühlingsgold' (1937) were developed and

Roses growing on arches in the garden of John Scarman of Cottage Garden Roses in Staffordshire. The climbing Bourbon rose 'Madame Isaac Pereire' is in the centre. This is a favourite with many rosarians because of its repeat flowering, its lavender-scented fully double flowers and the fact that it will grow either as a shrub or as a short climber.

The English Rose Grace, raised by David Austin, and showing how like an old rose it is in looks, but with the added advantage of a wide range of flower colour, reliable repeat-flowering and better disease resistance. Moreover, at least some English Roses grow well in pots, which makes them suitable candidates for modern small gardens. These virtues, together with scent (usually), are why English Roses are now so widely planted in English gardens open to the public.

work was done on perpetual-flowering climbing and pillar roses as well. These gradually took the place of once-flowering Ramblers, if there was an arch or pillar to clothe.

In the last thirty years of the twentieth century, however, new trends began to emerge. Two developments in particular made it much easier for gardeners to use roses in shrub or mixed plantings. The most important was the breeding of roses with the look and scent of the old roses but with the constitution, broad colour range and repeat-flowering of Hybrid Teas. The trail was blazed by David Austin from Albrighton in the West Midlands, in the 1960s, with the development of what he calls 'English Roses'.

It is almost impossible to overstate the influence that Austin has had on the development of rose growing and rose gardens in this country (indeed, all over the world, since his roses often do well also in the United States and Australia) and his work has spurred others to try to imitate him – always the highest form of flattery. His first success was Constance Spry, a wonderful climber but, alas, a single-season flowerer. It was really with Mary Rose, Graham Thomas and Heritage, in the early

1980s, that he hit his stride. Some cultivars have been allowed to go out of the catalogues, usually because of some weakness in constitution, and have been superseded. (English Roses can be rather prone to blackspot in damp climates.) But most have proved to be excellent garden plants, amongst them Gertrude Jekyll, Graham Thomas and The Alnwick Rose. David Austin introduces about six new roses each year; they are not all in the very first rank, and it is hard for the layman to distinguish some from earlier introductions, but, taken all in all, they are a remarkable achievement, and have contributed somewhat to the decline in popularity of the bedding rose and the bedding rose garden, as well as the fleeting and more delicate old roses.

The other breeding development which has had some small impact on English gardens in recent years has been to do with laxer types of rose which can be used as ground cover, such as the Flower Carpet series from the German breeders Noack, and the County series introduced by the English firm of Mattocks. Although they are most likely to be seen planted by the council on roundabouts, they have been taken up also by gardeners, and definitely have a place in gardens.

ABOVE One of the loveliest and most floriferous gardens for roses is Broughton Castle in Oxfordshire (see also pages 19 and 109). This is the Ladies' Garden, laid out originally in the 1880s. It has an impressive hedge of the Hybrid Musk 'Felicia' and the shorter-growing 'Ballerina' against the castle wall at the back. Hybrid Musks were developed by the Revd Joseph Pemberton in the 1920s, and their free-flowering, scent and comparative resistance to disease have made them very popular with gardeners who like the 'old-fashioned' look. In the centre, on the stone below the metal basket planter, full of *Verbena* 'Sissinghurst' and *V.* 'Silver Anne', is an inscription from *The Rubáiyát* of Omar Khayyám: 'I sometimes think that never blows so red the rose as where some buried Caesar bled.' That gives one pause for thought.

FOLLOWING PAGES The Queens' Garden at Sudeley Castle in Gloucestershire, designed by Jane Fearnley-Whittingstall and planted in 1989. The design is based on a parterre (there has been one here from the sixteenth century), with beds of equal shape and size divided into sections. The roses are of the 'old-fashioned' type and are accompanied by plenty of herbs. This garden pays due honour to the great historical importance of Sudeley, which at one time gave a home to not one but two queens (Katherine Parr and Lady Jane Grey). Fittingly, among the roses are to be found 'Reine Victoria', 'Königin von Dänemark' and 'Empress Josephine'.

Those people who like the 'old rose' look are better served when visiting gardens open to the public than those for whom the Hybrid Tea or Floribunda is the epitome of beauty. With the exception of educational display gardens such as Rosemoor in Devon, Wisley in Surrey and the Gardens of the Rose at Chiswell Green, Hertfordshire, it is hard to think of many gardens where large numbers of Hybrid Tea and Floribunda roses are treated respectfully and sympathetically. The best bet for seeing them is in public parks, where bedding roses, grown as single cultivars in separate beds without any other planting, are still the order of the day. One of the best of these is the admirable Queen Mary's Rose Garden in Regent's Park, London.

A hundred years ago, the typical country house rose garden, designed by Thomas Mawson or Inigo Triggs, would, most likely, have been square and bounded by a pergola on at least one side, and have had a central pool of water and a fountain, with roses either in beds radiating from it or in square beds. There would have been wooden or metal tripods and open-work supports, arches, and bowers with seats. It is interesting that there are a number of rose gardens still existing in England which conform to this pattern, in particular Mottisfont Abbey in Hampshire.

Owned by the National Trust, Mottisfont holds the indisputably finest collection in the country of 'heritage' roses. This is to be found in the red-brick walled garden built at some distance from the abbey (a Georgian

LEFT ABOVE A summer border, where roses predominate, at Coughton Court in Warwickshire. They are mostly English Roses.

LEFT BELOW The centrepiece rose arch in the 2-acre/0.8-hectare walled garden at Daylesford House, Gloucestershire, designed by Mary Keen. The rose is *Rosa mulliganii*.

ABOVE One of Graham Thomas's great legacies is the National Trust's rose garden at Mottisfont Abbey in Hampshire, which holds the National Collection of pre-1900 shrub roses. In this picture, you can see *Rosa x odorata* 'Mutabilis', the petals of which change colour – hence the name. They open yellow, then become pink and finish a pale crimson. This border shows how salutary was Graham Thomas's emphasis on mixing shrub roses with good herbaceous plantings. Prominent in this picture are a variety of garden pinks (*Dianthus*) as well as *Campanula persicifolia* and *C.p.* 'Alba', and the grey-leaved *Stachys byzantina*.

Rose Graham Thomas, bred by David Austin and named after the great rosarian Graham Stuart Thomas, who did so much to rehabilitate the fortunes of old roses after the Second World War.

house on the site of a medieval abbey). The collection belonged to the fine rosarian and rose historian Graham Stuart Thomas, who, for many years, was Gardens Consultant to the National Trust and who brought his long-hoarded collection here in 1972. Ten years later, an adjacent garden was planted up with old roses acquired by Graham Thomas from the famous German rose garden at Sangerhausen. There are some three hundred species and cultivars here, and some real rarities, underscoring this garden's choice as the National Collection of pre-1900 shrub roses.[1]

Because the roses are predominantly of the 'old-fashioned' type and colour – whites, pinks, crimsons and mauvish-purples (if you discount a remarkable planting of the perpetual-flowering, golden-yellow English Rose named after, and chosen by, Graham Thomas himself) – this is a garden to see in June and early July; indeed the garden is open well into the evening on occasions each June for visitors to appreciate the scents at their strongest. The layout is formal and symmetrical, with four main areas, divided by gravel paths and with a centrepiece circular lily pond, guarded by four clipped Irish yews and with an anarchic glowing pink-flowered 'Raubritter' cascading into it. The four areas consist of lawns surrounded by rose-rich borders. The roses tend to be grown in groupings according to their classification. For example, the Hybrid Rugosas are close to the entrance and the Hybrid Perpetuals in two lengthy borders, while the Ramblers are trained over archways. One of the finest sights is a pink Constance Spry planted against a wall and framing a white-painted garden seat.

The beauty of Mottisfont is enhanced by the way Graham Thomas combined roses with herbaceous perennials as companions in borders, as well as growing them on their own, showing not only what goes well with them when flowering but what will come to the fore once they go out of flower. He used certain key, low-growing plants such as alchemilla, pinks (*Dianthus*), campanulas and *Sisyrinchium striatum*, so that the view of the roses was not impeded. 'While it is my opinion that shrub roses are supremely beautiful and should dominate their places in the garden, they need a good blend of companion shapes and colours and should not be overdone,'[2] he wrote. Height is provided by Ramblers growing on wooden structures and, in the second garden, a brick-edged round central feature of oak posts and metal arches.

Another important heritage rose garden is to be found at Mannington Hall in Norfolk in the walled garden. It is carefully laid out to show how rose gardens looked at different periods in history, from the fifteenth century onwards, and what roses were popular at what times. It includes a twentieth-century rose garden, which is salutary. Some 1,500 cultivars grow there.

There are many reasons to visit Warwick Castle, in the centre of Warwick: the Norman castle itself, the 'Capability' Brown landscape which surrounds it, the handsome eighteenth-century orangery and its

Rose 'Madame Isaac Pereire' a repeat-flowering Bourbon rose grown as a climber at Wartnaby Gardens in Leicestershire. The once-flowering Gallica rose 'Charles de Mills' grows at its feet.

rose-filled parterre, and the James Backhouse Victorian rock garden. However, these days, there is also the restored 1868 formal rose garden, designed by Robert Marnock. It was swept away in the 1930s but re-created in 1986, following the discovery of Marnock's designs in the county record office. David Austin named a rose, Warwick Castle, in honour of this restoration.

In a rather different style – more prolific and romantic – is the Rose Garden at Sissinghurst, to be found on both sides of the monumental yew Rondel (see page 34). Here Vita Sackville-West had the space to express her passion for old roses and Hybrid Musks (as well as a few particularly patrician modern roses such as the single-flowered apricot 'Mrs Oakley Fisher'), especially those with velvety petals, like the incomparable purple 'Tuscany'; and her taste influenced a generation of gardeners – people who never missed her weekly missives from the garden, published in *The Observer* on Sundays between 1947 and 1961. In places, she mixed her roses with perennials and bulbs, as Graham Thomas was to do later at Mottisfont. Her choice of roses has been left substantially unchanged since her death in the early 1960s.

Two rose gardens which may well have been influenced by Sissinghurst are Wartnaby Gardens, Leicestershire, and Gunby Hall, Lincolnshire. The former has a rose garden with an extensive collection of modern and historic roses, including the lavender-scented 'Madame Isaac Pereire' growing as a climber.

ABOVE The ground-cover rose 'Pink Bells', grown on a support, close to the Climber 'Kahlsruhe' and *Clematis* 'Etoile Violette' at Wartnaby Gardens in Leicestershire.

RIGHT The Rose Garden at Wartnaby Gardens. The roses round the pond are the Rambler rose 'Félicité et Perpétue'. On the right-hand side at the front are 'Gruss an Aachen' (small) next to *R.* x *damascena* var. *semperflorens* ('Quatre Saisons'), 'La Ville de Bruxelles' and, on the far right in front, 'Honorine de Brabant'.

That is also a feature at Gunby Hall, which is noteworthy for the box-edged beds of 'Mrs Oakley Fisher' close to the house. There is also a rose walk. Roses are definitely companions to other plants at Gunby, not herded into their own enclosure.

These pictures show something of the range of colour and flower shape of David Austin's English Roses. The scent you will have to take on trust! These cultivars are some of the results of a breeding programme that involves growing about 250,000 seedlings annually, from which an average of six new varieties are introduced each year.

LEFT ABOVE *Rosa* Pegasus, deliciously scented.

LEFT BELOW *Rosa* The Alnwick Rose, strongly fragrant.

RIGHT ABOVE *Rosa* Sweet Juliet, lemon-scented.

RIGHT BELOW *Rosa* Pat Austin, which has a strong Tea rose scent.

There is a place in this chapter for the show garden at David Austin Roses near Wolverhampton, since it seems so much more than simply a trial garden. Obviously, for a garden which holds a National Collection (of English Roses, of course), there are a great many roses – some seven hundred different varieties in all – but it feels as if there are more even than that, particularly perhaps because it is divided up into several spaces, using formal yew hedges. The Long Garden contains the old roses, Modern Shrub roses and some English Roses to extend the flowering season. It is divided by grass and herringbone brick paths, with verticality achieved by pergolas and arches dripping with Climbers and Ramblers. Off the Long Garden is the Victorian Garden, planted with English Roses and other repeat-flowering shrub roses, with the beds delineated by dwarf box formal edgings. There is even a garden full of modern bedding roses; David Austin is completely even-handed, it would seem. What this garden lacks in the quality of its hard landscaping it more than makes up for in sheer flowering power and scent. As Charles and Brigid Quest-Ritson, the heritage rose experts, put it: 'It is quite simply the best rose garden in Britain, open every day of the year – and free.'[3]

OTHER ROSE GARDENS

Abbots Rippon Hall, Cambridgeshire
Chippenham Park, Cambridgeshire
Elton Hall, Cambridgeshire
Peckover House, Cambridgeshire
The Manor, Hemingford Grey, Cambridgeshire
Lanhydrock, Cornwall
Dalemain, Cumbria
Renishaw Hall, Derbyshire
Weston House, Dorset
Hodges Barn, Gloucestershire
Hunts Court, Gloucestershire
Kiftsgate Court, Gloucestershire
Moor Wood, Gloucestershire
Ozleworth Park, Gloucestershire
Farleigh House, Hampshire
Hinton Ampner, Hampshire
Chartwell, Kent
Mount Ephraim, Kent
Penshurst Place, Kent
Houghton Hall, Norfolk
Lexham Hall, Norfolk
Felley Priory, Nottinghamshire
Brook Cottage, Alkerton, Oxfordshire
Old Rectory, Farnborough, Oxfordshire
Lower Hall, Shropshire
Wyken Hall, Suffolk
Loseley Gardens, Surrey
Polesden Lacey, Surrey
Bateman's, Sussex
Frith Lodge, Sussex
Nymans, Sussex
Pashley Manor, Sussex
Wightwick Manor, West Midlands
Abbey House, Wiltshire
The Priory, Kington St Michael, Wiltshire
Wilton House, Wiltshire
Castle Howard, Yorkshire
Millgate House, Yorkshire
Nostell Priory, Yorkshire

10

THE
KITCHEN
GARDEN

Gardeners love kitchen gardens. This is partly for historical reasons since, until comparatively recently, they were the surest barrier against want for some people, and the source of variety and excellence in nutrition for many more. But only partly. We are also impressed, even awed, by the enormous skill and dedication shown by generations of mostly uneducated men in hundreds of country house gardens, which ensured a continuous supply of fruit, vegetables and flowers through the year, without the benefit of fridges, freezers or international freight carriers. Then there are aesthetic factors, since fruit blossom can rival any foreign exotic tree for beauty, in my opinion, while straight rows of coloured-leaf lettuces or peas in flower are as attractive and satisfying as a ribbon of alyssum and lobelia. Rather more so, in fact. As for a gnarled old apple tree in rosy-red fruit against a lowering purple sky . . . I rest my case.

True, many kitchen gardens can be scruffy, makeshift and too obviously utilitarian, but the Platonic ideal of the kitchen garden, which you can still find at, say, West Dean, West Sussex, or Clumber Park, Nottinghamshire, is a wonderful thing. And a great draw for garden visitors.

Edible crops and culinary and medicinal herbs have been grown in gardens since at least medieval times, of course, and kitchen gardens have been the almost invariable adjunct of any house, in town or country, which had space enough, since at least the seventeenth century. Even the eighteenth-century landscape garden was not without its kitchen garden, although it was banished from its earlier position close to the house to somewhere where it would not block the view. ('Capability' Brown did this at Basildon Park in Berkshire, for example.) The kitchen garden undoubtedly reached its apogee in complexity and productiveness from 1850 until 1914, in country estates where there was acreage enough for a walled enclosure. Here, with the help of glass structures – glasshouses, pits and frames – not only frost-hardy vegetables and fruit but tender ones as well could be grown successfully. Even tropical fruits, such as pineapples, were possible, if enough money was expended on heating and labour. The business of forcing and retarding fruit and vegetables to provide produce out of due season has never again reached such levels of sophistication, in private gardens at least.

OPPOSITE The kitchen garden at Hadspen in Somerset, showing part of the 700-foot/213-metre-long curved wall. The centre of the garden contains vegetables, with ornamentals against the wall.

BELOW Growing apples as 'goblets' is a technique gleaned by Victorian gardeners from the French. They are enjoying a renaissance in ornamental potagers. This is The Old Rectory at Sudborough in Northamptonshire.

The kitchen garden was also traditionally the place to grow flowers for decorating the interior of the house: both those which could be cut and those left growing in pots, which were moved inside while they flowered and taken back to the glasshouse when they were over. Again forcing was commonplace.

Kitchen gardens were, and are, not necessarily bounded by walls, but the most successful in the past were, because these created the all-important microclimates which ensured the success of fruit growing and enlarged the range of produce that could be grown. They also provided something to attach lean-to glasshouses to, and they could be secured against theft and the depredations of farm and wild animals. (Being solid barriers, unlike hedges, they could also create damaging wind swirl, but the most sophisticated had external buttresses to mitigate that.) In the north of England, they were essential for reliable crops of hardy fruits, whose blossom might otherwise be frosted, but they were a fixture of southern gardens too. Those walls which have remained are often things of beauty themselves, especially if built out of local stone, hand-made bricks or cob, and very tall (12 feet/4 metres being quite usual and 15 or 18 feet/4½ or 5½ metres not uncommon). Generally speaking, walled gardens were square or rectangular, although the lie of the land could turn them into trapezoids or other geometric shapes.[1] Always there was a south-facing, west-facing and north-facing wall to accommodate the requirements of fruit: vines, figs, peaches, nectarines and apricots on the south, apples and pears on the west, acid cherries, currants and gooseberries on the north. In fact, walled gardens were often not built on a completely straight north–south, east–west axis but, in the south of England at least, they were angled slightly east of south, and further north slightly west of south, to help prevent too rapid a thaw on a sunny morning after a frosty night in spring when the fruit trees were flowering.

Occasionally, kitchen gardens were oval, such as the one at William Robinson's garden, Gravetye Manor, in West Sussex (he said it suited the slope of the ground). One side of the Melon Yard at Heligan in Cornwall is curved, as is the wall in the walled garden at Hadspen, Somerset. Most intriguing are the serpentine or crinkle-crankle walls, such as those at Vann in Surrey, Lexham Hall in Norfolk, and Hopton Hall in Derbyshire. Zig-zag walls were also sometimes favoured, as with the south wall of the walled garden at West Dean. The advantage of these serpentine walls was that they did not require buttressing, and fruit trees could be trained in the concave curves and would benefit from extra exposure to the sun, because of the increased surface area. In some kitchen gardens, the walls had hot-water pipes running through them, which were used to heat the walls and promote even earlier flowering and fruiting; the holes can still be seen at, for example, Flintham Hall in Nottinghamshire.

Inside the walls, the glasshouses were built to high specifications: even the panes of glass were curved at the bottom so that the rain ran

An espalier pear on a crinkle-crankle wall at Vann in Surrey. Crinkle-crankle walls, either curved or zig-zag, were thought to encourage better flowers and fruiting than straight ones, because of the increased surface area. They were also stronger structurally than straight walls and could be built just one brick thick, so saving on materials.

to the middle and away from the glazing bars. Frame yards, with brick-built cold frames, and glazed frames which could be lifted to let in air, were extensive. These were where 'hot beds' were prepared for forcing carrots and other vegetables in the early spring; these used fresh manure, which heated up and was covered by soil so that it would not scorch the young vegetables.

The formal layout of the walled kitchen garden varied little from garden to garden, since a geometric shape was the most convenient for gardeners pushing barrows to and fro. The garden tended to have a central pond with a fountain, often the wellspring from which all-important water was drawn, and this could either be ornate or fairly simple. Four paths radiated from the centre. These paths were usually composed of hoggin – that is, gravel rolled in clay – and might well have trained fruit trees running along their sides. Fruit tree training was an art which reached its apogee in France in the nineteenth century, but English gardeners also became adept at making goblets, festoons, U cordons and the like. The borders under the walls contained the fruit trees, of course,

LEFT Cordon-trained pears in blossom on an old kitchen garden wall at The Priory, Kemerton, in Worcestershire. Cordons have long been popular because it is possible to grow a great number of varieties in a comparatively confined space.

ABOVE An apple cultivar grown as an espalier – a French technique originally. All these 'restricted forms' (cordon, espalier, 'step-over', fan) give the gardener the opportunity to control pests and prune more easily. They are also most ornamental. The flower growing close by is *Nicotiana sylvestris*. This is at Bourton House in Gloucestershire.

BELOW Pears look particularly good when trained on sturdy arches because of their naturally pendulous nature when maturing. These are at Westwell Manor in Oxfordshire.

ABOVE Flowers for picking, such as dahlias, *Malope*, sweet peas and statice, growing in the kitchen garden at Spetchley Park in Worcestershire, in July, together with spinach and other vegetables. It makes a very attractive mix.

OPPOSITE Heligan in Cornwall has a very fine and extensive traditional kitchen garden, where Victorian methods are frequently used. (Even pineapples are grown here.) The terracotta pots shown here are for forcing rhubarb into early growth in spring. The wall at the end is curved, which was quite common in Victorian times.

FOLLOWING PAGES West Dean in West Sussex, the *ne plus ultra* of walled kitchen gardens, runs on traditional lines. These are young pear trees trained into a variety of restricted forms, including 'four-winged pyramids' and 'goblets *à la Lorette*'. The plums and Morello cherries on the wall are trained as fans.

as well as cutting flowers and permanent crops such as rhubarb, seakale and cardoons.

Usually there would be a double herbaceous border, each side of the main path leading to the glasshouses. The ones at Clumber Park were intended to hide the workaday vegetables from the sight of the 'quality' on their way to inspect the ornamental plants in the conservatory, which formed the central portion of the run of glasshouses, set against one wall of the garden.

The good times for kitchen gardens could not last, sadly. The rot set in after the First World War, and was accelerated by economic stringencies in the 1930s and 1940s. The death knell was sounded by the post-Second World War social revolution; most countrymen and women no longer saw 'private service' as a desirable career. By the 1950s, aside from royal and ducal estates, there were few gardens operating at anything like the peak of activity of fifty years before. As a typical example, at Pylewell Park in Hampshire, whose story is minutely and admirably chronicled by Susan Campbell,[2] there were 16 full-time gardeners in 1930, 4 in 1968 and only 2 by the late 1970s.

Pylewell Park lasted longer than most. In the 1960s and 1970s, especially after the oil crisis of 1973 which shattered confidence, walled gardens all over the country were turned into car parks (in the case of National Trust gardens, in particular), leased to commercial nurseries and market gardens, became Christmas tree plantations or were simply allowed, slowly and steadily, to decay, with soil beautifully worked for generations becoming bramble patches in a short matter of years, and just the odd fig tree growing through the glasshouse roof, still defiantly fruiting, to indicate something of the glory of earlier days.

Remarkably, however, in the last twenty years, and partly as a result of the exposure to, and popularity of, Harry Dodson and his televised 'Victorian' kitchen garden, a number of walled gardens have been restored to something like their former magnificence. A few are enjoying a second, if slightly artificial, heyday, thanks to enormous efforts by both talented individuals and enlightened public bodies. I say 'artificial' because the produce grown is not usually destined for consumption in 'the Big House', but is either sold at the gate or, more often, ends up on the compost heap. (Heligan is one exception: the fruit and vegetables are eaten in the garden restaurant.) Despite all that, there is an abiding and lively interest from garden visitors in 'how things were done in the old days'.

Some of these walled gardens, such as Clumber Park, Heligan, and Normanby Hall Country Park in Lincolnshire, are self-conscious period pieces, where old varieties of seed and old methods of cultivation are used wherever possible, in the case of Clumber as a specific educational exercise by the National Trust. Others, such as West Dean, have an air of modern dynamism as well, since old varieties and techniques are used, but by no

means exclusively. No Victorian head gardener would have had, for example, such a range of tomatoes and chillies available to them as can be seen annually at festival events held there in late summer.

West Dean was once the home of Edward James, a surrealist painter and general all-round eccentric, who inherited the estate in 1912. It is now a centre for a range of educational courses promoting the arts. 'In 1992, work started on redeveloping the gardens with the aim of recapturing its turn-of-the-20th-century ambience,'[3] wrote Jim Buckland, gardens manager, who looks after the 2½-acre/1-hectare kitchen garden with only the help of his wife and one other. (There were eleven staff in James's day.) The kitchen garden is in two enclosures, the first containing thirteen glasshouses and three frames, and the second the fruit garden, with half-standard fruit trees growing in grass and fruit trees fan-trained along the mile length of sheltering wall. Fruit trees are also grown in a variety of intriguing restricted shapes, such as goblets, U cordons and four-winged pyramids.

The Victorian glasshouses by Foster and Pearson, which were the very last word when they were erected between 1891 and 1900, have all been immaculately restored and are in full working order. They comprise fig houses, vineries, peach houses and floral display houses, as well as houses growing gourds, peppers, tomatoes, melons and strawberries; all are grown to the very highest standard.

Out of doors is a wonderfully productive vegetable garden with a central double herbaceous border, known as the Hot Border, which is planted up with flowers at their most colourful, and best, in late summer when the produce is reaching harvest time. Many of the vegetables grown are from seed obtained from the Heritage Seed Library run by Garden Organic, but seed also arrives from gardens round the world. The atmosphere of neat and determined industry engendered by the gardeners at West Dean, in such an attractive, well-ordered setting, brings back to life the essential nature of the Victorian kitchen garden.

The walled garden at Normanby Hall Country Park, followed the traditional story of flourishing in Victorian times (it was built in 1817) and then suffering when the house was requisitioned in both world wars, finally being leased to the local council in the 1960s, when the glasshouses were pulled down. True to a growing trend, in the 1990s the walled garden was restored, using public grants. New, faithful-to-the-original glasshouses were erected on the old foundations, the only differences being that coated aluminium was used rather than wood for the glazing bars, and automatic ventilation added. There is a tall, narrow peach 'case' (lean-to greenhouse), a fernery, a vinery and a display house. The walled garden opened to visitors in 1997.

The garden is run on organic principles, which it would not have been in Victorian times, when a number of poisonous chemicals such as arsenic and Paris green were used, although some of the remedies which

are employed at Normanby, such as spraying vines with bicarbonate of soda to try to fend off mildew, are very old.

The design is conventional, the area being carved up into four large beds, with a central gazebo, herbaceous borders on each side of the central gravel path and narrower borders round the walls. As at West Dean, the walls are covered in trained fruit, and there are fruit arches, tunnels and goblet trees. There is an exuberant subtropical bedding display outside the vinery in the summer.

The 2-acre/0.8-hectare walled garden at Audley End in Essex, which dates from the 1750s, is another faithfully authentic restoration by English Heritage and Garden Organic – and is run entirely on organic principles too. Mercifully, this garden was never totally abandoned, having been a market garden until the late 1990s, so the soil had been left in good heart. This being a garden overseen by English Heritage, there is emphasis on using pre-1900 varieties. Striking here is the enormous vinery, which stretches most of the length of the south wall.

These walled kitchen gardens constitute a very important, but numerically very small, proportion of the productive gardens open to

ABOVE The restored 2-acre/0.8-hectare walled kitchen garden at Audley End in Essex, dating from the 1750s. This is an authentic restoration by English Heritage. Note the 170-foot/52-metre-long five-bay vine house, on the south wall, which dates from 1802. This garden is run entirely on organic lines by Garden Organic (formerly HDRA).

FOLLOWING PAGES A modern potager designed by Tom Stuart-Smith in a private garden, with the emphasis on good cultivation methods as well as attractive decorative elements. There are raised beds, to aid drainage, bordered by woven hazel hurdles, and hazel is used also for the bean 'wigwams' and as decorative support for lilies in pots. Chives have been allowed to flower to provide muted colour, and beds are edged by 'step-over' apples.

THE KITCHEN GARDEN

garden visitors these days. For the reality has been that, as after the Second World War gardens became progressively more the preserve of the owner rather than the employed gardener, the size of kitchen gardens generally shrank markedly. There was neither the need, nor the labour, to grow so much produce. That does not mean, however, that gardeners have lost the desire to grow comestibles – far from it. But they now do it in different ways.

Popular, because it is attuned both to the economics and to the pervading philosophy of our day, is the potager, the size of which can differ from an acre down to a few square yards. Potager is simply the French word for a vegetable garden but, thanks to our exposure to articles and programmes on the great potager at Villandry in France and its extraordinary aesthetic approach to kitchen gardening, the word has come to mean an ornamental kitchen garden, where looks are not sacrificed to utility, and where time and trouble are taken over the design. The allure of the potager in an era when no one in England is in much danger of starving, and looks matter nearly as much as taste, is obvious.

The potager is geometric in character, both for practical and aesthetic reasons, and often incorporates some degree of nostalgic installation such as a simple open knot garden (see page 15), whose compartments can be used for herbs. Fruit trees tend to be trained into restricted shapes, as they were in the large-scale walled gardens of old, but the availability of dwarfing and semi-dwarfing rootstocks has certainly been a boon to the would-be potagiste. In very small gardens, standard gooseberries play the same part of defining axial paths.

One of the greatest and most influential exponents of the potager was the late Rosemary Verey, whose potager at Barnsley House in Gloucestershire was laid out in the early 1980s and fortunately survives to this day; indeed the house is now an hotel and the potager has been extended recently to provide the restaurant with enough fresh produce. Rosemary Verey described how it came about. 'Looking back, I realize it was William Lawson who inspired me to change our vegetable patch . . . into a decorative potager, where, in his words, "*comely borders with herbs*" and "*abundance of roses and lavender [would] yield much profit and comfort to the senses*".'[4] Rosemary Verey was a collector of antiquarian gardening books and the book she is referring to here is *The New Orchard and Garden*, published first in 1618.

Her potager (a 'small area, about the size of a tennis court and its surround'[5]) is laid out in a part-walled, part-hedged enclosure, outside the garden proper, and close to grazing cows and a pony field. This was deliberate, the idea being that the visitor would come across the potager unexpectedly and it would be a delightful surprise. The garden is characterized by masses of narrow, straight, concrete-slab and second-hand-brick paths, sufficient for most work to be done from them and

Flowers and vegetables grown together for decorative effect, with purple curly kale, nasturtiums (which of course have edible flowers), and orange and yellow French marigolds (*Tagetes*). French marigolds are very strong-smelling and are widely thought to deter aphids, yet also attract beneficial insects, notably hoverflies.

The potager at Barnsley House in Gloucestershire, laid out by Rosemary Verey in a part-walled, part-hedged enclosure outside the garden proper. This garden has been widely copied. Vegetables were grown in blocks or interlocking patterns. Clipped yellow privet added a ray of artificial sunlight. The greatest difficulty for committed potagistes is picking produce without spoiling the visual effect. This potager is still well kept up and indeed has been enlarged by the present owners, who run a hotel and use the produce in the kitchens.

avoid treading on the soil. The bricks and slabs were laid without mortar so that they would have a countrified, informal look. 'No cement was used – it would make the paths difficult to move, and anyway I much preferred *the unprofessional look*'⁶ – my italics: this seems to me neatly to encompass the potager philosophy.

In the first half of the garden are two large squares, hedged with box, with diagonal paths to a centre circle containing four trained fruit trees, pears on one side, apples on the other. These are trained as goblets. Between these two squares runs a narrow path up to the centre of the potager, which contains a trained apple tree, surrounded by standards of the charmingly old-fashioned rose 'Little White Pet'.

Beyond this circle are two large square gardens, cut up into smaller ones, bounded by narrow paths and box hedges, with sturdy finials at the corners. Verticality is provided by trained fruit trees as well as simple bamboo structures for climbing beans and wooden trellis. In Rosemary Verey's day, vegetables were grown in blocks or interlocking patterns,

for example 'Lollo Rosso' red lettuces together with the glaucous-purple leaves of red cabbage, green-leaved lettuce and leek flags for vertical contrast. In places, clipped yellow privet added a ray of artificial sunlight. The vegetables were grown on a strict rotation system; there were no compromises with good cultivation requirements. 'Salad crops . . . are arranged wherever they can make exciting colour combinations.'[7]

Beyond these beds is a tunnel made from simple, curved, black plastic-coated metal arches, from which in high summer hang climbing marrows and fat, colourful gourds. To the two sides of the main planting areas are herb beds and arbours, one with a vine over it, the other a golden hop. Although the structural planting remained from year to year, Rosemary Verey changed the colour effects and the patterns frequently.

There is a rustic sturdiness about the potager in England. The vegetables and fruit may be ornamental in looks, but the hard landscaping must not look machine-made or too expensive. At Helmingham Hall, Suffolk, and Pine House, Leicestershire, as well as at

ABOVE A metal tunnel from which gourds appear to drip at Pine House in Leicestershire.

RIGHT Trimmed tumps of santolina and lavender in the potager at West Green House in Hampshire. In true potager tradition, there is a decorative, but productive, mix of flowers, herbs and vegetables, with sweet peas on hazel tripods, Swiss chard, red cabbage and onions in front of a rosemary hedge.

Barnsley, arches, from which gourds hang, are made of uncomplicated metalwork. At West Green House, Marylyn Abbott has two ornamental fruit cages of great charm, designed by Oliver Ford, in the centre of her large potager, but they do not feel too ornate for the setting.

Verticality can be achieved using standard gooseberries or honeysuckle or tripods of woven willow. Flowers, especially cutting flowers, are essential, usually growing in separate beds but sometimes mixed up amongst the vegetables. Rosemary Verey was very keen on flowers in the potager – with the right traditional feel, such as tulips in spring, and shrub roses in summer. Generally in potagers, sweet peas find a favoured place amongst the vegetables, since these must be picked as regularly as saladings. Vegetables in the potager are not always sown in straight lines but often instead in squares or drifts, depending on the layout of the beds. The key is to make it possible to get at them from the path, so as not to tread any more than necessary on the soil.

Rosemary Verey also designed the potager at The Old Rectory, Sudborough, although later amendments are the work of Rupert Golby, another fine potagiste and garden designer, along with the owner. The garden has narrow brick paths, leading to a central wrought-iron arbour; it is perfectly planted and carefully maintained.

There is no doubt that potagistes have been helped (though which is cause and which effect is difficult to untangle) by the upsurge in production of terracotta forcing and other pots. Although there is now a lively market in pre-war artifacts, such as pots and cloches, terracotta pots are also being made again. Rhubarb and seakale are right back in fashion.

There can be few kitchen gardens where herbs are not an important ingredient, and the

use of them has increased exponentially in recent years, since there is now such a public emphasis on healthy living. Much that was known 500 years ago is being rediscovered. Claims for herbs' efficicacy can be, and are sometimes, overdone, but most herbs have something to recommend them; certainly gardeners have learned to make herb gardens attractive and full of variety, as well as alluring to insects and birds.

Herb gardens can be made in pots or in a few raised beds, or they can be large and stately. At The Abbey House Gardens, in Malmesbury, Wiltshire, a garden on the site of a Benedictine monastery, and therefore a place where herbs would have been grown for many centuries, there is an attractive Herb Garden: circular, with many narrow, radiating paths and, between them, raised wooden beds of herbs and a central diamond-shaped wooden-sided pond with fountain. This treatment accords a seemly but not excessive regard to herbs and their attractiveness as garden plants.

There is a physic garden at Chenies Manor, Buckinghamshire, while at Acorn Bank in Cumbria, a National Trust property, an entire walled

OPPOSITE This is the Herb Garden at The Abbey House Gardens at Malmesbury, Wiltshire. This is an impressive part-formal, part-riverside and woodland garden, almost in the centre of the town, much of it in what had been the garden of a Benedictine monastery. The Herb Garden is in a 'clock' shape, made up of raised, timber-edged beds, such as the monks would have used. Note the quality of the workmanship in the herb beds, using wooden nails. Also the bamboo covers, which in the Far East keep chickens from straying, but are excellent for slightly tender plants or those vulnerable to bird damage. This is a garden very respectful of its distant, monastic past.

ABOVE The Abbey House Herb Garden is surrounded by a circular colonnade, made from steel hoops used for making polytunnels. There are 180 fruit cordons on the outer columns and clematis and roses on the inner supports. The owners reckon there are more roses in this 5-acre/2-hectare garden than anywhere else in England.

FOLLOWING PAGES A charming herb garden in Devon designed by Tessa Traeger and Patrick Kinmonth, with unpretentious 'hard' elements and topiary, as befits the intrinsically homely nature of herb growing. There are collapsible willow wigwams for sweet peas and nasturtiums, Victorian glass 'bell' cloches to protect young plants and slate edgings to the simple stone paths. The moss-covered stone seat flanked by box shapes is particularly charming. Yellow tree lupins and golden-leaved feverfew and chives lend colour to an otherwise green scene.

LEFT A very attractive herb garden, with other elements, such as variegated holly in pots, in a garden in Oxfordshire.

ABOVE A traditional vegetable plot in a cottage garden in Nottinghamshire – orderly, productive and unpretentious. Every inch is used and the approach is purely practical. The varying colours of leaf vegetables, however, give it a pleasant aspect.

garden has been turned over to a collection of 250 culinary and medicinal herbs. Here the favourable microclimate provided by the wall ensures that the northerly latitude is no obstacle.

I cannot leave this subject without saying something about more utilitarian gardens. Not everyone wishes to grow their vegetables for aesthetic effect, or refrain from picking them when they are *au point*, in order that the symmetry is not spoiled. Indeed, that is probably true of the vast majority of kitchen gardeners in this country. However, that is not to say that there cannot be a splendour about utilitarian plots at times. And at least they have the merit of being, in the proper sense of the phrase, down to earth, as well as very fruitful. Some are even open to the public.

OTHER KITCHEN GARDENS

Emmaus House, Bristol
South Farm, Cambridgeshire
Acorn Bank, Cumbria
Levens Hall, Cumbria
Calke Abbey, Derbyshire
Hardwick Hall, Derbyshire
Arlington Court, Devon
Clovelly Court, Devon
Tapeley Park, Devon
Edmondsham House, Dorset
Cerney House, Gloucestershire
Conholt Park, Hampshire
Abbey Dore, Herefordshire
Osborne House, Isle of Wight
Belmont, Kent
Leighton Hall, Lancashire
Gunby Hall, Lincolnshire
Fenton House, London
Castle Acre Priory, Norfolk
Felbrigg Hall, Norfolk
Houghton Hall, Norfolk
Lexham Hall, Norfolk
Sulgrave Manor, Northamptonshire
Kelmarsh Hall, Nottinghamshire
Bridewell Organic Garden, Oxfordshire
Hodnet Hall, Shropshire
Barrington Court, Somerset
Somerleyton Hall, Suffolk
Wyken Hall, Suffolk
Titsey Place, Surrey
Sarah Raven's Cutting Garden, Sussex
Bede's World, Tyneside
Upton House, Warwickshire
The Old Malt House, Wiltshire
Burton Agnes Hall, Yorkshire

In this final chapter, I come now to consider perhaps the most interesting (and difficult) question concerning the design of the English garden, namely, where are trends going? We have seen how strong and widespread was the Arts and Crafts garden in the twentieth century, and how persuasive to gardeners was, and is, the idea of informal and profuse planting within a formal framework. As a result, by the later years of the century, young garden designers were at their wits' end, caught between the conservatism of their clients and their own desire to do something different and exciting: something preferably with an intellectual underpinning to it. Whatever they managed to achieve in the show gardens at Chelsea Flower Show they found difficult to sell in the real world, so to speak. (At least the better ones had enough work; for by the 1990s it had become established amongst a sizeable tranche of the property-owning classes that garden design could be entrusted to professionals.) And, amongst creative amateur gardeners, too, there was a feeling that there were other voices, other rooms. They were beginning to have different things than Jekyllesque borders on their minds.

Contemporary garden designers found they were up against a powerful historicist movement, however, which was prompting the restoration of historic gardens at every turn. The public now had the opportunity to marvel at the rescue of an eighteenth-century masterpiece such as Stowe, the re-created Victorian carpet-bedding miracles at Waddesdon Manor and Harewood House, and Gertrude Jekyll's brilliance reinstated at The Manor House, Upton Grey and Hestercombe. The impact of these restorations on public attitudes can be imagined, but it was not entirely helpful to designers and amateur gardeners trying to look forward.

Contemporary designers had somehow to climb out from underneath this dead weight of tradition, and the story of the 1990s and beyond is that some of them have succeeded. In order to understand something of what they are about, we need to look back ourselves, if briefly, at the history of Modernism, as it translated into garden design in England.

Modernism arrived in England from the Continent in the 1920s. In architecture, Modernism was (to simplify grossly) concerned with functionalism and utility, the credo being that an object which performed the function for which it was made was also beautiful. This was not a million miles away from the Arts and Crafts philosophy but, added to

THE CONTEMPORARY GARDEN

OPPOSITE Conceptual art in gardens tends to be confined to garden shows, since it is not always very practical in gardens, and can also date quickly. This is Tony Heywood's *The Split*, enlivening the Westonbirt International Festival of the Garden in 2003. Heywood calls himself a 'horticultural intervention artist'.

BELOW At The Menagerie in Northamptonshire, built by the late owners, the architectural historian Gervase Jackson-Stops designed a thatched, rustic arbour with a Classical portico. There is a jolly aspect to it, the result of the scholarly owner having some highbrow fun.

349

this was a fascination with technological advances and new building materials. Followers of Modernism abhorred superfluous decoration (Adolf Loos said, demotically, that 'ornament was excrement') and Le Corbusier famously referred to the Modernist house as a 'machine'. As far as the design of gardens went, axial geometry, so important to the formal garden through the ages, was abandoned. Le Corbusier said that the landscape around a house should be 'Virgilian' – that is, placed amongst grass and trees. Asymmetry ruled. Gardens were made to be seen from a number of viewpoints. As for plants, they became more useful as individual 'sculptures' than as complex constituents of a dynamic scheme. Most importantly, perhaps (and this idea has been influential ever since), Modernist gardens were meant to be closely connected to the house, with interior and exterior linked.

Christopher Tunnard and Oliver Hill, both landscape architects, were the main exponents of the style in England. Tunnard was responsible for St Anne's Hill in Surrey and Bentley Wood in Sussex, and influenced others by publishing *Gardens in the Modern Landscape* in 1938. His avowed principles for the modern garden were, firstly, functionalism, which one has to say made eminent sense in the modern world; secondly, empathy – that is, the placing of the house and garden sensitively in the landscape; and thirdly, the importance of using abstract sculpture in the garden, actively rather than incidentally. He did not ignore plants, but he did not believe that they should be massed for effect.

But neither white, flat-roofed boxes on piloti, however well sited in the landscape, nor concrete terraces, acres of grass and clumps of birch trees had much popular appeal. Indeed, Tunnard completed just six commissions before he left for the United States in 1939. At his departure, the Modernist garden in England more or less died. People have since bemoaned the lack of its popularity, especially since it seemed, paradoxically, to be an approach with strong echoes of eighteenth-century landscape gardening – with the idea of the house set in its landscape, and the necessity to 'consult the genius of the place' – but the English seemingly could not be weaned from their passion for growing flowers. And, moreover, concrete soon showed itself to be a medium that did not age well outside in our soft, damp climate. In truth, Modernism in garden making was less articulate than in architecture and the result was, for the average garden maker, confusion and even repulsion.

Otherwise, pre- and post-war English garden designers as opposed to landscape architects were inclined to be eclectic, and less intolerant, in their approach. Men such as Percy Cane, Lanning Roper and Vernon Russell-Smith continued to provide garden owners with plant-rich, accomplished, but not immensely adventurous gardens. Percy Cane, for example, is, perhaps, best remembered for his trademark woodland glade and azalea-lined stone steps at Dartington Hall, Devon.

I have mentioned (see page 232) the professional landscape architects in England whom the Modernists Thomas Church, Garrett Eckbo and Roberto Burle Marx influenced. These English disciples only occasionally had the opportunity to be garden designers since, after the war, there was precious little private work around. (What is more, Modernist architects were often social improvers who considered public projects, such as the mushrooming New Towns, more worthy of their time than private gardens.) It has only been in the last two decades or so, as garden owners have become steadily more affluent, that there have been enough adventurous clients around prepared to experiment, and promote, home-grown talent, in a substantial way.

Sir Geoffrey Jellicoe had led the way, having been in the first wave of Modernists before the war, and he lived to see his two great private gardens – Shute House in Dorset and Sutton Place in Surrey – become highly admired (see pages 287 and 254–5). The influences on him seem to me, however, to have been very complex. His gardens had a highly symbolic quality, for they were at least partly explorations of the theme of life's journey. He maintained that the theme of his work at Sutton Place, for example, was 'Creation, Life and Aspiration', while at Shute House he provided a choice for the onlooker of two directions (as so often in life), where the River Nadder splits and flows two ways. Water is in places at Shute dark, murky, even subterranean, while in others it is light, sparkly and musical. He was also influenced by Jungian ideas, in particular the idea that gardens act on people's subconscious. Is there not here also an echo of eighteenth-century attitudes towards garden making?

John Brookes (who worked for a time with both Dame Sylvia Crowe and Brenda Colvin) continued, from the 1960s, to carry the torch for an humane species of Modernism, and has been influential, especially through his books, such as *Room Outside* (1969). His work is often abstract, but never ascetic, and gardeners have responded positively to it. Sadly, from our point of view, as with Jellicoe, some of his most interesting work has been for corporate or public clients, so it is not relevant here. Brookes also deserves the credit for addressing head on the potential difficulties faced by millions of post-war gardeners, with gardens severely restricted in size, when he published *The Small Garden* in 1979.

Other post-war Modernist designers who, like Brookes, managed to combine their progressive ideas about the manipulation of space with a skilful use of plants include Peter Aldington at Turn End, his house in Buckinghamshire, Preben Jacobsen and Sir Frederick Gibberd. The architect of Heathrow Airport, Liverpool Catholic Cathedral and Harlow New Town, Gibberd only ever designed one garden, his own, but it is a very interesting one. Without axial geometry, it is designed to be seen from a number of carefully thought-out viewpoints. It encompasses a

FOLLOWING PAGES An example of John Brookes's work in a garden in Sussex. He has carried the torch of an humane species of Modernism, without the self-denying austerity it can have, since the 1960s. This is a contemporary take on a traditional formal garden.

LEFT An example of Christopher Bradley-Hole's work in Wiltshire. The artfully placed stones are of Portland limestone. This garden sits well in its landscape, yet is a challenge to the pure agriculture with its field of wild flowers.

ABOVE A view of the same garden from another angle. The stones echo the curve of the bench and mown grass, and also refer to Stonehenge, which is also in Wiltshire.

sequence of different spaces: glades, an ultra-narrow lime avenue and pools, all enlivened by carefully placed modern sculptures as well as *objets trouvés* and fountains (see page 249).

But what about the young, or relatively young, contemporary designers working now? Nothing appears presently to be ruled in or out, but those making the waves, so to speak, are designers who combine a regard for minimalism with a close interest in plants. Minimalism in art began in the 1960s in New York as a reaction against the Abstract Expressionism of, for example, Jackson Pollock; it was influenced by Mies van der Rohe's seminal 'Less is More' slogan, and has been influential in art ever since. Its appeal as a way of dealing with the inherent difficulties posed by small gardens is obvious.

For designers such as Christopher Bradley-Hole, Minimalism means simplicity, purity of line, a strong geometry, as well as some spiritual quality inspired by Oriental religions. As he puts it: 'Minimalist designers cannot rely on decoration and therefore have to achieve results by manipulating space, proportion and materials.'[1] The problem with Minimalism is that, in its purest form, though cool and tranquil, it denies

both seasonality and the deep-seated desire of English gardeners to grow plants – and lots of them. The clean, pure lines can be very attractive but are too austere and unchanging for popular taste. That is why, although Bradley-Hole has written a book entitled *The Minimalist Garden*, his work, both for private clients and public bodies (like English Heritage at Portland Castle), shows a clever melding of pared-down layout, with a, frankly, pretty broad palette of plant form and colour. He has plainly not remained immune to the influence of the New Naturalism (see page 208), nor that of James van Sweden and Wolfgang Oehme in the United States, who have explored some of the same ideas as the Europeans in this matter. Together with Tom Stuart-Smith and Dan Pearson, in particular, Bradley-Hole has shown that a sophisticated refinement in the use of plants (they are all plantsmen as well as designers) within a spare, geometric and high-quality structure can be the way to the hearts of their clients.

It might be thought that uniting hard-edged modern materials with naturalistic planting would feel uncomfortable, but it is only a different way of providing informality within a formal framework, especially in a

LEFT ABOVE A modern amphitheatre, by Christopher Bradley-Hole in a private garden in Sussex, showing a classical influence but in a modern idiom. 'Minimalist designers cannot rely on decoration and therefore have to achieve results by manipulating space, proportion and materials.'

LEFT BELOW A stylish naturalism exhibited by Bradley-Hole in a garden in Sussex. There is a strong connection between house and garden, with a formal layout softened by the laxest planting, using a limited palette of plants.

ABOVE This is a rather more mainstream contemporary garden in Oxfordshire, designed by Jinny Blom. Although demonstrably a garden, it is careful of context. The planting is muted in colour and blends seamlessly into the countryside beyond. Amongst the plants used is a native elder, the purple-leaved form (seen flowering on the left).

ABOVE Tom Stuart-Smith's own garden in Hertfordshire, highly structured and profusely planted. To achieve the effective two-tone green, he has sown lettuce between the two L-shapes of yew.

RIGHT The thoroughly modern parterre at Broughton Grange in Oxfordshire, designed by Tom Stuart-Smith, where the wonderfully versatile dwarf box delineates the cell structure of a tree leaf. The bottom of three terraces, it is bedded-out twice a year, first with bulbs and then with tender annuals. The middle terrace can be seen on page 374.

This is the erstwhile farmyard of Bury Court in Hampshire, designed by Piet Oudolf. The wooden sculpture in the pond is by Paul Anderson. Again, traditional materials – brick, granite setts, yew hedging – are here used in a contemporary manner. The space is not divided up into 'rooms' but consists of several borders, surrounding a central grass garden.

post-modern age when irony and individualism are strong motivating forces. The result of such an approach is that some contemporary gardens look strikingly different from those made twenty years ago: Scampston Hall in Yorkshire, Broughton Grange in Oxfordshire (where Tom Stuart-Smith has, amongst many other things, laid out a parterre depicting the cell structure of a tree's leaf using dwarf box), and Bury Court in Hampshire. The feeling that the world was standing still has finally gone.

In the excitement of all this, however, we should not forget the work of landscape architects, such as Kim Wilkie, who restore and elaborate historic landscapes, but in a creative, rather than strictly historicist, way (admirable as that is in many circumstances, of course). In his case, his work at Heveningham Hall in Suffolk includes putting in place a 'Capability' Brown plan, which was never completely implemented 200 years ago, and digging 1¼ miles/2 kilometres of lake. A 130-feet/48-metre-wide, three-arched stone bridge is the next project. As interesting, I think, was the removal of a rather unsatisfactory Victorian garden from behind the hall and its replacement with a completely new garden of curving grass terraces. As he has put it: 'The terraces flow with the rising land, arcing in a Fibonacci series fan that encompasses the veteran trees and gives the house space to breathe.'[2]

At Great Fosters, a country house hotel in Surrey, he has, amongst other works, added a 20-feet/6-metre-high sculpted grass amphitheatre at the end of a lime avenue to screen off the motorway, together with earth 'bunds' to cut down the traffic noise. Apparently a string quartet concert was held in celebration on completion of this, just 82 feet/25 metres from the motorway, and the acoustics were 'perfect'. It was not

exactly silent when I visited but, undoubtedly, the decibel levels were lower than expected.

There has been a tradition of earth sculpting, off and on, since pre-historical times, and Wilkie is one of the most accomplished contemporary 'sculptors'. The great thing about modern land sculpting is that it can take advantage of advances in construction techniques, geotextile technology and mega machinery.

It would be nice to be able to describe other examples of this 'art', since some of the most exciting contemporary gardens have aspects of it; unfortunately, for the purposes of this book, the best ones are in Scotland (Charles Jencks' Garden of Cosmic Speculation, Dumfriesshire, and his serpentine mount at the Scottish National Gallery of Modern Art, Edinburgh) and many of the rest are public, rather than garden, projects. Land sculpture is usually seen as on too large a scale for gardens, although there is an interesting grass mound at the Blewbury Manor, Berkshire, and a square, flat-topped grass mound for viewing in the Walled Garden at Scampston Hall (see page 230).

Not quite in the same vein, but certainly an example of new designers working creatively in an old setting, is Trentham Gardens, Staffordshire, where Tom Stuart-Smith and Piet Oudolf have been recruited to redesign the Italian Gardens (see page 32). Within Barry's formal framework, Stuart-Smith has planted his signature meadow perennial plantings, including rivers of grasses through the beds, to echo, for those with particularly sharp eyes, the River Trent which flows near by.

Similar in philosophy are the 'Contemporary Heritage Gardens', created at a number of English Heritage properties. The idea was to

An example of earth sculpture in Oxfordshire. This is the spiral mound at Blewbury Manor, a 10-acre/4-hectare garden. Earth sculpture is not common in contemporary gardens, but there is also a mound at Scampston Hall, Yorkshire (see page 230). At Great Fosters, Surrey, and Heveningham Hall, Suffolk, Kim Wilkie has made grass amphitheatres. The spirit of eighteenth-century Claremont lives on.

LEFT Tom Stuart-Smith's garden for the *Daily Telegraph* at Chelsea Flower Show in 2006. The sharp-edged, rusty corten steel panels and tanks contrast markedly with the lax, dense planting of summer perennials and bulbs – *Allium* 'Purple Sensation', the blue *Nepeta racemosa* 'Walker's Low' and *Salvia* 'Mainacht' – and the white annual *Orlaya grandiflora*.

FOLLOWING PAGES The 'other' Hampton Court in Herefordshire, with a garden designed and laid out since 1996 by Simon Dorrell. This is a complex, geometric water garden in the old Victorian walled garden, the main features of which are two beautifully executed octagonal pavilions with connecting canals and water steps. The massive Victorian castle is in the background.

make gardens which took the best of contemporary design, but put it within the framework of historic gardens. These garden designs were put out to open competition. Isabelle van Groeningen won at Eltham Palace, London, designing the South Moat border and adjacent woodland. Rupert Golby at Osborne House, Isle of Wight, has made both formal and informal plantings within the walled garden, with modern galvanized metal arches for trained fruit, incorporating the initials V and A (since this is a royal property). At the Medieval Bishop's Palace in Lincoln, Mark Anthony Walker's innovative design uses intersecting brick paths, with stainless-steel tree grids and etched discs at the intersections, to make reference to the ribbed vaulting and bosses to be found on the ceiling of the nearby cathedral. Christopher Bradley-Hole has designed a Portland stone circular wall to act as both a performance and sitting area at Portland Castle in Dorset. The plantings are of grasses and other plants, which will withstand the salt winds.

At Bryan's Ground in Herefordshire, the owners have created a wonderfully ornate 'Arts and Crafts' garden to complement the Edwardian house, based on strict axial geometry but including many teasing and exuberant features, such as the Sulking House and the Rose Cabinet. Simon Dorrell, one of the owners, is also responsible for the design of the Hampton Court Gardens in Herefordshire where he created a complex, geometric water garden in the old Victorian

Great care has been taken by the owners at East Ruston Old Vicarage in Norfolk to provide the right conditions for agaves, aloes, cacti, puyas, dasylirion and other tender plants, in the area of the garden called Desert Wash. This is designed to imitate conditions in Arizona, where rain is rare but causes floods and creates channels when it comes. So free-draining is the soil (mainly consisting of gravel, topped by flint stones) that tender plants survive winter cold, when they would die in wetter conditions. So far 300 tonnes of flint have been used here, and the work is ongoing. Such care in providing a distinct plant habitat is unusual in England, but not unheard-of. The bridge looks like a skeleton lying in the desert, perhaps.

walled garden, with two open-sided octagonal wooden pavilions, and connecting canals and water steps. Also notable is the thatched hermitage, which has to be reached by a tunnel at the bottom of the Gothic stone tower, close by a Picturesque cascade and a purposely gloomy Sunken Garden. What saves this garden from any accusation of pastiche is the sheer quality of the craftsmanship and strength of conviction with which it has been designed and executed. Creating it must have been a lot of fun.

The difficulty – from the point of view of the visiting public – with much new design work is that it has been realized in gardens which are either not open to the public (since wealthy patrons in this country often value their privacy) or open only for groups by appointment. As these gardens reach maturity that may change, but one important and positive recent development to ensure that visitors can see some of those contemporary gardens that are pushing out the boundaries is the Modern Gardens weekend, held annually at the end of June.

Much of what motivates contemporary designers, and many gardeners, is respect for the environment, and an interest in biodiversity and sustainability. The New Naturalism movement has also sparked off a desire to create realistic habitats, even if they are not English (or perhaps, because, since our own flora is so relatively poor). I have mentioned Christopher Lloyd's American prairie at Dixter, for example, and the Gravel Garden, based on Mediterranean plants, made by Beth Chatto out of an old car park, and there is also both a Cretan-influenced Cottage Garden and a South African garden at The Garden House, Devon, and a number of disparate gardens laid out at East Ruston Old Vicarage. The Californian Border, Desert Wash, Mediterranean Garden and Meadow here all mimic specific conditions and habitats.

So much for country gardens. In an era when 90 per cent of the population live in towns or cities, it is both inevitable, as well as right and proper, that designers and amateur gardeners alike should concern

themselves with how to organize the spaces in city gardens and roof gardens. The latter have their champions amongst contemporary designers such as Arabella Lennox-Boyd and Stephen Woodhams, helped by advances in technology which solve a number of practical problems such as the need to waterproof effectively. Roof gardens, by

OPPOSITE ABOVE A roof garden in London by James Aldridge where the severely modern furniture and planters are complemented by the brilliant white stems of the birches, which have an unmistakably contemporary feel to them, as well as clipped lavender. The furniture is by Philippe Starck.

OPPOSITE BELOW A London roof terrace designed by Dan Pearson. Note the playful topiary, of a bird happy to nest in the city.

LEFT Another view of the same roof terrace. The plants are all heat- and drought-tolerant, as they need to be. Amongst them are thrift, houseleeks, *Cosmos atrosangineus* (in the bottom right-hand corner) and, in the galvanized planters, purple-leaved *Cotinus* and silver-leaved *Convolvulus cneorum* with the grass *Festuca glauca*.

ABOVE In small city gardens, more or less anything goes. Here is a classical take on a garden with an obelisk and water chute, as well as plenty of 'greens'. John Evelyn would surely have approved. Plants include *Yucca recurvifolia* and *Trochodendron aralioides* beside the pool, and *Pittosporum tobira* and pleached limes at the lower level. This is designed by James Aldridge and is a decided contrast to his roof garden shown on page 368.

RIGHT The designer Anthony Noel is known for his strongly ornamented and formal city gardens, and his delight in painting pots and other containers. In a typical small, rectangular London garden he has placed four large classical urns, achieving a strong impression by size and repetition. The planting is also strong and forthright: angel's trumpets (*Brugmansia*) and 'Stargazer' lilies, with variegated-leaved cordylines in the big pots.

their very nature, mainly are not open to the public, and the reader must be content to enjoy the pictures.[3]

In city gardens, there is a more adventurous use of modern materials, such as aluminium for decking and water features, Astroturf to escape from the tyranny of sparse, shaded grass, adventurous lighting, even canvas sails for shade. In roof gardens, particularly, the harsh conditions for plants have prompted much use of glass and concrete, with plant lovers seeking out spiky-leaved succulents or grey-leaved xerophytes.

It is in the cities that an imaginative eclecticism can be seen most clearly, perhaps

because the gardens are both smaller and also very enclosed. It is in the city that you will find, for instance, the Antipodean-style garden belonging to a New Zealander and designed by James Fraser, in an example of what one might call reverse colonization.

Finally, it would have been extraordinary, I suppose, if the ideas of conceptualism, so powerful in Britain from the 1980s in the other visual arts, should not have found their way into garden making; at least for some *avant-garde* designers who challenge even the conventional meaning of the concept 'garden', in ways that vary from the brilliantly inspired to the downright silly. In the process, gardens become as much art installations as conventional spaces for plants but, in England, as a garden visitor, you are most likely to see this at temporary garden shows, such as the Westonbirt International Festival of the Garden, rather than in permanent gardens. Many are in cities, and it is, unfortunately, a rare New Tech garden that is open to visitors.

Among the leading proponents of the 'style' are Paul Cooper who, with his most imaginative Floating Garden at Chelsea Flower Show in 1999, challenged the idea that gardens are static by having circular floating planters, propelled by submerged pumps, changing their relationship with each other constantly. He is happy to use plastics – preferably if they are brightly coloured. He is at home with new technologies generally (indeed, he has published a book entitled *The New Tech Garden*) and that seems to be true of a lot of designers who started out life as artists. Stephen Woodhams – he of the signature galvanized steel, cone-shaped planters – is another. Indeed, their approach seems often to be a way of taking sculpture outdoors.

OPPOSITE The entrance to a London garden, designed by James Fraser, which is filled with New Zealand plants, including the drooping leaves of *Pseudopanax*, silver-leaved *Astelia* and gourds twining round the gatepost. This is an example of reverse colonialism of the most benign kind. The use of recycled materials is imaginative – note the uneven lengths of the gate struts. The choice of flamboyant, mainly evergreen plants, also ensures privacy.

ABOVE Paul Cooper is a designer who likes to push out the boundaries of what we accept constitutes a garden. He is happy working with hard-edged, modern materials. These are his extremely jolly floating planters at the 1999 Chelsea Flower Show, which moved around the pool, changing the aspect of the 'flower beds' as they did so. I particularly like the use of lupins, denizens of the traditional herbaceous border.

The top terrace at Broughton Grange in Oxfordshire. It seems to me that what Tom Stuart-Smith has done is take a traditional partly walled space and put a Modernist spin on it, using clean, asymmetric lines. The planting is also unusual: for example, there is the highly individualistic placing of a traditional formal garden element – topiary. The top terrace has Irish yews, the middle terrace bobbles of beech, which turn rusty brown in winter. Serpentine paths, hidden by plant material, run through the terrace left and right from the stepping stone in the canal.

The champion of what he calls 'horticultural intervention art' is Tony Heywood, a garden designer and 'horticultural installation creator' who challenges the idea of the garden as 'rural' escape. For him, garden design should be much more unashamedly urban, of the street, embracing new technologies, rather than a retreat, an opportunity for empirical experimentation or a 'validation of gracious living'. 'The HIA is urban-based and proud of it; takes as its starting point not nature in its organic sense but the media-focused world of popular culture, film and music in which it finds itself; is interested in the artificial; makes no claims to classic status; looks like hard work; and its taste is questionable, even provocative.'[4]

Gardens by these designers are forward-looking, often edgy and always unpredictable, but they can provide a shock of surprise and delight in the onlooker; their designs are very much a matter of 'nothing ventured, nothing gained'. Astroturf, galvanized steel, coloured Plexiglas, gaily painted rocks, plastic mobiles, synthetic fabrics, acid-etched glass, mirrors, innovative lighting turning night into day (since many urban clients do that, anyway), *trompes l'oeil*, as well as mist machines and outdoor stereo music systems – all these have been recruited to the cause. The effects are not always successful, since some manufactured modern materials can soon look dated, and the shock of surprise can be short-lived; but these designers are also experimenting in volumes and spaces, as every garden designer has done since time immemorial, and the results can be both aesthetically satisfying and fit for purpose. And at least these designers are not just going through the motions.

Interesting, thought-provoking and often amusing as all this is, it does not represent the mainstream way forward, since it does not suit the majority of garden owners. What will happen to gardens in the next few years is harder to predict, in our fragmented society. Garden designers are mixed in their attitudes, many feeling that there is still too much harking back to the past Arts and Crafts glory (although that is a view held most firmly by people who do not properly appreciate how history can be usefully reinterpreted), while others think we are in a 1980s timewarp, reworking modular, design-led solutions, based on geometric patterns and too much brickwork, time and time again, since they make commercial sense and do not entirely prohibit the cultivation of plants. More still are anxious as to whether shrinking garden size may be the ultimate limiting factor.

What is heartening, and could not have been confidently predicted fifty years ago, is how well contemporary garden owners have dealt with the disappearance of skilled gardening help, embracing technical advances and raising their own skill levels and commitment to compensate.

My feeling is that there are still many new lovely gardens to be made in the future, but that, in a time of ineluctable climate change, they will carry an increasingly heavy responsibility to be sustainable and promote biodiversity. Which is good news for plant lovers, of course. The polluting qualities of cement and concrete will rule these materials out, *deo volente*, and the exploitative use of foreign stone and scarce materials will seem increasingly unacceptable. Gardens will depend far more on recycled materials, living sculptures of, for example, willow, and swimming ponds, rather than pools. There need be no aesthetic falling away, however, for English designers and garden owners are capable of rising to the challenge, as they have always done in the past.

OTHER CONTEMPORARY GARDENS

The Manor House, Stevington, Bedfordshire
Waltham Place Gardens, Berkshire
Turn End, Haddenham, Buckinghamshire
Castle Hill, Devon
Scypen, Devon
Stanbridge Mill, Dorset
Marks Hall, Essex
Ozleworth Park, Gloucestershire
Througham Court, Gloucestershire
Conholt Park, Hampshire
Vineyard Manor, Hertfordshire
The Old Zoo Garden, Lancashire
7 The Butts, London
66A East Dulwich Road, London
Eltham Palace, London
70 Gloucester Crescent, London
7 St George's Road, Twickenham, London
82 Wood Vale, London
17 Poplar Grove, Manchester
Corpusty Mill, Norfolk
The Exotic Garden, Norfolk
Althorp House, Northamptonshire
Richmond Castle, Yorkshire

NOTES

1 FORMAL BONES (PAGES 12—71)

1 Christopher Thacker, *The Genius of Gardening* (Weidenfeld and Nicolson, 1994), p. 14.
2 James van Sweden, *Architecture in the Garden* (Frances Lincoln, 2002), p. 31.
3 John Evelyn, *Sylva*, 1662.
4 Roy Strong, *The Laskett: The Story of a Garden* (Bantam, 2003).
5 Ibid., pp. 48–9.

2 FLORAL EXUBERANCE (PAGES 72—123)

1 George Fleming, the imaginative head gardener to the Duke of Sutherland at Trentham Park (see page 32) from 1841, is credited with this innovation.
2 Gertrude Jekyll, *Colour Schemes for the Flower Garden* (Antique Collectors' Club), pp. 128–30.
3 Ibid.
4 The owner, Ros Wallinger, wrote about this in *Gertrude Jekyll's Lost Garden: The Restoration of an Edwardian Masterpiece* (Garden Art Press, 2000).
5 Margery Fish, *We Made a Garden* (Collingridge, 1956).
6 Nori and Sandra Pope, *Planting with Colour* (Conran Octopus, 2002) and *Colour by Design: Planting the Contemporary Garden* (Conran Octopus, 1998).
7 The garden designer and author Penelope Hobhouse moved there in the 1960s and, in the twelve years she was there, made a lovely garden. She moved on to Tintinhull, where she was similarly successful, and now gardens at the Coach House, Dorset (see page 105).
8 Some of these have been bred or selected in the garden, including *Anemone* 'Hadspen Abundance', *Astrantia* 'Hadspen Blood' and *Brunnera* 'Hadspen Cream'.
9 Nori and Sandra Pope, *Colour by Design: Planting the Contemporary Garden* (Conran Octopus, 1998), p. 11.
10 Ibid.
11 West Green House guidebook.
12 Marylyn Abbott, *Gardening with Light and Colour* (Kyle Cathie, 1999), and *Marylyn Abbott's Thoughts on Garden Design* (Kyle Cathie, 2004).
13 Tim Richardson, *The English Garden in the Twentieth Century* (Aurum Press, 2005), p. 80.
14 For the most part, that is. In 1987, there was snow, frost and cold winds at Tresco, which destroyed many of the plantings, and, in 1990, fierce gales felled most of the shelterbelt. However, the gardens have recovered well and quickly, partly because of the speedy growth of many subtropical plants.
15 Christopher Holliday, *Sharp Gardening* (Frances Lincoln, 2005).
16 Sylvia Crowe, *Garden Design* (Country Life, 1958), p. 106.

3 THE LANDSCAPE TRADITION (PAGES 124—53)

1 Joseph Addison wrote in *The Spectator* in 1712: '. . . there is generally in Nature something more grand and August than what we meet with in the curiosities of Art.'
2 William Shenstone, *Unconnected Thoughts on Gardening* (1764).
3 His employment by county landowners to improve grounds was satirized by Jane Austen in *Mansfield Park*.

4 THE COUNTRY GARDEN (PAGES 154—89)

1 A solitary, enormous monkey puzzle still to be seen in the front gardens of Victorian villas is an example that survives of the Gardenesque.
2 Gertrude Jekyll, *Wood and Garden* (Antique Collectors' Club, 1981), p. 18.
3 Vita Sackville-West, *Even More for Your Garden* (Michael Joseph, 1958), p. 81.
4 Margery Fish, *Cottage Garden Flowers* (Collingridge, 1961).
5 Jane Brown, *Tales of the Rose Tree* (HarperCollins, 2004), p. 170.
6 Dan Pearson, *The Garden: A Year at Home Farm* (Ebury Press, 2001).
7 Ibid.
8 Ibid., p. 17.
9 *Beth Chatto's Gravel Garden* (Frances Lincoln, 2000), p. 12.
10 Ibid., p. 13.

5 GARDENING WITH NATURE (PAGES 190—215)

1 The conservatory at Chiswick House built by the 6th Duke of Devonshire in 1812 housed newly imported camellias.

2 Pam Lewis, *Sticky Wicket: Gardening in Tune with Nature* (Frances Lincoln, 2005) and *Making Wildflower Meadows* (Frances Lincoln, 2003).

3 Christopher Lloyd, *Meadows* (Cassell, 2004), p. 28.

4 Tim Richardson and Noël Kingsbury (eds), *Vista: The Culture and Politics of Gardens* (Frances Lincoln, 2005), pp. 100–110.

5 Keith Wiley, *On the Wild Side: Experiments in the New Naturalism* (Timber Press, 2004).

7 ORNAMENT IN THE GARDEN (PAGES 238—269)

1 Ivan Hicks, *Favourite Gardens Newsletter*, Spring 2002, Tourism South East.

2 Roy Strong, *The Laskett: The Story of a Garden* (Bantam Press, 2003).

3 *Derek Jarman's Garden* (Thames and Hudson, 1995), p. 47.

4 Ibid.

5 Ibid.

6 Frederick Gibberd, *The Englishman's Garden*, ed. Alvilde Lees-Milne and Rosemary Verey (Allen Lane, 1983), p. 70.

7 www.mythicgarden.eclipse.co.uk

8 WATER, WATER EVERYWHERE (PAGES 270—99)

1 Dan Pearson, *The Garden: A Year at Home Farm* (Ebury Press, 2001), p. 34.

2 The yews at Westbury Court have suffered lately from attack by *Phytophthora* (a disease most prevalent in waterlogged soil), and the National Trust has warned that, in a time of climate change, the garden is increasingly vulnerable to flooding. Notwithstanding, it is a remarkable garden.

3 Michael Spens, *Jellicoe at Shute* (Academy Editions, 1993), p. 7.

4 Ibid., p. 55.

9 THE ENGLISH ROSE (PAGES 300—319)

1 National Collections are held under the auspices of the National Council for the Conservation of Plants and Gardens.

2 Graham Stuart Thomas, *An English Rose Garden* (Michael Joseph, 1991), p. 14.

3 Charles and Brigid Quest-Ritson, *The Royal Horticultural Society Encyclopedia of Roses* (Dorling Kindersley, 2003), p. 45.

10 THE KITCHEN GARDEN (PAGES 320—47)

1 For example, hexagonal in the case of Tyringham in Buckinghamshire.

2 Susan Campbell, *A History of Kitchen Gardening* (Frances Lincoln, 2005), *passim*.

3 Jim Buckland, 'Careful Training Bears Fruit', *The Garden*, March 2002.

4 *Rosemary Verey's Making of a Garden* (Frances Lincoln, 1995), p. 145.

5 Ibid., p. 150.

6 Ibid., p. 147.

7 Ibid.

11 THE CONTEMPORARY GARDEN (PAGES 348—75)

1 Christopher Bradley-Hole, *The Minimalist Garden* (Mitchell Beazley, 1999), p. 131.

2 Kim Wilkie, *Garden Design Journal*, March 2006, p. 35. The Fibonacci series is a mathematical progression whereby the sum of two numbers becomes the next number in the series. This makes a spiral, when plotted on a graph, and has for some time been thought to govern the arrangement of leaves and branches on a tree, the spirals on a sunflower head and pineapple scales. These spirals are said to counteract the stress of growth. The Fibonacci series is, not surprisingly, popular with gardeners who are interested in both mathematics and philosophy. Scypen in Devon is another garden where the Fibonacci series is used.

3 Anyone who wishes to experience one long-established one, of course, need go no further than High Street, Kensington, London, where Ralph Hancock's 1930s roof garden (often still called Derry and Toms after the department store then below) includes a 'Tudor garden', 'woodland' and a formal Spanish garden, complete with Moorish pool.

4 Tony Heywood, 'Horticultural Intervention Art', Tim Richardson and Noël Kingsbury (eds), *Vista: The Culture and Politics of Gardens* (Frances Lincoln, 2005).

No reader who enjoys visiting gardens should be without:
King, P., and Lambert, K. (eds), *The Daily Telegraph Good Gardens Guide*, Frances Lincoln, published annually
The Gardens of England and Wales Open for Charity (also known as the 'Yellow Book'), The National Gardens Scheme, published annually
Patrick Taylor, *The Gardens of Britain and Ireland*, Dorling Kindersley, 2003

BOOKS
Abbott, M., *Gardening with Light and Colour*, Kyle Cathie, 1999
—, *Marylyn Abbott's Thoughts on Garden Design*, Kyle Cathie, 2004
Batey, M., *Jane Austen and the English Landscape*, Barn Elms, 1996
—, *Alexander Pope: The Poet and the Landscape*, Barn Elms, 1999
Batey, M., and Lambert, D., *The English Garden Tour: A View into the Past*, John Murray, 1990
Billington, J., *London's Parks and Gardens*, Frances Lincoln, 2003
Bisgrove, R., *The National Trust Book of the English Garden*, Viking, 1990
—, *The Gardens of Gertrude Jekyll*, Frances Lincoln, 1992
Bradley-Hole, C., *The Minimalist Garden*, Mitchell Beazley, 1999
Brown, J., *The Art and Architecture of English Gardens*, Weidenfeld and Nicolson, 1989
—, *The English Garden through the 20th Century*, Garden Art Press, 1999
—, *The Pursuit of Paradise: A Social History of Gardens and Gardening*, HarperCollins, 1999
—, *Tales of the Rose Tree*, HarperCollins, 2004
Buchan, U., *An Anthology of Garden Writing*, Croom Helm, 1986
Campbell, S., *A History of Kitchen Gardening*, Frances Lincoln, 2005
Chatto, B., *Beth Chatto's Gravel Garden*, Frances Lincoln, 2000
Cooper, G., and Taylor, G., *English Herb Gardens*, Weidenfeld and Nicolson, 1986
—, *Paradise Transformed*, Monacelli, 1997
Cooper, P., *The New Tech Garden*, Mitchell Beazley, 2001
Crowder, C., *The Garden at Levens*, Frances Lincoln, 2005
Davies, J., *The Victorian Kitchen Garden*, BBC Books, 1987
Devonshire, the Duchess of, *The Estate: A View from Chatsworth by the Duchess of Devonshire*, Macmillan, 1990
Dickey, P., *Breaking Ground: Garden Design Solutions from Ten Contemporary Masters*, Artisan, 1997
Elliott, B., *Victorian Gardens*, Batsford, 1986

Fearnley-Whittingstall, F., *The Garden: An English Love Affair*, Weidenfeld and Nicolson, 2004
Fish, M., *We Made a Garden*, Collingridge, 1956
—, *Cottage Garden Flowers*, Collingridge, 1961
Gibson, M., *The English Rose Garden*, Shire Books, 2000
Hadfield, M., *A History of British Gardening*, John Murray, 1979
Hall, M., *Waddesdon Manor: The Heritage of a Rothschild House*, Harry N. Abrams, 2002
Harvey, J., *Mediaeval Gardens*, Batsford, 1990
Holliday, C., *Sharp Gardening*, Frances Lincoln, 2005
Hunningher, E. (ed.), *Making Gardens: A Celebration of Gardens and Gardening in England and Wales from the National Gardens Scheme*, Cassell, 2001
Hyams, E., *The English Garden*, Thames and Hudson, 1966
Jarman, D., *Derek Jarman's Garden*, Thames and Hudson, 1995
Jekyll, G., *Colour Schemes for the Flower Garden*, Antique Collectors' Club, 1995
—, *Roses for English Gardens*, Antique Collectors' Club, 1982
—, *Wood and Garden*, Antique Collectors' Club, 1981
Keen, M., *The Glory of the English Garden*, Barrie and Jenkins, 1989
Kingsbury, N., *The New Perennial Garden*, Frances Lincoln, 1996
Lacey, S., *Gardens of the National Trust*, The National Trust, 1996
Lawson, A., *The Gardener's Book of Colour*, Frances Lincoln, 1996
le Rougetel, H., *A Heritage of Roses*, Unwin Hyman, 1988
Lees-Milne, A., and Verey, R., *The Englishman's Garden*, Allen Lane, 1982
Lennox-Boyd, A., *Designing Gardens*, Frances Lincoln, 2002
Lewis, P., *Making Wildflower Meadows*, Frances Lincoln, 2003
—, *Sticky Wicket: Gardening in Tune with Nature*, Frances Lincoln, 2005
Lloyd, C., *Meadows*, Cassell, 2004
—, *Succession Planting for Adventurous Gardeners*, BBC Books, 2005
Longstaffe-Gowan, T., *The Gardens and Parks at Hampton Court Palace*, Frances Lincoln, 2005
Lord, T., *et al* (eds), *RHS Plant Finder, 2006–2007*, Dorling Kindersley, 2006
Lord, T., *Gardening at Sissinghurst*, Frances Lincoln, 1995
Maitland, S., and Matthews, P., *Gardens of Illusion*, Cassell, 2000
Maynard, A., with Seddon, S., *Gardens with Atmosphere: Creating Gardens with a Sense of Place*, Conran Octopus, 2001

Oudolf, P., and Kingsbury, N., *Planting Design: Gardens in Time and Space*, Timber Press, 2005

Page, R., *The Education of a Gardener*, Harvill, 1995

Pavord, A., *Hidcote Manor Garden*, National Trust Enterprises, 1993

—, *The Tulip*, Bloomsbury, 1999

Pearson, D., *The Garden: A Year at Home Farm*, Ebury Press, 2001

Plumptre, G., *The Latest Country Gardens*, The Bodley Head, 1988

—, *Great Gardens, Great Designers*, Ward Lock, 1994

—, *Garden Ornament*, Thames and Hudson, 1989

Pope, N. and S., *Colour by Design: Planting the Contemporary Garden*, Conran Octopus, 1998

—, *Planting with Colour*, Conran Octopus, 2002

Quest-Ritson, C., *Climbing Roses of the World*, Timber Press, 2003

—, *The English Garden: A Social History*, Penguin, 2003

Quest-Ritson, C. and B., *The Royal Horticultural Society Encyclopedia of Roses*, Dorling Kindersley, 2003

Richardson, T., *English Gardens in the Twentieth Century*, Aurum Press, 2005

Richardson, T., and Kingsbury, N. (eds), *Vista: The Culture and Politics of Gardens*, Frances Lincoln, 2005

Sackville-West, V., *Even More for Your Garden*, Michael Joseph, 1958

Sanecki, K., *History of the English Herb Garden*, Ward Lock, 1992

Snell, S., *The Gardens at Hatfield*, Frances Lincoln, 2005

Spens, M., *Jellicoe at Shute*, Academy Editions, 1993

Strong, R., *The Laskett: The Story of a Garden*, Bantam, 2003

—, *The Renaissance Garden in England*, Thames and Hudson, 1979

Taylor, C., *Parks and Gardens of Britain: A Landscape History from the Air*, Edinburgh University Press, 1988

Taylor, P., *One Hundred English Gardens*, Headline, 1995

Taylor, P. (ed.), *The Oxford Companion to the Garden*, Oxford University Press, 2006

Thacker, C., *The Genius of Gardening*, Weidenfeld and Nicolson, 1994

Thomas, G.S., *An English Rose Garden*, Michael Joseph, 1991

—, *The Graham Stuart Thomas Rose Book*, John Murray, 1994; Frances Lincoln, 2004

Thompson, P., *The Self-Sustaining Garden*, Batsford, 1997

Turner, T., *English Garden Design*, Antique Collectors' Club, 1986

—, *Garden History: Philosophy and Design 2000 BC–2000 AD*, Spon Press, 2005

van Sweden, J., *Architecture in the Garden*, Frances Lincoln, 2002

Verey, R., *Rosemary Verey's Making of a Garden*, Frances Lincoln, 1995

Wales, HRH The Prince of, and Lycett-Green, C., *The Garden at Highgrove*, Weidenfeld and Nicolson, 2000

Wallinger, R., *Gertrude Jekyll's Lost Garden: The Restoration of an Edwardian Masterpiece*, Garden Art Press, 2000

Waymark, J., *Modern Garden Design: Innovation since 1900*, Thames and Hudson, 2003

Whalley, R., and Jennings, A., *Knot Gardens and Parterres*, Barn Elms, 1998

Wiley, K., *On the Wild Side: Experiments in the New Naturalism*, Timber Press, 2004

ARTICLES AND PERIODICALS

Bisgrove, R., 'A Walk on Jekyll's Wild Side', *The Garden*, April, 2004, pp. 282–7

Brookes, J., 'Happy Medium', *The Garden*, May, 1998, pp. 372–3

—, 'Naturally Relaxed', *The Garden*, 2001

Buckland, J., 'Careful Training Bears Fruit', *The Garden*, March 2002, pp. 178–81

—, 'I Don't Get to Share Horticultural Pillow Talk with Other Colleagues', *The Garden*, 2002, pp. 562–3

—, 'Playing with Fire', *The Garden*, 2004, pp. 600–603

Cleveley, A., 'Maximise Your Potential', *The Garden*, February 2003, pp. 124–9

Garbutt, S., 'A Return to Victorian Values', *The Garden*, pp. 628–31

McArdle, C., 'East Lambrook Manor, Somerset', *The Garden*, January 2002, pp. 18–23

Roberts, J., 'The Organic Kitchen Garden', *Gardens Illustrated*, December 2002

van Groeningen, I., 'Gifts from a Giant', *The Garden*, May 1998, pp. 367–71

Verey, R., 'The Priory at Kemerton', *The Garden*, 1984, pp. 302–9

Watkins, J., 'Haseley Court Gardens', *The Garden*, October 1990, pp. 520–25

Wilkie, K., *Garden Design Journal*, March 2006, page 131

INDEX

Gardens are in **bold** type if they are open to visitors, regularly in the season, one or two days a year for charity or by appointment. They are mostly listed in *The Good Gardens Guide* or the 'Yellow Book'; if not, you may find opening details in the local press or on the Internet. As gardens sometimes close for a year or longer – for restoration, for personal reasons or because of a change of ownership – only gardens open in 2006 are in bold, since the future status of garden openings cannot be predicted.

Page numbers in *italic* type refer to the captions to the illustrations.

ACKNOWLEDGEMENTS

URSULA BUCHAN

I acknowledge with sincere thanks the help I have received from a number of people in the preparation of this book, in particular Andrew Lawson, of course, whose knowledge of gardens has been absolutely invaluable, as well as all those at Andrew Lawson Photography, especially Judy Dod, for their enthusiastic assistance. Dr Brent Elliott and his staff at the Royal Horticultural Society's Lindley Library were most helpful and I am grateful to them. I should also like to thank all those who have patiently answered a variety of questions: Marylyn Abbott, Jane Allhusen, Stephen Anderton, Mark Bradshaw, Kathy Brown, Jim Buckland, Susie Lewis, Mike Nelhams, Mary Keen, Lady King, Lord Neidpath, Sir Roy Strong and Xa Tollemache. Jane Brown kindly read and commented upon part of the typescript. I should also like to thank Joan Darbyshire, Briony Lawson and Jane Otter for their hospitality while I was on the road. On the home front, I am most grateful for the unflagging support and interest of my family, not to mention some very bright suggestions; and to Cynthia Ogilvie for looking after the garden so expertly while I was tied to my desk or away on garden visits. Finally, I should like to thank all those involved with the book at Frances Lincoln: John Nicoll, whose idea this was, Jo Christian, Becky Clarke and, in particular, Anne Askwith, who edited the typescript so skilfully. My thanks are, as always, due to Anthea Morton-Saner at Curtis Brown.

I and the publishers have done our best to ensure the accuracy of information in the book, but the publishers would be happy to correct errors, if any there be, in later editions.

ANDREW LAWSON

Special thanks to the garden owners who have welcomed me to their gardens and permitted me to take pictures. Their kindness and hospitality have always taken account of a garden photographer's unsocial hours, and have often extended to breakfast or lunch and even an overnight stay. I am most grateful to HRH The Prince of Wales for permission to use pictures of Highgrove. Also to the National Trust and to English Heritage for granting permission for me to publish pictures of gardens in their care. And many thanks to my friend Marianne Majerus for permitting me to use her picture of East Ruston on the far coast of Norfolk which I have not, so far, managed to reach.